ANTHROPOLOGY, DEVELOPMENT AND THE POST-MODERN CHALLENGE

D0104615

Anthropology, Culture and Society

Series Editors:
Dr Richard A. Wilson, University of Sussex
Professor Thomas Hylland Eriksen, University of Oslo

ANTHROPOLOGY, DEVELOPMENT AND THE POST-MODERN CHALLENGE

KATY GARDNER AND DAVID LEWIS

Pluto Press

LONDON • STERLING, VIRGINIA

First published 1996 by Pluto Press
345 Archway Road, London N6 5AA
and 22883 Quicksilver Drive,
Sterling, VA 20166–2012, USA

British Library Cataloguing in Publication Data
A catalogue record for this book is available from
the British Library.

ISBN 0 7453 0746 9 (hbk)
ISBN 0 7453 0747 7 (pbk)

Library of Congress Cataloging in Publication Data are available

Impression: 05   04   03   02   01   7   6   5

Designed and Produced for Pluto Press by
Chase Publishing Services
Typeset from disk by
Stanford DTP Services, Northampton
Printed in the European Union by
Antony Rowe, Chippenham, England

CONTENTS

Figures

PREFACE

We have chosen to write this book for two main reasons. The first is that, to our knowledge at least, there is no single book in existence which attempts to bring together the various histories, opinions and debates which have emerged during the relationships between development people and anthropologists in the contemporary period. Lucy Mair's path-breaking *Anthropology and Development*, published in 1984, has certainly made our task much easier, but Mair's book was written well before both subjects embarked upon their respective periods of intensive self-reflection, as the debates around post-modernism raged during the late 1980s and early 1990s. It is therefore our modest hope that this book fulfils a need among students, teachers, researchers and practitioners.

Our second reason is a more personal one. Both of us have for some time wished for an opportunity to try to make sense of disparate experiences working (over the past decade or so) at different times as anthropologists, researchers and development practitioners – in the field, at universities and research institutes, behind desks in development agencies and within interdisciplinary consultancy teams.

It might be useful to provide the reader with some short biographical notes before they embark on reading the text, in order that he or she knows something of the personal career trajectories of both authors. Katy Gardner and David Lewis both studied social anthropology as a first degree in the early 1980s. Katy Gardner's PhD research involved fieldwork in a Bangladeshi migrant village. After completing her dissertation, she spent a year working for the British Overseas Development Administration (ODA) as an assistant social advisor. During this period she was involved in short visits to various projects in South Asia as well as administrative work in London. Since leaving the ODA Katy has worked as a full-time lecturer in anthropology and development at the Universities of Kent and Sussex. She has also been involved in a range of consultancy work for both private and governmental agencies. She is the author of *Songs at the River's Edge: Stories from a Bangladeshi Village* (Virago, 1991) and *Global Migrants, Local Lives: Travel and Transformation in Rural Bangladesh* (Oxford University Press, 1995).

David Lewis moved from anthropology into a more interdisciplinary study of development. After a postgraduate course in development studies, he completed a PhD in rural sociology, in which he studied the effects of rural technological change in a Bangladeshi village. A five-year period of freelance research and consultancy work followed, during which he worked as a Research Associate at the Overseas Development Institute in London and as a Visiting Fellow at the Centre for Development Studies at the University of Bath. He undertook research and consultancy work for a number of government and non-governmental agencies in Bangladesh, India, Nepal, Sri Lanka and Albania before becoming a full-time lecturer at the Centre for Voluntary Organisation, Department of Social Policy and Administration at the London School of Economics and Political Science. He is the author of *Technologies and Transactions: A Study of the Interaction between Agrarian Structure and New Technology in Bangladesh* (Centre for Social Studies, Dhaka, 1991); co-editor of *Non-Governmental Organisations and the State in Asia: Rethinking Roles in Sustainable Agricultural Development*; and a co-author of *Reluctant Partners?: NGOs, the State and Sustainable Agricultural Development* (both Routledge, 1993), and of *Trading the Silver Seed: Local Knowledge and Market Moralities in Aquacultural Development* (Intermediate Technology Publications, 1996).

Of course, everyone's experience of this varied field will be different, and no doubt there are many perspectives which others might equally seek to reflect in a book such as this. We make no claims to comprehensiveness, though we have tried to provide at least an indication of the wide terrain which might be covered. We have for example largely left out (due to the limitations of our own training and expertise) a detailed discussion of areas such as medical anthropology, ethnicity, macro-economic development issues, population studies, the environmental movement and refugee resettlement. Nor have we reflected, at least in any direct sense, the opinions of those 'acted upon' in the name of development.

It might be useful to finish with a few words about our overall intentions. We believe that many of the current assumptions about and approaches to development are flawed or basically wrong-headed, but we do not see much value in simply being critical without trying to offer any creative alternatives. Instead, we favour the creation of options which are rooted in reality rather than simply in rhetoric, in breaking down the barriers which exist between the 'developers' and the 'developed' and in the need for a full and critical discussion about 'development' which reflects a true multiplicity of voices.

We believe that there is a pressing moral and political responsibility to work towards improving the quality of life for the bulk of the world's population, and that in general a poor job has so far been made of this task. We are not arguing here that anthropology can somehow 'save' the development industry, or necessarily make the process of planned change a more benign one. However, we do believe that anthropologists and development practitioners may have something to learn from each other, in order that better futures may be imagined and, perhaps, brought into being.

Katy Gardner
David Lewis   May 1995

Note: In writing about some of these experiences as ethnography (and this has been attempted in Chapter 6 in particular) we have, for obvious reasons, disguised the particulars of these accounts in terms of places and organisations, in keeping with the anthropological tradition of preserving the anonymity of their informants.

ACKNOWLEDGEMENTS

David Lewis and Katy Gardner would like to thank Eric Worby, Dina Siddiqi, Ben Crow, Sushila Zeitlyn, B.K. Jahangir, S.M. Nurul Alam, Sue Phillips and Emma Crewe for their stimulating discussions about many of these issues and for their encouragement during the long period of writing.

We would both like to thank Richard Wilson for commissioning the book and for useful editorial comments and support. And James Fairburn for reading the original manuscript and providing valuable insights. Thanks also to Hamish Arnott for help with proofreading.

We would like to dedicate this book to the memory of Jonathan Zeitlyn, whose open mind, personal warmth and commitment to working towards a fairer world will continue to inspire both of us.

GLOSSARY

Development jargon

accountability making development interventions more responsive to the people they seek to assist; also used by donors to mean making sure that money is used for the purpose for which it was intended

applied anthropology the application of anthropological research to solving practical problems in development, public health, administration, industry, etc.

appropriate technology the idea of viewing technology in the context of people's needs, drawn originally from the work of E.F. Schumacher in the 1970s, in reaction to Western 'hi-tech' solutions to problems of poverty

basic needs a development strategy devised in the 1970s by governments and UN agencies in reaction to disillusionment with 'trickle down'

beneficiaries those people whom a development project is intended to assist

bottom-up interventions which come from the grassroots as opposed to government planners or development agencies

community development the attempt to strengthen the institutions of local communities in order that they will sustain the gains brought about by a development project

conditionality the imposition of terms by an aid giver upon a government or an organisation receiving the assistance (e.g. a bilateral donor gives a loan to an NGO provided it is used to support particular activities)

donor usually refers to government agencies such as the UK Overseas Development Administration (ODA) or United States Agency for International Development (USAID), or to multilateral agencies such as the World Bank, but also includes NGOs such as Oxfam who fund partner organisations in the countries where they work

empowerment the transformative potential of people to achieve positive changes in their lives by asserting their rights as women, citizens, etc., usually by group action, and thereby gaining greater power to solve problems

evaluation the task of assessing whether or not a development project has been successful in meeting its objectives

non-governmental organisation there are many types: international, national and local; large and small; specialised (e.g. health, agriculture) or general (combining many sectors of activity); membership or non-membership. NGOs are non-profit development organisations, many of which depend on donations from members, the public or development agencies. In the US, NGOs are often known as private voluntary organisations (PVOs)

the North along with 'the South', the term originated recently as less pejorative alternatives to 'First World' and 'Third World'. But both terms continue to cause problems by insisting that poverty can be geographically specified

participation used to describe greater involvement by 'beneficiaries' in deciding the type of development projects they need, and how they are run. The degree of this involvement can, however, vary greatly

project an intervention aimed at promoting social change usually by, or with the support of, an outside agency for a finite period (anything from a few years to several decades)

social development a new term used in the UK to describe the 'softer' elements of the development process as distinct from economic and technical issues – education, health-care, human rights, etc.

social movements groups around the world taking issue-based action in a variety of areas (human rights, environment, access to land, gender rights, peace, etc.) usually local, without outside assistance at least in the first instance

the South see entry for 'the North'

structural adjustment policies which became common during the 1980s, introduced by the World Bank, as conditionality on loans, aimed at improving efficiency by reducing public spending, cutting state subsidies and rationalising bureaucracy

sustainability the desire by planners and agencies to avoid creating projects which depend on their continued support for success; also used in its environmental sense to ensure renewal of natural resources

targeting the attempt to ensure that the benefits of a project reach a particular section of the population – women, farmers with no land, squatters, etc.

Third World originally designated the poorest areas of the world after the Second World War (as distinct from the capitalist First World and the communist Second World)

top-down interventions imposed on local people by those in authority – the opposite of bottom-up

trickle down the assumption, which comes from neo-classical economics, that if economic growth is achieved then benefits will eventually 'trickle down' from the 'wealth producers' to the poorer sections of the population

Anthropological jargon

acculturation originally used to refer to changes in cultures as they came into contact wth each other, the term later became synonymous among US anthropologists with the idea that non-Western or 'indigenous' cultures went into decline after contact with industrialised ones

applied anthropology the application of anthropological knowledge and research methodologies to practical issues, born out of anthropologists' involvement in colonial administration and development policy in the 1930s and 1940s

cultural relativism derived from the work of Franz Boas (1858–1942), this concept encouraged anthropologists to understand each culture on its own terms, instead of making evolutionary or ethnocentric generalisations

diffusionism a term associated with E.B. Tylor (1832–1917), used to explain the transmission of cultural traits across space, through culture contact or migration

discourse based on the ideas of Michel Foucault, discourse theory refers to the idea that the terms in which we speak, write and think about the world are a reflection of wider relations of power and, since they are also linked to practice, are themselves important in maintaining that power structure

ethnocentricity the idea that a tendency exists to interpret other cultures according to the values of one's own, a term first used by William Sumner (1840–1910)

ethnography a term which means both the study of a community or ethnic group at close quarters and the text (usually known as a monograph) which results

evolutionism in contrast to diffusionists (see above), evolutionists believe that universal human psychological characteristics eventually produce similar cultural traits all over the world, although these evolve at different rates in different places

functionalism a theory which tries to explain social and cultural institutions and relations in terms of the functions they perform within the system; heavily criticised because it fails to take account of historical factors such as change, conflict and disintegration

indigenous used instead of the more pejorative 'native' to refer to the original inhabitants of an area which has been occupied by migrants; but still brings problems in many situations by implying that there are somehow 'legitimate' inhabitants of land with greater rights than newcomers

participant observation the foundation of anthropological field research since the pioneering work of Malinowski (1884–1942), in which the anthropologist seeks to immerse herself as fully and as unobtrusively as possible in the life of a community under study

post-modernism the wider cultural and epistimological rejection of modernity in favour of a broader pluri-cultural range of styles, techniques and voices, including the rejection of unitary theories of progress and scientific rationality. In anthropology in particular, post-modernism has led to the questioning of the authority of the ethnographic text and in part to a crisis of representation

structural-functionalism a theoretical perspective associated with the British anthropologist Radcliffe-Brown (1881–1955), which stressed the importance of social relations and institutions in forming the framework of society, while at the same time functioning to preserve society as a stable whole

structuralism following from the work in linguistics of Saussure and Jakobson, the anthropologist Levi Strauss (1908–) argued that that culture is a superficial manifestation of deeper structural principles, based on the universal human imperative to classify experience and phenomena

ACRONYMS

BRAC	Bangladesh Rural Advancement Committee
ECLA	Economic Commission of Latin America
FAO	Food and Agricultural Organisations
FSR	farming systems research
GAD	gender and development
IBRD	International Bank for Reconstruction and Development
IFAD	International Fund for Agricultural Development
IMF	International Monetary Fund
ITDG	Intermediate Technology and Development Group
NGO	non-governmental organisation
ODA	Overseas Development Administration
OECD	Organisation for Economic Co-operation and Development
PRA	participatory rural appraisal
SDA	social development advisor
SIDA	Swedish International Development Authority
UNDP	United Nations Development Programme
UNICEF	United Nations Children's Fund
USAID	United States Agency for International Development
WID	women in development

1 ANTHROPOLOGY, DEVELOPMENT AND THE CRISIS OF MODERNITY

Development in ruins

Like a towering lighthouse guiding sailors towards the coast, 'development' stood as THE idea which oriented emerging nations in their journey through post-war history ... Today, the lighthouse shows cracks and is starting to crumble. The idea of development stands like a ruin on the intellectual landscape. Delusion and disappointment, failures and crimes have been the steady companions of development and they tell a common story: it did not work. (Sachs, 1992: 1)

Within some intellectual circles, the concept of development has been declared dead. It has become a non-word, to be used only with the inverted commas of the deconstructed 1990s. 'Development', the argument goes, represents the world as in a state of linear progression and change in which the North is 'advanced', and the South locked into static traditionalism which only modern technology and capitalist relations of production can transform. We now know that these understandings of the globe's shared history and shared future are deeply flawed. By the mid-1990s it has become clear that the supposed benefits of modernisation are largely an illusion: over much of the globe the progressive benefits of economic growth, technological change and scientific-rationality have failed to materialise. Combined with this, it has been suggested that the concept is embedded in neo-colonial constructions of the world and is a key ideological tool in global power relations (Escobar, 1988; 1995). Sachs, for example, talks of development's 'ethnocentric and even violent nature' (1992: 5). In this view, it is a construct rather than an objective state, a dream perhaps, but one which many people assert has justified a starkly political project of continued Northern dominance over the South.

1

And yet, so persuasive is development as a concept that many people discussing global poverty continue to use the term as a working tool, even if deriding it philosophically. This is not simply because notions of development are deeply interwoven with our understandings of the world – although in many post-industrial societies this is certainly true. As well as being a series of interlinked concepts and ideals, it is also a set of practices and relationships. Development agencies are actual institutions, which affect the world around them and spend billions of dollars a year. Likewise, development plans, workers and policies are all objective entities. We cannot simply will them into non-existence by insisting that they are constructs, however questionable the premisses on which they rest may be. In what follows, we therefore assume that development is an enormously powerful set of ideas which has guided thought and action across the world over the second part of the twentieth century; it involves deliberately planned change, and continues to affect the lives of many millions of people across the world. In speaking of development we take its highly problematic nature as a given, using the term to describe a set of activities, relationships and exchanges as well as ideas.

This book is concerned with anthropology's relationship with these interconnected and problematic domains. In the chapters that follow we shall argue that both development and anthropology have been recently facing what are often referred to as 'post-modern' crises. Rather than throwing up our hands in horror, however, we suggest that both have much to offer each other in overcoming the problems which they face and in moving forward. Anthropological insights can provide a dynamic critique of development and help push thought and practice away from oversystemic models and dualities (traditional as opposed to modern; formal as opposed to informal; developed versus undeveloped) and in more creative directions. Likewise, critical engagement with processes of planned and non-planned change offers considerable potential for anthropologists interested in understanding the workings of discourse, knowledge and power, and in social transformation. It is a domain for 'studying up' instead of the discipline's traditional focus on the less powerful. Lastly, it suggests one way forward for a more politically engaged anthropology. In sum, as anthropologists, activists and radical development workers approach the era of 'post-development' there are many ways in which they can work together to transform the existing status quo. The different roles may even be performed by the same individual.

In the rest of this chapter we shall briefly trace the trajectories of the contemporary intellectual quagmires facing both development and anthropology. We shall outline and critique conventional theories of development, discuss recent challenges facing anthropology and begin to set the questions which throughout the rest of the book we shall be attempting to answer.

Development: history and meanings

Arturo Escobar argues that as a set of ideas and practices 'development' has historically functioned over the twentieth century as a mechanism for the colonial and neo-colonial domination of the South by the North[1]. Its emergence was contingent upon particular historical conjunctions. Some of the most important of these are shifting global relations after the Second World War, the decline of colonialism, the Cold War, the need for capitalism to find new markets, and the Northern nations' faith in science and technology (Escobar, 1995: 26–39). Those using the term and working within development institutions are therefore helping to reproduce neo-colonial power relations even while many believe themselves to be engaged in processes of empowerment or the redistribution of the world's riches. To appreciate this more fully, let us examine the roots of the term.

In virtually all its usages, development implies positive change or progress. It also evokes natural metaphors of organic growth and evolution. The *Oxford Dictionary of Current English* defines it as 'stage of growth or advancement' (1988: 200). As a verb it refers to activities required to bring these changes about, while as an adjective it is inherently judgemental, for it involves a standard against which things are compared. While 'they' in the South are undeveloped, or in the process of being developed, we in the North (it is implied) have already reached that coveted state. When the term was first officially used by President Truman in 1949, vast areas of the world were therefore suddenly labelled 'underdeveloped' (Esteva, 1993: 7). A new problem was created, and with it the solutions; all of which depended upon the rational-scientific knowledge of the so-called developed powers (Hobart, 1993: 2).

Capitalism and colonialism: 1700–1949

The notion of development goes back further than 1949, however. Larrain has argued that while there has always been economic and social change throughout history, consciousness of 'progress', and the belief that this should be promoted, arose only within specific historical circumstances in northern Europe. Such ideas were first generated during what he terms the 'age of competitive capitalism' (1700–1860): an era of radical social and political struggles in which feudalism was increasingly undermined (Larrain, 1989: 1).

Concurrent with the profound economic and political changes which characterised these years was the emergence of what is often referred to as the 'Enlightenment'. This social and cultural movement, which was arguably to dominate Western thought[2] until the late twentieth century, stressed tolerance, reason and common sense. These sentiments were accompanied by the rise of technology and science, which were heralded as ushering in a new age of rationality and enlightenment for humankind, as opposed to what were now increasingly viewed as the superstitious and ignorant 'Dark Ages'. Rational knowledge, based on empirical information, was deemed to be the way forward (Jordanova, 1980: 45). During this era polarities between 'primitive' and 'civilised', 'backward' and 'advanced', 'superstitious' and 'scientific', 'nature' and 'culture' became commonplace (Bloch and Bloch, 1980: 27). Such dichotomies have their contemporary equivalents in notions of undeveloped and developed.

Larrain links particular types of development theory with different phases in capitalism. While the period 1700–1860 was characterised by the classical political economy of Smith and Ricardo and the historical materialism of Marx and Engels, the age of imperialism (1860–1945) spawned neo-classical political economy and classical theories of imperialism. Meanwhile, the subsequent expansionary age of late capitalism (1945–66) was marked by theories of modernisation, and the crises of 1966–80 by neo-Marxist theories of unequal exchange and dependency (Larrain, 1989: 4). We shall elaborate on these later theories further on in this chapter.

While capitalist expansion and crisis are clearly crucial to the history of development theory, the latter is also related to rapid leaps in scientific knowledge and social theory over the nineteenth and early twentieth centuries. A key moment in this was the publication of Darwin's *Origin of Species* in 1859. This was to have a huge influence on the social and political sciences in the West. Inspired by Darwin's arguments about the evolution of biological species, many political economists now theorised social change in similar terms. In *The Division of Labour* (originally published in 1893), for instance, Durkheim – who is now widely considered one of the founding fathers of sociology – compared 'primitive' and 'modern' society, basing his models on organic analogies. The former, he suggested, is characterised by 'mechanical solidarity', in which there is a low division of labour, a segmentary structure and strong collective consciousness. In contrast, modern societies exhibit 'organic solidarity'. This involves a greater interdependence between component parts and a highly specialised division of labour: production involves many different tasks, performed by different people; social structure is differentiated, and there is a high level of individual consciousness.

Although their work was quite different from Durkheim's, Marx and Engels also acknowledged a debt to Darwin (Giddens, 1971: 66). Marx argued that societies were transformed through changes in the mode of production. This was assumed to evolve in a series of stages, or modes of production, which Marx believed all societies would eventually pass through. Nineteenth-century Britain, for example, had already experienced the transformation from a feudal to a capitalist mode of production. When capitalism was sufficiently developed, Marx argued, the system would break down and the next stage – of socialism – would be reached. We shall discuss below the influence of Marxism on theories of development.

Closely associated with the history of capitalism is of course that of colonialism. Particularly over later colonial periods (say, 1850–1950), notions of progress and enlightenment were key to colonial discourses, where the 'natives' were constructed as backward or childlike, and the colonisers as rational agents of progress (Said, 1978: 40). Thus while economic gain was the main motivation for imperial conquest, colonial rule in the nineteenth and twentieth centuries also involved attempts to change local society with the introduction of European-style education, Christianity and new political and bureaucratic systems. Notions of moral duty were central to this, often expressed in terms of the relationship between a trustee and a minor (Mair, 1984: 2). While rarely phrased in such racist terms, development discourse in the 1990s often involves similar themes: 'good government', institution building and gender training are just three currently fashionable concerns which promote 'desirable' social and political change. From these dubious beginnings, it is hardly surprising that many people today regard such concepts with suspicion.

By the early twentieth century the relationship between colonial practice, planned change and welfarism became more direct. In 1939 the British government changed its Law of Development of the Colonies to the Law of Development and Welfare of the Colonies, insisting that the colonial power should maintain a minimum level of health, education and nutrition for its subjects. Colonial authorities were now to be responsible for the economic development of a conquered territory, as well as the well-being of its inhabitants (Esteva, 1993: 10).

The post-colonial era: 1949 onwards

Notions of development are clearly linked to the history of capitalism, colonialism and the emergence of particular European epistimologies from the eighteenth century onwards. In the latter part of the twentieth century, however, the term has taken on a range of specific, although often contested, meanings. Escobar argues that it has become a discourse: a particular mode of thinking, and a source of practice designed to instil in 'underdeveloped' countries the desire to strive towards industrial and economic growth (1988; 1995). It has also become professionalised, with a range of concepts, categories and techniques through which the generation and diffusion of particular forms of knowledge are organised, managed and controlled (ibid.). We shall be returning to Escobar's views of development as a form of discourse, and thus of power, later on in this book. For now, let us examine what these more contemporary post-Second World War meanings of development involved.

When President Truman referred in 1949 to his 'bold new programme for making the benefits of our scientific advances and industrial progress available for the improvement and growth of underdeveloped areas' (cited in Esteva, 1993: 6) he was keen to distance his project from old-style imperialism. Instead, this new project was located in terms of economic growth and modernity. During a mission of the newly formed International Bank for Reconstruction and Development (IBRD) to Colombia, for example, integrated strategies to improve and reform the economy were called for, rather than social or political changes.

Defining development as economic growth is still common today. Indeed, after the debt crises of the 1980s and subsequent structural adjustment programmes,[3] economic reform and growth are very much at the top of the 1990s agenda for organisations such as the World Bank. Behind these aims is the assumption that growth involves technological sophistication, urbanisation, high levels of consumption and a range of social and cultural changes. For many governments and experts the route to this state was, and is, industrialisation. As we shall shortly see, this is closely linked to theories of modernisation. Successful development is measured by economic indices such as the Gross National Product (GNP) or per capita income. It is usually assumed that this will automatically lead to positive changes in other indices, such as rates of infant mortality, illiteracy, malnourishment and so on. Even if not everyone benefits directly from growth, the 'trickle down effect' will ensure that the riches of those at the top of the economic scale will eventually benefit the rest of society through increased production and thus employment. In this understanding of development, if people become better fed, better educated, better housed and healthier, this is the indirect result of policies aimed at stimulating higher rates of productivity and consumption, rather than of policies directly tackling the problems of poverty. Development is quantifiable, and reducible to economics.[4]

One major drawback to defining development as economic growth is that in reality the 'trickle-down effect' rarely takes place; growth does not necessarily lead to enhanced standards of living. As societies in the affluent North demonstrate, the increased use of highly sophisticated technology or a fast-growing GNP does not necessarily eradicate poverty, illiteracy or homelessness, although it may well alter the ways these ills are experienced. In contrast, neo-Marxist theory, which was increasingly to dominate academic debates surrounding development in the 1970s, understands capitalism as inherently inegalitarian. Economic growth thus by definition means that some parts of the world, and some social groups, are actively underdeveloped. Viewed in these terms, development is an essentially political process; when we talk of 'underdevelopment' we are referring to unequal global power relations.

Although the modernisation paradigm continued to dominate mainstream thought, this definition of development – as resulting from macro and micro inequality – was increasingly promoted during the 1970s and, within some quarters, throughout the 1980s. It can be linked to what became termed the 'basic needs' movement, which stressed the importance of combating poverty rather than promoting industrialisation and modernisation. Development work, it was argued, should aim first and foremost at satisfying people's basic needs; it should be poverty-focused. For some, this did not involve challenging wider notions of the ultimate importance of economic growth, but instead involved an amended agenda in which vulnerable groups such as 'small farmers' or 'women-headed households' were targeted for aid.[5] Many of these projects were strongly welfare-orientated and did not challenge existing political structures (Mosley, 1987: 29–31).

In the 1990s, the desirability of technological progress is being further questioned. Environmental destruction is an increasingly pressing issue. Cases where technological change has been matched by growing inequality and the breakdown of traditional networks of support are now so well documented as to be standard reading on most undergraduate courses on development. It is becoming clear that mechanisation and industrialisation are mixed blessings, to say the least. Combined with this, the optimism of the 1960s and early 1970s, when many newly independent states were striving for rapid economic growth, was replaced by increasing pessimism during the 1980s. Faced by debt, the inequality of international trading relations and in many cases political insecurity, many governments, particularly those in Africa and Latin America, have been forced to accept the rigorous structural adjustment programmes insisted upon by the World Bank and International Monetary Fund (IMF).

Development in the post-war period has of course involved the construction not only of particular ideas, but also of a set of specific practices and institutions. Before turning to the various theories which have been offered since 1949 to explain development and underdevelopment, let us therefore briefly turn to what is often referred to as 'the aid industry'.

The 'aid industry'

As we have already indicated, aid from the North to the South was without doubt a continuation of colonial relations, rather than a radical break from them (Mosley, 1987: 21). Donors today tend to give most aid to countries which they previously colonised: British aid is concentrated mostly upon South Asia and Africa, while the Dutch are heavily involved in South East Asia, for example. Although planning is a basic human activity, the roots of planned development were planted during colonial times, through the establishment of bodies such as the Empire Marketing Board in 1926 and the setting up of Development Boards in colonies such as Uganda (Robertson, 1984: 16). The concept of aid transfers being made for the sake of development first appeared in the 1930s, however. Notions of mutual benefit, still prevalent today, were key, for the aim was primarily to stimulate markets in the colonies, thus boosting the economy at home (Mosley, 1987: 21).

Despite these initial beginnings, the real start of the main processes of aid transfer is usually taken to be the end of the Second World War, when the major multilateral agencies were established. The IMF and the International Bank for Reconstruction and Development (later to become the World Bank) were set up during the Bretton Woods Conference in 1944, while the Food and Agricultural

Organisation (FAO) was created as a branch of the United Nations in 1945. In contrast to what became known as 'bilateral aid', which was a transfer from one government to another, 'multilateral aid' came to involve a number of different donors acting in combination, none of whom (supposedly) directly controls policy. However, from the outset donors such as the World Bank were heavily influenced by the US and tended to encourage centralised, democratic governments with a strong bias towards the free market (Robertson, 1984: 23). Meanwhile, various bilateral agencies were also established by the wealthier nations. These are the governmental organisations, such as the United States Agency for International Development (USAID; set up in 1961) or the British Overseas Development Administration (the ODA; established as the Overseas Development Ministry in 1964), both of which are involved in project and programme aid with partner countries. Figure 1.1 shows the inter-relationships and resource flows between these different actors.

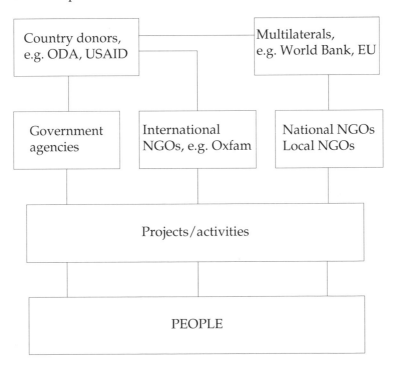

Figure 1.1: Resource flows and potential partnership links between different types of development agencies

Considerable amounts of aid were initially directed at areas in Europe which were devastated after the Second World War. By the early 1950s the Cold War made aid politically attractive for governments anxious to stem the flow of communism in the South. During this period the World Bank changed its focus from reconstruction to development. By the late 1960s, after many previously French and British colonies had gained independence, aid programmes expanded rapidly. Indeed, rich donor countries actually began to come into competition with each other in their efforts to provide assistance to poor countries, a clear sign of the economic and political benefits which accompanied aid. Keen to improve their product, many now stressed development, instigating grandiose and prestigious schemes. The 1960s also saw the first UN Decade for Development, with a stated aim of 5 per cent growth rates, and 0.7 per cent of donor countries' GNP being given in aid. Today few countries give this much: in 1984–5 the US gave 0.24 per cent, the UK 0.34 per cent, and Norway 1.04 per cent (Cassen et al., 1986: 8).

Since the earliest days of the aid industry, there have been significant shifts in those countries giving and receiving the most aid. Increasingly, for example, sub-Saharan Africa is receiving the largest proportion of aid, whereas earlier India was the largest recipient. Likewise, some countries have been so successful that they are now becoming influential donors: Japan and Saudi Arabia are examples. In the 1990s, new countries have also entered the aid arena, especially those which were previously considered to be communist, such as China and Vietnam.

While the individual players may have changed, aid continues to play a major role in the economies of many countries of the South, accounting for one third of all capital in-flows to the Third World in 1980–83 and worth approximately US$35 billion (Mosley, 1987). In 1988 the 18 Northern nations who belong to the Development Assistance Committee of the Organisation for Economic Co-operation and Development (OECD) gave US$48.1 billion (Madeley, 1991: 1). One quarter of this is multilateral aid; the rest is direct, government-to-government assistance.

Whether or not aid is a form of 'neo-imperialism' has been a moot point in development studies. Some writers argue that aid is simply another way in which the political and economic power of the North continues to be asserted over the South, developing only the dependency of recipients on their donors (for example, Hayter, 1971; Sobhan, 1989); but others stress that while there are undoubted benefits to donors (political influence perhaps, or the creation of markets for domestically produced products), aid cannot simply be understood as exploitative.[6] Most aid, for example, is aimed at the neediest countries, rather than the biggest potential markets and allies, and many projects and programmes are planned with good intentions and genuine aims to promote desirable change (Mosley, 1987). Indeed, rather than the wholly negative picture presented by polemicists such as Hancock in his attack on the aid industry (1989), some writers have argued that most aid is successful in terms of its own objectives (Cassen et al., 1986). Others maintain a middle line, pointing out the complex reasons why aid projects fail and constructively suggesting how they could help, rather than accusing them all of being neo-imperial façades, and thus all 'bad' (Mosley, 1987; Madeley, 1991).

An interesting twist to these debates is given by Ferguson (1990) in his account of the development regime in Lesotho, part of which we discuss below in Chapter 3. Ferguson argues that, rather than deliberately setting out to perpetuate neo-colonial relationships between the North and South (for example, by bringing peasants into the global market under unfavourable terms of exchange, as some political economists have argued, or by securing markets for goods produced in the donor country), the role of aid projects is actually far more subtle:

Whatever interests may be at work, and whatever they may think they are doing, they can only operate through a complex set of social and cultural structures so deeply embedded and so ill-perceived that the outcome may be only a baroque and unrecognisable tranformation of the original intention. The approach adopted here treats such an outcome as neither an inexplicable mistake, nor the trace of a yet-undiscovered intention, but as a riddle, a problem to be solved, an anthropological puzzle. (Ferguson, 1990: 17)

Ferguson's contribution is therefore to distinguish between the *intentions* of those working in the aid industry and the *effects* of their work. As such it provides a very useful way of moving beyond the simple rhetoric of the 'aid as imperialism' school of thought.

Following on from Ferguson's approach, we do not think it worthwhile to spend too much time considering whether aid is or is not a 'good' thing.[7] Instead, we assume that it exists and shall continue to exist for some time. Rather than simply condemning aid and development work, what we are concerned with is how anthropology might be used to critique, improve and suggest alternatives to it. How this might be done is a central theme of this book. Before exploring these issues further, let us turn to a brief summary of the different theoretical perspectives informing developmental work.

Theories of development

Conventionally, development theory is described in terms of two oppositional paradigms, both of which involve a range of different measures. These have been discussed in detail elsewhere.[8] Like most 'grand theories', neither has stood up well to the onslaught of 1990s post-modernism. Today, there is no single theoretical model which is commonly used to explain development, nor is there any one 'solution' to the problems of underdevelopment. Indeed, contemporary understandings tend to draw from a variety of theoretical sources and suggest a variety of strategies.

Modernisation

What can be labelled 'modernisation theory' is a collection of perspectives which, while at their most intellectually influential in the 1950s and 1960s, continues to dominate development practice today. Many of the technicians and administrators involved in project planning are still essentially modernisers, even if their jargon is more sophisticated than that of their predecessors in the 1960s. Likewise, many development economists today still pin their hopes to the promises of modernisation. As Norman Long puts it, modernisation 'visualises development in terms of a progressive movement towards technologically more complex and integrated forms of "modern" society' (Long and Long, 1992: 18).

Industrialisation, the transition from subsistence agriculture to cash-cropping, and urbanisation are all keys to this process. Modernisation is essentially evolutionary; countries are envisaged as being at different stages of a linear path which leads ultimately to an industrialised, urban and ordered society. Much emphasis is put upon rationality, in both its economic and moral senses. While modern, developed societies are seen as secular, universalistic and profit-motivated, undeveloped societies are understood as steeped in tradition, particularistic and unmotivated to profit, a view exemplified by G. Foster's work on the 'peasant's image of the limited good' (1962).

As we have already seen, these ideas have roots in nineteenth- and early twentieth-century political economy, much of which sought to theorise the sweeping social and economic changes associated with industrialisation. Durkheim's model of an industrialised 'organic' society, Simmel's thoughts on the money economy and Weber's discussion of the relationship between Protestantism and industrial capitalism are all examples. More recently, the work of economist W.W. Rostow illustrates the concept of modernisation par excellence. In his works on economic growth (Rostow, 1960a; 1960b), the forms of growth already experienced in the North are taken as a model for the rest of the world. While economies are situated at different stages of development, all are assumed to be moving in the same direction. Traditional society is poor, irrational and rural. The 'take-off' stage requires a leap forward, based on technology and high levels of investment; preconditions for this are the development of infrastructure, manufacturing and effective government. After this societies reach a stage of 'self-sustaining' growth; in its 'mature' stage, technology pervades the whole economy, leading to 'the age of high mass consumption', high productivity and high levels of urbanisation (Robertson, 1984: 25).

Some writers have attached particular social characteristics to the different stages, often with evolutionary overtones. For example, Talcott Parsons has argued that nuclear families are best suited to the highly mobile, industrialised world (Parsons, 1949). Others associate industrial society with (again) rational political systems, realism and the death of ideology (Kerr et al., 1973; cited in Robertson, 1984: 33). Interestingly, early feminist work on the relationship between capitalist growth and gender, while usually critical of development, also sometimes implied that stages in the development process were associated with particular forms of gender relations, most notably to do with changes in the division of labour (for example, Boserup, 1970; Sacks, 1975).

If one believes that life is generally better in the Northern countries than in their poorer neighbours in the South (which in terms of material standards of living cannot easily be denied), modernisation is an inherently optimistic concept, for it assumes that all countries will eventually experience economic growth. This optimism must be understood in the historical context of post-war prosperity and growth in the North, and independence for many Southern colonies in the 1950s and 1960s. The governments of many newly independent countries, like their ex-colonisers, often believed that – with a little help – development would come swiftly, and many launched ambitious five-year plans to this effect (for example, India's First Five-Year Plan in 1951, and Tanzania's First Five-Year Plan in 1964). Truman's speech embodies this initial optimism.

Another reason why modernisation can be described as optimistic is that it presents development as a relatively easy process. Enduring underdevelopment is explained in terms of 'obstacles'. These are internal to the countries concerned, ideologically neutral, and can generally be dealt with pragmatically.

Inadequate infrastructure is a good example. Factors conventionally used to explain this are lack of capital, weak or corrupt management and lack of local expertise (both of which might cause roads and bridges not to get built, or to be badly maintained) and, perhaps, difficult environmental conditions (mountainous terrain, continuous flooding). The solutions to these problems are straight-forward: roads and bridges can be built with external capital and expertise in the form of aid donated by the developed North; local technicians and bureaucrats can be trained, and 'good government' supported (an explicit policy of the British Overseas Development Administration since the late 1980s). Another strategy to improve infrastructure might be the introduction of information technology to local institutions, or the training of personnel to use new technology. In both scenarios, various changes are understood as necessary for a country or region to 'take-off'. With more efficient infrastructure, economic growth is encouraged and, it is hoped barring other obstacles, the country will move on to the next stage. Development agencies and practitioners are thus cast in the role of trouble-shooters, creating a range of policies aimed at 'improve-ment' (Long, 1977).

By the late 1960s it was becoming obvious that despite attempts to remove obstacles to development, often involving considerable foreign capital investment, economic growth rates in developing countries were disappointing; in some cases there were even signs that poverty was increasing. The failure of several large-scale devel-opment projects, which should have prompted 'take-off', increasingly indicated that simplistic notions of modernisation were inadequate. One now notorious case is the Groundnut Scheme of southern Tanzania.[9] This latter project received £20 million in 1946–52 (the total British aid budget in 1946–56 was £120 million) and had a return of zero (Mosley, 1987: 22). Unquestioning faith in the desirability of cash crops on behalf of planners, together with inadequate research into local farmers' needs and into the appropri-ateness of different crops to the local environment, was central to the scheme's failure.

Modernisation, as both a theory and a set of strategies, is open to criticism on virtually every front. Its assumption that all change inevitably follows the Western model is both breathtakingly ethno-centric and empirically incorrect, a fact which anthropologists should have little difficulty in spotting. Indeed, anthropological research has continually shown that economic development comes in many shapes and forms; we cannot generalise about transitions from one 'type' of society to another. Religious revivalism is just one example of this, and has been interpreted as a reaction to modernity (see, for example, Ahmed, 1992). Combined with this, while theories of modernisation assume that local cultures and 'peasant' traditionalism are obstacles to development, what Norman Long calls 'actor-oriented research' (1992) has consistently found that, far from being 'irrational', people in poor countries are open to change if they perceive it to be in their interest. They often know far better than development planners how to strategise to get the best from difficult circumstances, yet modernisation strategies rarely, if ever, pay heed to local knowledge. Indeed, local culture is generally either ignored by planners or treated as a 'constraint'. This is a grave failing, for anthropologists such as Mair (1984) and Hill (1986) have shown in detail how an understanding of local culture is vital for more appropriate development projects. We shall spend much of this book discussing such insights.

Modernisation also ignores the political implications of growth on the micro level. Premissed on the notion of 'trickle down', it assumes that once economic growth has been attained, the whole population will reap the rewards. Again, anthropologists and sociologists have repeatedly shown that life is not so simple. Even in regions of substantial economic growth, poverty levels often remain the same, or even deteriorate further (Mosley, 1987: 155). Evidence from areas which have experienced the so-called Green Revolution illustrates how even when many of the signs of economic development are present, localised poverty and inequality can persist (see Pearse, 1980). Disastrously (for the poorest or for some minorities), modernisation theory does not distinguish between different groups within societies, either because it assumes these to be homogeneous (the 'mass poor') or because it believes that eventually the benefits of growth are enjoyed by all. The communities which are at the receiving end of development plans are, however, composed of a mixture of people, all with different amounts of power, access to resources and interests (Hill, 1986: 16–29). Heterogeneity exists not only between households, but also within them. The marginalisation of women by development projects which treat households as equal and homogeneous units is a case in point (Whitehead, 1981; Rogers, 1980; Ostergaard, 1992).

The most fundamental criticism of theories of modernisation, however, is that they fail to understand the real causes of underdevelopment and poverty. By presenting all countries as being on the same linear path, they completely neglect historical and political factors which have made the playing field very far from level. Europe during the Industrial Revolution and Africa or South Asia in the second half of the twentieth century are not, therefore, comparable. These points have been forcibly made by what is generally referred to as dependency, or neo-Marxist, theory. This school of thought was radically to affect development studies during the 1970s.

Dependency Theory

One of the first groups to explain development in terms of political and historical structures was the Economic Commission of Latin America (ECLA). Established in 1948 by the United Nations, by the 1950s this had become a group of radical scholars whose outlook was deeply influenced by Marxism. The work of the ECLA drew attention to the structure of underdevelopment: unequal relations between the North and South, especially in terms of trade, the protectionism of many Northern economies and the dependency on export markets of many countries within Latin America. These notions of dependency and underdevelopment (as opposed to undevelopment) gained widespread recognition with the work of A.G. Frank (1969).[10]

Drawing from Marxist concepts of capitalism as inherently exploitative, dependency theorists argue that development is an essentially unequalising process: while rich nations get richer, the rest inevitably get poorer. Like most Marxist analysis, their work is primarily historical and tends to focus upon the political structures which shape the world. Rather than being undeveloped, they argue, countries in the South have been underdeveloped by the processes of imperial and post-imperial exploitation. One model which is used to describe this process is that of the centre and periphery (Wallerstein, 1974). This presents the North as the centre, or 'core' of capitalism, and the South as its periphery. Through imperial conquest, it is argued, peripheral economies were integrated into capitalism, but on an inherently unequal basis. Supplying raw materials, which fed manufacturing industries in the core, peripheral regions became dependent upon foreign markets and failed to develop their own manufacturing bases. The infrastructure provided by colonial powers is wholly geared towards export; in many cases an economy might be dependent upon a single product. Dependency is thus

a continuing situation in which the economies of one group of countries are conditioned by the development and expansion of others. A relationship of interdependence between two or more economies or between such economies and the world trading system becomes a dependent relationship when some countries can expand through self-impulsion while others, being in a dependent position, can only expand as a reflection of the expansion of the dominant countries, which may have positive or negative effects on their immediate position. (Dos Santos, 1973)

Closely related to theories of dependency are those presenting the globe as a single interrelated system in which each country is understood in terms of its relationship to the whole. Immanuel Wallerstein's 'world system' (1974) and Worsley's notion of 'one world' (1984) are central to these ideas. It is from this context that notions of 'Third World' and 'First World' have developed; these terms explicitly recognise the way in which the world is divided into different and yet interdependent parts. The Third World, it suggests, is not natural, but created through economic and political processes.

Structures of dependency, the argument goes, are also repeated internally. Just as on an international level the centre exploits the periphery, within peripheral regions metropolitan areas attract the bulk of scarce local resources and services. They are occupied by the local elite, who, through their links with the centre, spend considerable time taking profit out of the country (by investing, for example, in costly education abroad). Like international relations between centre and periphery, they also exploit surrounding rural areas, through unequal exchange, for example in terms of trade between rural farmers and urban markets. Capital accumulation in the periphery is therefore unlikely to occur, both because of processes which suck it into the metropolitan centre, and because of wider international processes which take it outside the country.

Dependency theory therefore understands underdevelopment as embedded within particular political structures. In this view the improvement policies advocated by modernisation theory can never work, for they do not tackle the root causes of the problem. Rather than development projects which ease the short-term miseries of underdevelopment, or support the status quo, dependency theory suggests that the only solution possible is radical, structural change. There are of course examples of this solution being followed. The radical internal restructuring of countries embracing socialism (China and Cuba are key examples) and the subsequent problems faced by them demonstrate that this is a route fraught with difficulty, however. Not only is state socialism often associated with extreme political repression, but by the 1990s, with the breakdown of communism in the Soviet Union and Eastern Europe, the new openness of China to world trade, aid and other manifestations of capitalism, and the economic crisis facing Cuba, its long-term viability appears limited.

The international political backlash against state socialism which gathered force during the 1980s has been matched by similarly forceful revocation of neo-Marxist analysis within academia. The generalisations of Marxist analysis, its inability to deal with empirical variation and its insistence on pushing all human experience into the narrow strictures of a single theory are fundamental problems. Analytically, it appears to be of limited help, for its explanatory framework is too simplistic. It is also attacked from within orthodox Marxism. Bill Warren has argued that dependency theory failed to understand the nature of imperialism and capitalist development in the previously colonised South. Rather than remaining stagnant and perpetually underdeveloped, the ex-colonies are moving forward in a way largely in keeping with Marx's original ideas about the progressive (though destructive and contradictory) force of captalism within his theory of historical materialism (Warren, 1980).

One of the main problems with dependency theory is that it tends to treat peripheral states and populations as passive, being blind to everything but their exploitation. While it is certainly important to analyse the structures which perpetuate underdevelopment, however, we must also recognise the ways in which individuals and societies strategise to maximise opportunities, how they resist structures which subordinate them and, in some cases, how they successfully embrace capitalist development.

Rather than offering solutions to societies in the capitalist world, dependency theory is in danger of creating despondency in its insistence that without radical structural change, underdevelopment is unavoidable. This does not mean that it has not had pervasive and continuing influence on developmental practice. It has contributed to the politicisation of development, which can no longer be presented as neutral. Internationally, this politicisation is expressed by the formation of alliances of Third World countries against the North, such as the Non-Aligned Movement, which since its inception following the Bandung Conference in 1955 has acted as a kind of international pressure group for Third World countries. Out of this emerged the Group of 77 countries (G77) which functions as a counterbalance to the influence of the Northern industrial nations within the UN and its associated agencies (McGrew, 1992).

Notions of dependency have also contributed to, and reflect, the increasing politicisation of 'development' in the South at both grassroots and state levels. As an intellectual movement, its proponents were mostly situated in the South, in particular Latin America. Most fundamentally, neo-Marxist analysis raises a question largely ignored by theories of modernisation, but of crucial importance: who gets what from development? By focusing upon the ways in which profit for some is connected to loss for others, neo-Marxist analysis remains an important contribution to the understanding of development, even if as an analytical tool it is sometimes a little blunt.

While modernisation and dependency theory are politically polar opposites (one liberal and the other radical), they have a surprising amount in common. Both are essentially evolutionary, assuming that countries progress in a linear fashion and that it is capitalism which propels them from one stage to the next. Both assume that change comes 'top-down' from the state; they ignore the ways in which people negotiate these changes and, indeed, initiate their own. Both are fundamentally deterministic and are based upon the same fundamental rationalist epistimology (Hobart, 1993: 5; Long and Long, 1992: 20). Most crucially for those at the receiving end of underdevelopment, neither offers a realistic solution. Modernisation's improvement policies, which wrongly assume 'trickle down' from profit-making elites to the rest, often do little to help the poorest and most vulnerable. Meanwhile the radical change suggested by dependency theory is often impossible to achieve.

In the mid-1990s, we can discern the influence of both modernisation and dependency theory in current practice and thinking. Notions of modernisation survive in much contemporary developmental thought. As we have already mentioned, agencies such as the World Bank remain committed first and foremost to promoting economic growth. Meanwhile statements such as the following, from a Food and Agriculture Organisation report on the sociocultural aspects of a multimillion dollar aquaculture project, are still surprisingly common:

It may be that attempting to inculcate 'modern' values and practices may be easier with villagers who are already more 'modernised' ... However, this principle, if carried too far, could lead to concentration of effort on the 'best prospects' and neglect of those with manifestly better need of assistance. (FAO, 1987)

The only thing which differentiates this from earlier statements of modernisation is the rather self-conscious use of inverted commas.

Dependency theory also continues to influence thought and practice. It can be located, for example, alongside notions of empowerment which reject aid as a form of neo-imperialism and argue that postive change can only come from within Southern societies. Paolo Friere's work on functional education, which has had a huge influence on some areas of developmental practice, in particular upon non-governmental organisations (NGOs), is an example of the practical application of neo-Marxist theory; first and foremost, he suggests, people need to develop political consciousness, and the route to this is through pedagogic techniques of empowerment (Friere, 1968). Debates on gender and development have also increasingly involved awareness of the structural influences of global inequality and colonialism on gender relations, and of the need for women in the South to empower themselves rather than be recipients of Northern benevolence (Sen and Grown, 1987).

The demise of development theory

Despite these lingering influences, it was increasingly argued during the 1980s that the age of the 'grand narrative'[11] was largely over. By the 1990s, neither modernisation nor dependency theory have survived intact as a viable paradigm for understanding change and transformation, or processes of poverty and inequality. There are various interconnected reasons for this. We have already suggested that neither theory can realistically explain the problems of global inequality and poverty. The strategies they offer for redressing such problems are also flawed. But there are wider factors operating too.

Politically, as since the late 1980s the old polarities of the Cold War have become obsolete, there is much talk of a 'New Global Order'. Although this concept is contested,[12] the global and polarised struggle between the two opposing socioeconomic systems of capitalism and communism is clearly at an end. It is no longer so easy to speak of the 'Third World', for the boundaries between the First and the Second have largely collapsed. Within the New Global Order there is also no easy division between states on the periphery and those in the centre; the economic dynamism of Eastern Asia, for example, which is overtaking traditional centres of capitalism in North America and Europe, appears wholly to disprove dependency theory. Combined with this, religious and ethnic revivalism, and the conflict with which both are often associated, have vividly indicated that understanding modernity is not nearly so simple a matter as was once assumed.

The 1990s: the age of post-modernity?

Arguably then, in the 1990s we have entered the age of post-modernism. While this term has various meanings, it is most simply explained as a cultural and intellectual rejection of modernity. Culturally, post-modern tendencies in the North can be traced back to the 1940s and 1950s, wherein the arts have increasingly moved beyond modernism to a broader, more pluralistic range of styles and techniques; eclecticism, parody and multimedia forms are now common. Likewise, the boundaries between 'high' and 'low' culture are increasingly broken down: in some quarters the works of Madonna or television soap operas are considered to be as valid subjects for critical analysis and attention as Shakespeare or classical opera. Intellectually, post-modernism involves the end of the dominance of unitary theories of progress and belief in scientific rationality. Objective 'truth' has been replaced by emphasis on signs, images and the plurality of viewpoints: there is no single, objective account of reality, for everyone experiences things differently. Post-modernism is thus characterised by a multiplicity of voices.

Post-modernism involves both conservative and subversive political tendencies. By insisting upon diversity and cultural relativity, it disregards the possibility of common problems and thus common solutions. So revolutionary movements which advocate blanket remedies for social ills such as state socialism are not on the agenda. In its insistence upon locating particular voices and deconstructing what they say, however, it is inherently subversive. Edward Said's brilliant analysis of *Orientalism* (1978), for example, deconstructs Northern writings on the 'orient' to show how they homogenise and exoticise the 'East' and by doing this function as the ideological backbone of imperialism. Following Foucault, since the late 1970s and 1980s there has been an increasing awareness of the relationship between discourse (fields of knowledge, statements and practice, such as development) and power. From this, all categories which lump peoples or experiences together become politically suspect. One sign of the increasing acceptance of such views is that the 'Third World', 'women' or the 'poor' are more often than not accompanied by inverted commas to show our awareness of the problematic nature of such categories. These arguments have had a radical effect on the authority of 'experts', fundamentally undermining many of the earlier assumptions which came out of the colonial, and post-colonial, North.

The influence of such arguments should not of course be exaggerated. The majority of people working within development are largely unaware of post-modernism and are certainly not interested in problematising the discourses within which they work. We suggest, however, that development theory has reached a profound impasse, and that this is partly a result of post-modern tendencies.

Emphasis on diversity, the primacy of localised experience and the colonial roots of discourses of progress, or the problems of the Third World, have radically undermined any attempt at generalisation. To a degree, this is reflected in practice. Over recent decades there have been many different approaches, which rather than being based upon one single theoretical creed, promising all-encompassing solutions in a single package, attempt to deal with specific problems. It is best to discuss these as strategies rather than theories, for many draw on several theoretical sources. The new trends also relate more directly to practice and policy rather than theory.

In the abandonment of generalised and deterministic theory, there is an increasing tendency to focus upon specific groups and issues ('women', 'the landless'),[13] a more reflexive attitude towards aid and development and a new stress upon 'bottom-up', grassroots initiatives. These perspectives were already emerging in the 1970s, when stress upon 'basic needs', rather than macro level policy aimed at industrialisation, was increasingly fashionable within aid circles. Instead of being radical, these strategies are inherently populist. As part of a general trend which places people more directly on the developmental stage, they are closer to liberal ideologies of individualism, self-reliance and participation than Marxist ones of revolution or socialism. Other trends include human development,[14] the use of cost-benefit analysis and the concept of 'good government', or institution building. We shall return to some of these new directions in Chapter 5. For now, we need only note that they do not comprise a body of homogeneous thought and practice. Indeed, we suggest that development, both as theory and as practice, is increasingly polarised. While multilateral agencies such as the World Bank or United Nations agencies embrace neo-liberal agendas of structural adjustment, free trade and 'human development', others stress empowerment and the primacy of indigenous social movements. As the notion of development loses credibility, development practice is becoming increasingly eclectic. This can be both confusing and directionless, and liberating: a source of potential creativity.

Post-modernism and anthropology

Just as post-modernist approaches have problematised concepts and theories of development, they are also associated with a crisis in anthropology (Grimshaw and Hart, 1993). While the degree of this is contested, there can be little doubt that since the mid-1980s many conventional tenets of the discipline have been rigorously queried, both within and outside the professional establishment. To a degree, anthropology has always had some post-modern tendencies. Cultural relativism, one of the discipline's central tenets, insists upon recognising the inner logic of different societies. The world is thus presented as culturally diverse and composed of many different realities. What anthropologists have not tended to question till recently, however, is the status of the knowledge that they gather. Ahistorical generalisations, based upon the observations of the 'objective' anthropologist, have been made in many 'classic' ethnographies which disguise heterogeneity within local culture. Theoretical frameworks such as functionalism and structuralism (which continued to influence some branches of anthropology up until the late 1970s)[15] tend to reduce societies to a series of commonalities, whether these be the notion of interdependent institutions which function to maintain the workings of the overall social system, as in functionalism, or the idea of common binary oppositions which underlie all social forms and to which all cultures can be reduced, as in structuralism.

In many ways then, anthropology's claim to represent and understand the diverse societies of the world is an easy target for post-modern critiques. One area in which it has been attacked is the claim of so-called objective generalisation, or what Jonathan Spencer calls 'ethnographic naturalism' (1989: 153–4). This confers authority on the anthropologist by suppressing the historical specificity of the ethnographic experience. Given post-modern emphasis on local and diverse voices, the intellectual authority of the anthropologist who is supposedly providing an 'objective' account of exotic peoples is easily criticised.

Unease about the quasi-scientific paradigms of anthropology, and textual conventions which construct anthropologist-authors as experts, was expressed by a series of publications over the 1980s, such as Clifford and Marcus's *Writing Culture* (1986), Marcus and Fischer's *Anthropology as Cultural Critique* (1986) and Clifford's *The Predicament of Culture* (1988). Writing conventions are not, however, the only problem. Growing reflexivity about the colonial heritage of anthropology[16] and its contribution to imperialist discourses about the Southern 'other' have contributed to increasing introspection concerning the subject's assumptions. Objectification of other peoples, we now realise, is linked to political hierarchy (Grimshaw and Hart, 1993: 8). Anthropological representations are not neutral, but embedded in power relations between North and South. This has led to what in feminist theory has been termed the 'politics of location' (Cornwall and Lindisfarne, 1994: 44–5) – the notion that one has no right to 'speak' for other groups, and the ascribing of legitimacy only to 'authentic' voices.

These arguments have led to various reactions. Some anthropologists have moved away from ethnography and retreated into the analysis and deconstruction of text; others have experimented with different styles of writing. A considerable number have retained their interest in ethnography, but turned their attention to their own societies, or to others in the North. Rabinow (1986: 259) has argued that one solution to the 'crisis of representation' facing anthropology is to 'study up' and research the powerful rather than the powerless. This might involve studying colonial authorities, planners, government – and development agencies too. Connected to this is the call to 'anthropologise the West' (ibid.: 241). Anthropologists, it is suggested, need to turn their attention away from the exotic 'other' and focus instead upon the assumptions of their own societies. While suffering considerable self-doubt and anxiety, since the late 1980s anthropology has therefore moved in various new directions.

Anthropology and post-development: moving on

Arturo Escobar has attacked anthropologists working in development for failing to react to changes taking place within anthropology, for questionable methodological practices and – most damningly – for reproducing discourses of modernisation and development (1991: 677). In a later work he suggests that development makes anthropological encounters with Third World others possible – just as colonialism once did. Rather than challenging it, anthropologists 'overlook the ways in which development operates as an arena of cultural contestation and identity construction' (1995: 15). There are indeed grave problems facing anthropologists engaged with development. If we accept that it functions as a hegemonic discourse, in which the world is represented, ordered and controlled in particular ways, how can those working within it not be ethically compromised?

In the rest of this book we hope to show that while the relationship between development and anthropology is highly problematic, anthropologists should not simply retreat. Discourses are not static but can be changed, both by those working within them (who can help to challenge and unpick central assumptions and practices) and by those working outside (by revealing alternative understandings of the world and alternative processes of change). We shall suggest that these processes are already underway, and have been for some time. While it is undeniably true that anthropologists in development are often compromised, their insights coopted and neutralised by the dominant discourse, their work practices changed and their critical faculties numbed, this need not necessarily be the case.

If both anthropology and development are facing crisis in the 1990s, both too contain the possibilities for positive engagement and change. Anthropology can contribute to more positive forms of developmental thought and practice, both by working *in* development and also by providing a critical account *of* development. As we shall argue, this distinction is often blurred: those that produce critiques of development often influence development practice, even if unintentionally. Meanwhile the study of development is a fertile area for anthropologists wishing to answer Rabinow's call to 'study up'. It is also a way in which we can move beyond the silencing of identity politics to a more politically engaged anthropology. Some feminists have argued that there must be post-modern 'stopping points' rather than endless cultural relativism (Nicholson, 1990: 8), and that one such point is gender. We suggest that another is the politics of poverty.

What, then, do we mean by development? We use the term here to refer to processes of social and economic change which have been precipitated by economic growth, and/or specific policies and plans, whether at the level of the state, donor agencies or indigenous social movements. These can have either positive or negative effects on the people who experience them. Development is a series of events and actions, as well as a particular discourse and ideological construct. We assume that these are inherently problematic; indeed, some aspects of development are actively destructive and disempowering.

Rather than promoting development per se, what we are interested in is challenging the social and political relations of poverty, through generating and applying anthropological insights. We define poverty as a state in which people are denied access to the material, social and emotional necessities of life. While there are 'basic needs' (water, sufficient calorific intake for survival and shelter), many of these necessities are culturally determined. Poverty is first and foremost a social relationship, the result of inequality, marginalisation and disempowerment. It occurs in the North as well as the South (although much of our attention in this book will be confined to the South). We suggest that while we need to move beyond the language and assumptions of development, the application of anthropology in attempting to construct a better world is as vital as ever in the post-modern, and post-development, era. Before discussing how this might be done, let us turn to the history of applied anthropology.

2 APPLYING ANTHROPOLOGY – AN HISTORICAL BACKGROUND

Since the earliest days of British, French and US anthropology, some anthropologists have been interested in using their knowledge for practical purposes. This branch of the discipline became known as 'applied anthropology'. From the 1930s onwards, many academic anthropologists collaborated – formally or informally – with professionals engaged in public administration, social work and agriculture. Others sought careers outside academia in sectors where their skills could be utilised on a longer-term basis, working in fields as diverse as industry, agriculture, conservation and defence.

One of the main areas in which these 'applied' anthropologists have long been active is that of development.[1] Some of the earliest applied work was carried out for the British colonial administrations in Africa, where anthropologists undertook research into areas of specific interest to administrators, provided information or advice to officials (either on request or of a less specific, unsolicited kind) or participated in the training of government servants. In the US, opportunities for applied anthropology originated through the Bureau of Indian Affairs, which became a sponsoring body for research into local customs, political institutions and landholding patterns and rights.

The concerns of applied anthropologists grew more wide-ranging as opportunities were taken up for work in areas as diverse as inner-city community health-care, company management within private industry and involvement in US government counter-insurgency activities. Anthropology was seen at this time as a tool which gave administrators or business people an ability to understand, and therefore to some extent control, the behaviour of the people with whom they were dealing, whether they were 'natives', employees or consumers in the market place. The gradual professionalisation and institutionalisation of development after the Second World War led to the creation of formal opportunities for applied anthropologists to work in development agencies or as private development consultants.

This chapter begins with a brief history of applied anthropology before moving on to a discussion of the different roles in which applied anthropologists have worked in development. We conclude by considering the various ways in which anthropologists have been deployed within development (as consultants, advisors and researchers) and we suggest the direction that applied anthropology might take in the future.

Anthropologists, social change and cultural relativism

Early anthropologists were engaged in debating two major sets of theoretical issues which bore directly on the practical application of anthropological knowledge. The first of these was the notion of change itself. Within anthropology, social change was initially debated between diffusionists (such as the German Kulturkreise school, which included Fritz Graebner and Martin Gusinde), who saw change as gradually spreading across cultures from a common point, and evolutionists (including Lewis H. Morgan and Herbert Spencer), whose ideas rested on the assumption that all societies, if left alone, would evolve through broadly similar stages. In time the diffusionist arguments, which recognised that cultures interact with each other and are thereby altered, gradually replaced those of the evolutionists. With the growth of functionalism, anthropology began to concern itself more with the means through which societies maintained themselves than with the ways in which they changed.[2]

During the 1930s, the functionalist perspective of modern British social anthropology, personified by the work of A.R. Radcliffe-Brown and Bronislaw Malinowski, emphasised the relationships between different elements of a society and the ways in which it reproduced and maintained itself. The functionalists paid very little attention to how communities changed over time. The tendency to study societies as if they were static remained strong in the period up to the Second World War, but was challenged by anthropologists interested in what was termed 'culture contact' in the colonial territories. Gradually anthropological work began to take account of the historical context of communities and explanations of social and political change, in contrast to influential but ahistorical ethnographic monographs such as Evans-Pritchard's *The Nuer* and

Malinowski's *Argonauts of the Western Pacific*. Although this seems obvious from the vantage point of the 1990s, Beattie's observation has not always been reflected in the work of functionalist anthropologists:

Change is taking place in all human societies all the time. Sometimes it is sudden and catastrophic, as when a system of government is destroyed by revolution and replaced by a different one; sometimes it is gradual and hardly perceptible, so that even the members of the society themselves scarcely notice it. (1964: 241)

Increasingly, change came to be seen as inseparable from society itself, and the realisation and acceptance of this by anthropologists underpin a continuing relationship between anthropology and development. Nevertheless, it remains the case even today that anthropology retains a residual reluctance to involve itself with certain aspects of change. An interesting example of this trait (and one which we discuss later, in Chapter 5) is anthropology's lateness in contributing to recent debates in the social sciences about what have been termed the 'new social movements' and particularly to questions about people's political and cultural struggles in pursuit of social and economic goals (Escobar, 1992: 397).

A second obstacle which stood in the way of developing an applied anthropology was the issue of cultural relativism, which was stronger in the US than in Britain. Relativism raised the problem of the ethics of intervention by anthropologists in the communities in which they worked, a dilemma which has never been satisfactorily resolved and which continues as a topic for discussion today. The ethical choice of making practical use of anthropology became a complex one for many anthropologists. If a culture was to be understood on its own terms, as Ruth Benedict's influential 1934 book, *Patterns of Culture*, had convincingly argued, what business did members of one culture have telling those of another what to do? Eric Wolf has pointed out that: 'Applied anthropology, by definition, represents a reaction against cultural relativism, since it does not regard the culture that is applying anthropology as the equal of the culture to which anthropology is to be applied' (1964: 24).

The implications of this debate are still being felt among many anthropologists in academic departments around the world: between those who favour a more open-ended theoretical development of the discipline through prolonged fieldwork, and those who, crudely speaking, might see anthropology as a tool for social engineering or, as we ourselves might prefer to put it, are trying to help raise living standards – not only in material terms, but with regard to legal rights, freedom of expression, quality of life – for the poorer sections of the world's population.

The origins of applied anthropology in the UK

Colonial administrations created structures and institutions which profoundly influenced the societies, politics and cultures of the 'indigenous' peoples over which they assumed control in Africa and Asia. Many pre-war anthropologists gained opportunities for fieldwork within this framework, and there was a growing interest on both sides in the possibility that anthropology might play a role in assisting the colonial administrations with their work. The notion of an 'applied anthropology', in which anthropological skills could be deployed in order to produce a desired outcome in the encounter between communities and the state, arose from this realisation. The British anthropologist Lane Fox Pitt-Rivers had used the term 'applied anthropology' in 1881 (Howard, 1993: 369) and Sir Richard Temple had been urging the use of anthropology as a 'practical science' in the colonial context since 1914 (Grillo, 1985: 5). One of the best-known early advocates of 'applied anthropology' was Radcliffe-Brown during the 1920s, in the context of discussions under the UK colonial administrations concerning social change and contact between cultures.

The question of a practical role for anthropology provoked considerable controversy among anthropologists, activists and officials. Some colonial administrators saw anthropologists as other-worldly, non-practical types with little of value to contribute to the day-to-day administrative problems of the territories. The anthropologists, particularly those with liberal or anti-imperialist views, tended to view local, non-Western culture as something to be preserved, almost at all costs, against the ravages of colonialism. There was considerable scope for disagreement and misunderstanding on all sides. But despite these hurdles, there were anthropologists (some of whom were very influential) who decided that anthropology *did* have some practical value and could therefore be applied within an administrative context. For example, Radcliffe-Brown began courses in 'applied anthropology' after his appointment as Professor of Social Anthropology at the University of Cape Town in the early 1920s and set up a School of African Studies based on the study of anthropology. One of Radcliffe-Brown's main motivations was the reduction of conflict between whites and blacks in South Africa and he emphasised a potential role for anthropology in contributing to better cultural understanding between communities (Kuper, 1983).

From this period onwards, it became possible for a number of anthropologists to find fieldwork opportunities and funding within the British colonial system, usually in the African territories, where they worked on issues such as local land tenure systems and proposed reforms, succession to authority in particular tribes, labour migration and customary law. Similar processes were underway among French anthropologists in their government's colonial territories. Some anthropologists were commissioned to undertake specific research on prescribed areas of government interest, others provided information and suggestions on a regular or haphazard basis and out of a variety of motivations, ranging from critical support for colonial administrations to the attempted subversion of the 'system' from within.

The origins of applied anthropology in the US

In the US, evolutionary ideas about culture were gradually displaced after the First World War by those of the 'cultural anthropologists', whose outlook drew on the relativist ideas of their founder Franz Boas. In contrast to the evolutionists, who saw social change in terms of culture's adaptation to environment, Boas's work among the Eskimos (Inuit) had led him to adopt a view of culture as being completely independent of 'natural' circumstances, and in a sense this opened the way for anthropological intervention in societies. As Bloch (1983: 126–8) has argued, the view of culture held by these anthropologists led to the predominance of a 'cultural relativism', which held that 'it is wrong to evaluate one culture in terms of the values or knowledge of another'. Bloch goes on to point out that the dominance of cultural anthropology in the US in the period up to the 1950s squared with prevailing American political ideas. While recognising the existence of cultural differences, cultural relativism made possible the coexistence of different ethnic groups within one society, at the same time justifying non-interference by the state in people's lives.

US anthropologists did not have the same opportunities for foreign travel as did their counterparts in Britain and France. Although a few (such as Margaret Mead and Robert Redfield) did travel further afield during the 1920s and 1930s, most cultural anthropologists concerned themselves with documenting the ruined cultures of the Native Americans, whose communities provided opportunities for fieldwork 'in their own backyards'

(Wolf, 1964: 13). Much of this work was 'applied' in nature. The 1934 Indian Reorganization Act was passed by the US Congress with the aim of providing the means for the Office of Indian Affairs to gain access to local information in its attempts to reverse resource depletion on Indian lands and increase Indian participation in the management of their own economic affairs. An Applied Anthropology Unit was set up in order to look into the creation of self-governing bodies, settlement patterns on newly acquired lands, education policies, local morale and the use of existing local institutions for bringing about 'economic rehabilitation and social control'. The aim was for research to inform administrative action on these issues under the new Act (H.G. Barnett, 1956: 37).

In the late 1930s the Bureau of Indian Affairs embarked upon a large-scale natural resource survey with the Department of Agriculture in which anthropologists also played a role. The results of this intervention included recommendations which emphasised 'the necessity of taking persistent Indian attitudes into account in planning for their social and economic adjustment to dominant American values' (ibid.).

The American Society for Applied Anthropology was founded in 1941 (far earlier than any comparable body in the UK or France) and published a wide range of articles in its quarterly journal, *Human Organisation*. As well as documenting work with Native Americans, the journal covered issues such as the application of anthropology to industry, mental health, health programmes in general, and social work and social welfare. However, although it is clear that anthropologists in the US had begun to adopt a sense of responsibility towards addressing some of the issues of wider society, as an editorial pointed out some 15 years later, applied work in the early 1940s still tended towards a static perspective, with anthropologists rarely seeking to try to explain social change (*Human Organisation*, 1956: 1–3).

The relationship created between anthropologists and policy-makers in the world of 'Indian affairs' exercised a wider influence on the ideas and the institutions of US anthropology. For example, the term 'acculturation' was coined by US anthropologists to explain how 'groups of individuals having different cultures come into intensive firsthand contact, with subsequent major changes in the original culture patterns of one or both groups' (Haviland, 1975: 366). This idea led anthropologists to examine change in terms of contacts between cultures, which led to such new ideas as 'syncretism', where old features blended with the new, or 'deculturation', where aspects of culture were lost altogether.

Acculturation was a useful concept in that it provided anthropologists with a framework for analysing change, but it also contained certain crucial limitations. In presenting cultural change mainly in terms of the reorganisation of different components across cultures, emergent aspects of culture, as well as the more subtle changes in relationships between different institutions, tended to be given less consideration. The emphasis on firsthand contact also overlooked the tremendous power of the media to influence culture without the need for any direct contact.

When the US entered the Second World War in 1941 all this was set to change. During the war, the government made extensive use of professional anthropologists and as many as 90 per cent of anthropologists may have been involved in war activities (Mead, 1977). Some worked in areas occupied by US forces, such as the Trust Territory of the Pacific Islands, and were charged with facilitating the cooperation of the local population with the authorities in organised activities such as construction work. Training was given to military officers and administrators in anticipation of future roles administering territories taken from the enemy (H.G. Barnett, 1956: 12). Other anthropologists worked at home in centres for the relocation of Japanese Americans. The US war effort was, according to Eric Wolf (1964: 14), 'a lesson in cultural dominance on a scale never seen before', and this was to have a profound effect on US anthropology: a consciousness grew in which society was seen as far more powerful than individuals.

The result was that many anthropologists withdrew from an involvement in wider social issues through their work, retreating towards a more strictly delineated arena of 'academic' ethnographic and theoretical research – a position which we will consider in more detail later in this chapter.

Anthropology, colonialism and asymmetrical power

The utilisation by anthropologists of opportunities for fieldwork within colonial administrations has subsequently been subject to considerable criticism. The best-known critique is by Talal Asad and colleagues (Asad, 1973), who mounted a powerful retrospective attack on the aims and motivations of these anthropologists and indeed upon anthropology itself, based upon what Asad sees as the subject's colonial origins. It was the unequal encounter between Europe and the Third World, it was argued, which gave the West the opportunity to gain access to the types of cultural information upon which anthropology depends. Anthropology itself became part of this act of domination, though Asad recognises that anthropology simultaneously – as part of what he terms 'bourgeois consciousness' – provided ideas and activities which did not reflect the ideology of the colonial admininistration.

While it would be wrong to judge the actions of those anthropologists who worked for colonial administrators by the criteria of another age, it is also naive to assume that anthropology's relationship with colonialism was not itself the subject of considerable debate within the discipline and soul-searching among individual anthropologists. For instance, P.H. Gulliver has subsequently reviewed his work among the Arusha people for the colonial government in what used to be Tanganyika in East Africa during the 1950s (Gulliver, 1985). Gulliver's job had been to identify issues of importance and provide relevant information to the government. While some of his recommendations were rejected or ignored, others, such as the need to make more land available for Arusha settlement to relieve pressure on heavily cultivated existing lands, and the reorganisation of Arusha local government to include an elected tribal council with legislative responsibilities, were accepted. He writes:

it has been generally acknowledged that many of us in social anthropology were critical of colonial regimes, both for what they represented – an arm of Western metropolitan exploitation and paternalism, tinged with racialism – and for their inequities and inefficiencies and the downright oppression by particular regimes in particular conflicts. With such a critical attitude, it nevertheless seemed to me in 1952, when I applied for the appointment in Tanganyika, that colonialism was the going regime and it seemed reasonable and attractive to try and work within it, to contribute towards amelioration and improvement and even, just a little, to hasten its end (ibid.: 45).

Alongside those who are critical of anthropology's role in the colonial era, and those who justify their involvement on the basis of their ability to play a role in improving conditions for colonised peoples, there is a third view which argues that in fact the whole relationship, for better or for worse, has been exaggerated. Kuper (1983) suggests that many colonial administrators were sceptical of anthropologists and hostile in general to scholarship, which was regarded as irrelevant to day-to-day issues of administration.[3] Evans-Pritchard, in an article written in 1946, bemoaned the fact that in the previous 15 years of work in the Sudan he had never once been asked his opinion about anything by the authorities there.

The British academic establishment in its allocation of research funding during the 1940s and 1950s tended to reward scholarship rather than applied or practical research. This simultaneously served to widen the gulf between the anthropologists and colonial administrations (Kuper, 1983: 114–15). Demand from the UK Foreign Office for applied anthropology was weak, and anthropologists themselves did little to counter the views of those who saw them as 'romantic reactionaries' or unworldly, even untrustworthy, eccentrics who all too often 'went native'. Indeed, Kuper points out that: 'anthropologists failed to develop a coherent view of the structure of colonial societies, and so, with their functionalist orientation, they were easily cast into the mould of the stereotype' (ibid.).

Many anthropologists were uninterested in the role which the authorities wanted them to undertake: that of organising people in practical ways to make the task of administration more effective, which as James (1973) points out, would have made anthropology the real 'tool of imperialism'. This was a different type of anthropology from that which most practitioners were prepared to undertake.

Many of these issues continue to be debated within the field of development, with anthropologists worrying about being coopted and compromised and administrators being concerned that anthropologists cannot deliver useful outputs. Gulliver's comments, particularly towards the end of the passage quoted above, also reflect continuing tensions within the discipline between theory and practice and illustrate the dilemma which still haunts many anthropologists considering working in development today.

There have also been long-standing critiques of anthropology's asymmetrical power relations at the micro level, where anthropology has been accused of speaking *about* indigenous peoples but only rarely communicating *with* them (Sponsel, 1992). The data acquired by anthropologists (which depends on their informants' cooperation, hospitality and goodwill) is often hierarchically controlled within professional or commercial institutions, from which it can easily be manipulated, while ethnography tends to be written in languages to which informants may have little or no access. These critiques, as we shall see, have been responded to with varying degrees of success within applied anthropology.

Post-war applied anthropology

Applied anthropology emerged into the post-war era with its reputation somewhat tarnished. Many of the new nationalist leaders in newly independent countries identified anthropologists with the old order.[4] In the US, the dubious activities of many anthropologists during the Second World War undermined the legitimacy of applied work among academic anthropologists. There was therefore a general reaction among social scientists against government and its interventionist foreign policy, though some anthropologists did contribute to counter-insurgency activities (Hoben, 1982). Project Camelot, for example, initiated in 1964, was a US army social science project focusing on issues of social conflict in the US and countries such as Chile (Belshaw, 1976). There were clear links with dubious US foreign policy objectives: Project Camelot caused furious debate in academic circles and was widely discredited. In Britain, anthropology was withdrawing from its remaining colonial links and with these changes lost a major source of applied funding. Furthermore, anthropology's official influence in the post-colonial world faded as the British Foreign Office was reorganised during the 1950s and there were no anthropologists involved when the Overseas Development Ministry was established in 1964 (Grillo, 1985: 16).

Some anthropologists were able to expand their applied roles in the post-war period in the US by taking up positions in official policy circles and by advising on the Truman government's new programme of foreign aid, which, as noted in Chapter 1, effectively launched the concept of development assistance to the South. New agencies and institutions were rapidly established for this purpose. However, the impact of these anthropologists on development theory and practice was not sustained, and the new science of development economics held more sway than anthropology. For those anthropologists who continued to work in applied fields, problems and tensions remained in their relationships with the bureaucrats and the policy-makers. Anthropologists tended to lack status within the administrative hierarchy, especially when compared with engineers and economists. H.G. Barnett (1956: 49) wrote at the time: 'No matter how tactfully it is phrased, the truth is that anthropologists and administrators do not, on the whole, get along well together.'

These difficulties had surfaced particularly in the case of anthropologists working in association with government agencies, where prejudices, preconceptions and doubts on both sides tended to make attempted collaboration a rather marginal endeavour. By the early 1970s, very few anthropologists remained among the members of the International Co-operation Administration (ICA), which was the forerunner of USAID, even though this had once been the country's main employer of anthropologists (Hoben, 1982: 354).

Applied anthropologists did not receive much respect from their more academic colleagues either. Although their status within the discipline as a whole had never been particularly high in either Britain or the US, in some academic departments the pursuit of applied anthropology now came to be considered, in Lucy Mair's (1969: 8) oft-quoted words, as an 'occupation for the half-baked'. A continuing divergence between mainstream academic anthropology and applied anthropology promoted a feeling among many university-based staff that only the second-rate anthropologists carried out applied work, while the 'real' anthropologists worked on loftier, self-determined subject matter.

These changes did not only occur in the development-related areas of applied anthropology. Montgomery and Bennett (1979) describe a general move in the US away from practical anthropological concerns in the fields of domestic food and nutrition studies after the Second World War; areas where Mead and Redfield had made important contributions during the 1940s. Instead there was a 'return voyage to tribal ethnology and theoretical interests' away from applied concerns (Montgomery and Bennett, cited in Rhoades, 1984: 3). At the same time, many new anthropology departments were created after the war and a number of anthropologists took the opportunity in the 1950s and 1960s to enter academia and gain 'respectability'.

In India, the traditional concerns of anthropology with minority or 'tribal' communities (as they are still known locally) led to the institutionalisation of anthropology within the newly independent state. Anthropological texts formed part of the training given to Indian civil servants. Anthropology was seen as having a specialised contribution to make in the task of national social and economic development, and a government Department of Anthropology established in 1948 became a Central Advisory Board for Anthropology in 1958, charged with furthering the economic development of the 'tribal' areas. Nevertheless a distrust of anthropologists' motives continued in some quarters of Indian society, where they were (not without evidence) suspected of being more interested in keeping 'tribal' people 'in a zoo' than in helping to address their real problems (Mathur, 1989: 43). In Africa, another 15 years or so of colonial government had to be endured before anthropology began to find a place within newly independent countries.[5]

In the West at least, few anthropologists had attempted to forge links with professionals in other fields. This isolationist stance stood in stark contrast to their counterparts in economics, whose practitioners were far more prepared to put themselves at the service of wider society. In contrast, anthropology remained largely rooted within the academic establishment, and in the US was based within liberal arts colleges as opposed to science campuses, isolated from the practical concerns of economics, management and agriculture.

Anthropologists in general gained a reputation for being overconcerned with the intellectual independence of their academic agendas and unrealistically inhibited about the dangers of 'selling out'.

This tendency was particularly true in the case of agriculture. While agricultural economists had shown a readiness to place themselves within practical development situations, anthropologists had not, despite the relevance of their concerns. The discipline of agricultural economics benefited from the wider model of a 'client relationship with society' which had been pursued by the economics establishment (Thurow, 1977, cited in Rhoades, 1984: 4). However, some agricultural anthropologists in the US in the 1950s and 1960s did give serious attention to applied issues, but these tended to be individuals who were only occasionally successful in making a significant impact in practical terms. As Rhoades (1984: ix) points out, while Redfield and Warner had written as long ago as 1940 of anthropology's potential problem-solving role in agriculture through its ability to provide insights into the social and environmental aspects of farmers' lives:

> Over the four decades since the article appeared, the paths of anthropologists and agricultural scientists rarely crossed, a most surprising circumstance since anthropologists have dealt more directly and intimately with farming peoples than any other group of social or biological scientists.

Of course, as we shall see in Chapter 3, there were important exceptions. Geertz explored development issues in Indonesia from a contextual, historical perspective and his work was written in a form which was accessible to non-anthropologists. For instance, *Peddlers and Princes* (1963) tells the story of the differing histories of entrepreneurship in two Indonesian towns, which he related, drawing upon Weber's ideas about religion and economics, to historical and cultural factors. *Agricultural Involution*, published by Geertz in the same year, was widely read and cited by agricultural economists and others working on Indonesia, since it engaged with agricultural production issues, ecology and agrarian change. From our vantage point in the 1990s, many of the assumptions contained within these studies now seem tainted with a modernisation perspective on development, such as the reliance on concepts such as 'take-off'. But there can be no doubt that Geertz's work played an important role in continuing to develop links between the concerns of anthropology and development, while producing work which remained at the forefront of wider academic debate.

If anthropologists in the US had by this stage lost their 'political innocence', as Hoben (1982: 356) has pointed out, a number of new doors did open for the revitalisation of applied anthropology. For example, the concept of 'action anthropology' evolved from the work of Sol Tax and his colleagues among Native American communities and attempted to move beyond the confines of both academic and applied anthropology by pursuing a responsibility to the members of a community side by side with the acquisition of knowledge (Polgar, 1979: 409). According to Tax (Blanchard, 1979: 438), the anthropologist undertaking action anthropology has two goals: 'He [sic] wants to help a group of people to solve a problem, and he [sic] wants to learn something in the process.'

As well as allowing for the explicit involvement of the anthropologist in community problem-solving, this approach emphasised the need for the anthropologist to present his or her findings to both the academic and the 'native' community. This was a new idea: whereas the Bureau of American Ethnology had been established as an arm of US Congress to generate information for policy implementation towards indigenous people, no comparable information flow had been provided for those people themselves (Sponsel, 1992).

By the 1960s, anthropologists who were belatedly adopting an anti-colonial stance found theoretical support for a more practical involvement in radical developmental activities through the emergence of 'dependency theory' (see Chapter 1). A number of anthropologists produced work which drew on the ideas of political economy to locate ethnographies within the wider international economic relationships affecting communities under capitalist transformation. Two influential examples of this type of work are Eric Wolf's *Europe and the People without History* (1982), which is discussed in Chapter 3, and Sidney Mintz's *Sweetness and Power* (1985).

Many anthropologists within the US mainstream had become more interested in the effects of economic change on social differentiation within communities, were more open to sampling and quantitative methodologies and had begun to generate bodies of work on issues such as health-care delivery, technology adoption and education, and a number of these joined USAID (Hoben, 1982: 356). Development agencies were at last reflecting long-standing applied anthropological concerns, and more attention was being paid to the social and cultural context of USAID projects.

Anthropologists from the 1970s onwards were therefore able to make some impact on the allocation of development resources to low-income groups, as official policy gradually recognised the limitations of the 'trickle-down' approach; but they cannot be said to have successfully challenged the dominant development paradigm. The tradition of applied anthropology at home was continued by, among others, Cyril Belshaw, whose book *The Sorceror's Apprentice* (1976) advocated closer ties with policy-makers by elaborating a concept of 'social performance' which could evaluate the effectiveness of a social system in delivering goods, services and 'satisfactions' in the eyes of its people.

Despite a loyal commitment to applied anthropology among small numbers of anthropologists throughout the previous decades, it was not until the late 1960s and early 1970s in the UK that larger numbers of anthropologists began engaging once again with policy issues and needs-based research. Activist or socially concerned anthropologists began to reject the confines of a purely academic job and sought to apply anthropological knowledge to the important domestic social issues of the day. For instance, during this period anthropologists became involved with 'race relations' (Grillo, 1985: 2). One of the earliest and most basic insights which anthropologists provided at this time was, according to Beattie (1964: 271), a set of ideas about how recognisable physical differences between different peoples can be manipulated on a symbolic level by those wishing to exploit or perpetuate social, economic and cultural differences.

Some UK anthropologists began once more to turn their attention to development issues in the South, inspired by the new dependency perspectives with their critique of neo-classical economic assumptions and their assault on modernisation theory, which many anthropologists had long regarded as being crudely generalised and ethnocentric (T. Barnett, 1977). Other anthropologists opted to work within mainstream development agencies, as occasional consultants in development projects. Robertson's (1984) work advocated more involvement and responsibility among anthropologists in the administrative issues of planned development, rather than simply working with members of small-scale rural communities. Somewhat later than in the US, the British Overseas Development Administration began to appoint full-time 'social development advisors', many of whom were anthropologists, but it was not until the 1980s that the concerns of 'social development' began to be reflected more strongly in ODA policy and practice (Rew, 1985; Grillo, 1985).

Along with a resurgence in applied anthropology in the UK during this time, and no doubt related to it, was the growing problem of academic unemployment from the early 1980s onwards. Social science research funding in particular and higher education spending in general were cut back severely under the Conservative government of Margaret Thatcher. There were few teaching jobs or research openings for trained anthropologists within the university system and opportunities outside academia for working anthropologists suddenly became a pressing issue within Britain's professional associations. The dangers of academic research agendas becoming determined wholly or in part by the demands of the market place under conditions of reduced public expenditure during the 1980s led to fears about the academic credibility of applied anthropology.[6]

The status distinction between 'academic' and 'applied' work lives on in some UK academic departments; while in Canada, applied work is taught alongside generalist courses in order to try to avoid the dangers of separating the two (Warry, 1992: 155). The American Anthropological Association, the main professional body for anthropologists in the US, lists 'applied anthropology' as a legitimate field of the discipline (this is somewhat less apparent in corresponding UK literature). Applied anthropologists have continued to undertake work and publish on a wide range of important social issues. Recent articles in *Human Organisation* have included studies on the relationship between AIDS knowledge and behavioural change (Vincke et al., 1993), the perceptions of economic realities among drug dealers (Dembo et al., 1993), and the adaptive problems of General Motors personnel and their families during overseas assignments (Briody and Chrisman, 1992). Work in 'radical anthropology' and 'action anthropology' has continued, though outside the mainstream, to explore issues of political action.[7]

As we have already noted in Chapter 1, mainstream anthropology embarked upon a period of re-evaluation during the 1980s, with discussions about representation and textuality, based mainly on the critique set in motion by the work of Clifford and Marcus (1986). This post-modern anthropology concerned itself primarily with the need for a reflexive approach to ethnographic writing. The concept of practice was to some extent relegated to the back burner again, despite its centrality to issues such as anthropology's relationship to development and the growing interest among sociologists and political scientists about the new social movements which were beginning to challenge and change social and political realities at the local level (Escobar, 1992). The realisation that much of applied anthropology had been taking place within what Escobar (1995) calls the 'dominant discourse' began to stimulate discussion about anthropology's potential to challege its hegemony and to draw attention to other, less visible discourses. These themes are returned to in subsequent chapters.

There are signs that the insights of post-modernism could lead applied anthropology towards new approaches in keeping with radical development perspectives. A recent article by Johannsen (1992: 79) suggests the continuation of Tax's tradition of action anthropology in which anthropology provides

an infrastructure for sustained self-reflection by the people being studied, which will ultimately produce a process of self-assessment. It aims at empowering people by providing a context that better enables them to represent themselves, their culture and concerns.

Johannsen advocates steering a new path between trying to solve posed problems (applied anthropology) and representing a cultural system by one's own writing (interpretative anthropology). Both types of approach recognise that the practice of anthropology is essentially an *intervention* of some kind, either intentionally or unintentionally. By accepting this and making it explicit, a post-modern applied anthropology can provide the means by which people within a community represent themselves and identify the nature and solutions of their problems. It remains to be seen how this could work in practice, but these ideas come close to the types of action research being undertaken by some NGOs and other grass-roots organisations. We will be discussing this in more detail in Chapters 4 and 5.

Applied development roles for anthropologists

The preceding sections have dealt briefly with the history of applied anthropology. Now we need to turn to what it is that anthropologists have to offer, and what they actually do. What follows is an exploration of the various types of activities which applied anthropologists have undertaken in the development field.

The traditional methodology of social anthropology is what is known rather vaguely as 'participant observation': that is, the principle of living within a community for a substantial period of time – 'fieldwork', which might be expected to take one or two years – and immersing oneself in the local culture, work, food and language, while remaining as unobtrusive as possible. Many of the earliest anthropologists recorded their observations in a fieldwork diary, taking copious notes on all aspects of life, to be written up later as a monograph or ethnographic text, and without necessarily having a sense of the particular research questions they wished to address until they were well into their period of study or even until after they had returned home.

What resulted from this approach (and many of anthropology's classic texts fall into this category) tended to be highly personalised accounts voiced as objective accounts, with little explicit discussion of research methodology. This, coupled with the convention of changing names of people and places, meant there was very little opportunity for others subsequently to verify the more controversial aspects of anthropological accounts. In one of the more famous examples of anthropological revisionism, elements of Margaret Mead's work in Western Samoa were challenged in a controversial book by Derek Freeman (1983), who alleged that some of Mead's key findings on gender and sex differences were based on misleading information which had been provided by Samoan adolescents who had found it amusing to mislead an anthropologist with stories of fictional sexual exploits. As noted in the previous chapter, this questioning of 'classic' anthropology reached a more serious crisis point during the mid-1980s when post-modern critiques (e.g. Clifford and Marcus, 1986) cast severe doubts upon the authority of the anthropologist and the texts he or she produced.

The blandness of participant observation as a technical methodological term in the 1960s and 1970s was gradually addressed by the growing body of more defined data collection techniques which anthropologists began to use under the general category of participant observation: case study collection, questionnaire surveys, structured and semi-structured interviewing, even computer modelling and the supplementing of qualitative material with quantitative data. Nevertheless, participant observation has retained its centrality to the work of many anthropologists, and anthropologists have in general retained their fondness for qualitative rather than quantitative data.

Applied anthropologists have drawn upon a number of key insights from wider anthropology in order to equip themselves for their work. In terms of research methodologies, the main change is that participant obervation must normally now be undertaken within a tightly circumscribed time-frame, with a set of key questions (provided by the agency commissioning the research) replacing the more open-ended 'blank notebook' approach. Furthermore, the applied anthropologist knows that his or her findings will be appreciated far more if they can be presented concisely and made to include at least an element of quantification.

At a more theoretical level, applied anthropologists have tried to use an awareness of Western bias and ethnocentrism to provide a counterweight to the less culturally sensitive perspectives of planners and technicians. Applied anthropologists have utilised the once-influential distinction between the 'emic' (internal cultural or linguistic cultural categories) and the 'etic' (objective or universal categories) in order to highlight to development people the importance and variety of people's own categories of thought and action.[8] In other words, what people say they are doing may not be the same as what they are actually doing, and what projects set out to do may in practice have very different outcomes.

Anthropology's 'actor-oriented' perspective (Long, 1977; Long and Long, 1992) provides a valuable entry point and a 'way of seeing' which is appropriate to specific development projects, particularly in rural areas or with specific sections of the community. Development projects can themselves be viewed as 'communities'. Combined with this, participant observation, with the direct contact with local people which it involves, might be seen as less 'top-down' than other methods, such as the survey or questionnaire. Finally, applied anthropologists have drawn upon anthropology's holistic approach to social and economic life, which stresses an interrelatedness that is often missed by other practitioners. This was seen as having the potential to make useful links between the micro and the macro perspectives, as well as revealing hidden, complex realities which have a bearing on project-based work.

Equipped with these general insights, anthropologists have set about their applied work in a considerable number of different roles. Firth (1981) has set out a general typology and his list forms a useful starting point for our discussion. Perhaps the most common role is that of mediation by the anthropologist between a community and outsiders and, following from this, the attempt to interpret a culture to outsiders. Anthropologists can sometimes contribute to the formation of public opinion on issues relating to a small-scale community, such as through journalism or participation in other media. A more active level of participation might include helping to provide direct aid during times of crisis for a society being studied. Finally, anthropologists can undertake client-oriented research either as commissioned academics or as professional consultants.

Since applied anthropology, as we have seen, began its life within the arena of public administration, many applied anthropologists have continued to concern themselves with planned development. Lucy Mair's *Anthropology and Development* (1984) provides an overview of the anthropologist's role as intermediary between 'the developers' and 'the developed': in which anthropologists should act as go-betweens between the top-down developers and the voiceless communities. If a development intervention is to achieve its objectives, then the anthropologist has a responsibility to become involved to try to ensure that certain kinds of problems are avoided. Mair recounts hair-raising stories of planners foisting inappropriate projects on hapless rural people, which include resettlement schemes where people are moved without adequate compensation, and new technology resulting in economic benefits being captured by men within the household at the expense of women. But Mair's is essentially an optimistic view of the potential of anthropology to render development more people-centred, and she reassures us that 'if I concentrate on the disasters, it is because they are what anthropological knowledge might help to prevent on later occasions' (1984: 111).

Applied anthropologists and development projects

Anthropologists are also increasingly being employed by development agencies to help with project design, appraisal and evaluation. Since the Second World War the notion of the 'project' has become central to mainstream development activity, whether centred on large-scale infrastructural work such as the building of a dam or bridge, or 'softer' areas such as health or education provision. Projects tend to pass through a series of staged activities, often known as the 'project cycle', and this process is depicted in Figure 2.1.

By the 1960s and 1970s, the World Bank and the United Nations were promoting what they termed 'integrated rural development', in which conventional planning methods were cast aside in favour of a measure of community participation (at least at the level of intention) in setting needs and a more comprehensive approach to tackling problems on a number of sectoral fronts simultaneously – for example, agriculture, health-care provision and education components might be linked in one large project. Many of these projects unfortunately remained conservative in character as large bureaucracies proved themselves incapable (or unwilling) to involve local people in decision-making (Black, 1991).

As Pottier (1993) points out, the idea that economic and social change can be framed within projects is central to the top-down, controlling urge of development activity. When questions are asked within the conceptual framework of a project, it is all too easy to submit to the idea of 'social engineering' and to forget that most 'complications' involve real people in real-life situations around which straightforward decision-making boundaries cannot be drawn.

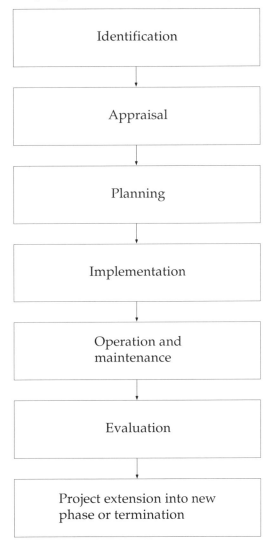

Figure 2.1: The project cycle

But it should not be surprising to find that many applied anthropologists have ventured into the world of development projects in the sincere hope that better results can be achieved. They have been invited to carry out 'impact studies' among the local community to assess whether or not the project's objectives have been met. Sometimes these studies can be combined with academic, longer-term research concerns in familiar cultural contexts, while others are 'one-offs' in less familar areas of the world for the anthropologist. Many anthropologists have formed part of interdisciplinary teams assembled for short periods in order to undertake time-bound consultancies which investigate these sets of issues.

Lucy Mair (1984) fully endorses the interventionist approach and argues that the applied anthropologist is in a position to warn those active in development of the 'likely resistance to be met' with regard to development projects from among the communities for which such projects are designed. He or she is also well placed to try to 'register the discontent' of people bypassed by development processes and to pass this information to those in a position to make improvements. The danger of Mair's position is that it retains a tendency to treat communities as being 'acted upon' in the development process, instead of actively determining the direction and conditions of change through a more bottom-up, participatory involvement. There are other pitfalls: anthropologists can be viewed by donors as the representatives of the local people and asked simply to provide certificates of social acceptability for projects. Another area of difficulty has been the tendency to bring in the anthropologists only when things begin to go wrong, rather than having them involved from the start. As Robertson has put it, anthropologists have often been used only as 'pathologists picking over project corpses', with little involvement in planning (1984: 294).

Applied anthropology and advocacy

These issues have led some anthropologists away from mediation and project-based work towards advocacy. Given contemporary post-modern debates surrounding 'voice', and the legitimacy of the pronouncements of outsiders about 'disadvantaged' groups which were mentioned in the last chapter, this role is not without its problems. Some of the pitfalls of advocacy are exemplified by the work of Oscar Lewis, who in research in a slum in the 1950s in Mexico saw himself as both a 'student and a spokesman' for the poor, who (it was assumed) were unable to speak for themselves. The publication in Spanish of Lewis's book about the 'culture of poverty' in a slum in Mexico (*The Children of Sanchez*) caused a political storm and he was accused by the government of having insulted the culture of the people of Mexico (Belshaw, 1976).

In spite of these problems, advocacy has a long tradition in applied anthropology. During the 1960s, in the field of resettlement issues, Thayer Scudder and others struggled to influence the authorities and agencies involved to take the needs of relocatees more seriously. Scudder was a pioneer of what became known as 'resettlement anthropology', though the advocacy role often adopted by the anthropologist in this context brings with it many risks and responsibilities (De Wet, 1991). Advocacy has now developed into a relatively well-established tradition within anthropology, at least within the US, where activities have included lobbying in state legislatures for increases in welfare rights, fighting to improve conditions in women's prisons and testifying before congressional committees to support child health-care programmes (M. Harris, 1991).

The appearance of what has been termed 'advocacy anthropology' by its practitioners (such as that practised by the Cultural Survival group – see Miller, 1995) has involved itself with the efforts of 'indigenous' people to gain more control over their lives (Escobar, 1992). For example, the right of people to retain their own cultural identities and to maintain access to their local natural resources (particularly land) is being contested in the United States, Canada, Australia, Brazil and many other countries. Anthropologists have played a role in organisations such as Survival International and the International Work Group for Indigenous Affairs (IWGIA). These concerns have also generated a broader form of what has been called 'committed anthropology', which may extend outside the formal academic career environment or the development mainstream in order to bring to public attention cases of genocide and ethnocide, taking action in campaigning about such abuses and making requests for material help for communities under threat (Polgar, 1979: 416). There have also been calls for anthropologists to pay more attention to issues of conflict resolution, which might allow a 'fusion of social commitment and critical insight' (Deshen, 1992: 184).

In the development context, the advocacy role has tended to be more associated with resistance to outside interventions rather than prima facie agenda-building; for example, supporting opposition from local communities to the building of a dam, or the preservation of local culture in the face of change and repression. The new emphasis on the idea of 'participation' within development (which we discuss further in Chapter 5), along with soul-searching within anthropology itself, has meant that anthropologists are now keener to see themselves as facilitating disadvantaged groups within a community in finding their voices, rather than speaking on behalf of them. A shift may be underway which takes the anthropologist away from mediating between people and projects towards facilitating better communication between communities and outsiders. To some extent these advocacy and 'social mobilisation' roles are ones which many NGOs and community groups already fulfil themselves. There has been a tremendous growth in recent years of NGO activities, with advocacy and lobbying an important part of the agenda. The case for anthropologists' involvement here may be weakened in many contexts, and this will be discussed in Chapter 7. Nevertheless, anthropologists are in a good position from which to contribute: helping to facilitate or create situations in which, say, hitherto 'voiceless' low-income farmers can put across their views to policy-makers through their own forms of local organisation, and helping to network information and lobbying policy-makers in the North, are perhaps some of the key roles which remain for the applied anthropologist in the development context.[9]

Conclusion

Various other approaches to development issues have been taken by anthropologists. For example, although anthropologists such as Lucy Mair explicitly reject the dependency school of development theory with its implication that only by revolution, not evolutionary change, can real development take place, more radical anthropologists have sought to develop explicitly just such a 'revolutionary anthropology' (Stavenhagen, 1971).

Rather than standing apart from the subjects of study, some anthropologists have therefore accepted various degrees of involvement with the people among whom they have worked. Sometimes this takes the form of helping out in various ways with local problems (such as providing medical supplies or taking a member of the community for treatment outside the locality), or trying to help the community through providing resources, such as contributing to the building of a new school. Other anthropologists have taken a more active role in community affairs, adopting the view that their research implies wider responsibilities for bringing about change, as debates about empowerment and participation within development have begun to cross-fertilise with the post-modern questioning of conventional anthropological theory and practice.

In subsequent chapters of this book we shall further explore the difficult issues faced by anthropologists working in development in the 1990s. Is anthropology hopelessly compromised by its involvement in mainstream development or can anthropologists offer an effective challenge to the dominant paradigms of development? We will argue that anthropologists can suggest alternative ways of seeing and thus step outside the discourse, both by supporting resistance to development and by working within the discourse to challenge and unpick its assumptions. The anthropological critique of development is often a piecemeal task, resembling a constant chipping away at a giant rock, but the rock is not immovable.

3 THE ANTHROPOLOGY OF DEVELOPMENT

Anthropologists, change and development

While anthropologists have long made practical contributions to planned change and policy, many have also studied development as a field of academic enquiry in itself. Although much of this work has 'applied' uses, its primary objective has been to contribute to wider theoretical debates within anthropology and development studies. In this chapter we shall explore some of this work, and attempt to show how the distinction between what Norman Long calls 'knowledge for understanding' versus 'knowledge for action' is largely false. In other words, the 'anthropology of development' cannot easily be separated from 'development anthropology' (i.e. applied anthropology). As Long points out, such a dichotomy obscures the inextricability of both types of knowledge, thus encouraging practitioners to view everything not written in report form as 'irrelevant' and researchers to ignore the practical implications of their findings (Long and Long, 1992: 3). As we shall see in this and the next chapter, the insights gleaned from knowledge produced primarily for academic purposes can have important effects upon the ways in which development is understood. This in turn can affect practical action and policy.

Rather than necessarily being trapped within the dominant discourses of development, we shall also suggest that the anthropology of development can be used to challenge its key assumptions and representations, both working within it towards constructive change, and providing alternative ways of seeing which question the very foundations of developmental thought. Research which focuses upon local resistance to development activities, or which contradicts static and dualistic notions of traditional and modern domains, are just two examples. As we hope to show too, the relationship between anthropology and development is not necessarily one-way: the study of development has proved to be fertile ground for anthropology, influenced by and feeding into wider debates within the discipline.

Since no society is static, change should be inherent in all anthropological analysis. However, this has not always been the case. While in its earliest phases the discipline was based upon models of evolutionary change, from the 1920s until the 1950s British social anthropology was dominated by the functionalist paradigms of Malinowski and Radcliffe-Brown (Grimshaw and Hart, 1993: 14–29). These presented the 'exotic' peoples studied as isolated and self-sufficient; social institutions were functionally integrated and each contributed in different ways to social reproduction. Rather than continually changing according to wider political or economic circumstances, such societies were therefore presented in ahistorical terms, functionally bound together by the sum of their customs and social institutions.

By the 1960s and early 1970s, structural-functionalism was increasingly superseded by the structuralism of Levi-Strauss.[1] While based on quite different theoretical premises from those of structural-functionalism, this too was largely uninterested in change, seeking out the binary oppositions which, the structuralists argued, underlie all human culture. Although structural-functionalism and structuralism were not the only paradigms in anthropology over these periods, and writers such as Leach challenged the static nature of structural-functionalist accounts,[2] in general history and economic change were not given much consideration by the mainstream. This tendency continues today in the work of some anthropologists. Indeed, cultural units are often portrayed in ethnography as isolates; if the forces of market or state are mentioned, they are presented as autonomous forces, impinging from the outside (Marcus and Fischer, 1986: 77).

In spite of these trends, individual anthropologists have long been studying the effects of economic change, development projects and global capitalism. Within some branches of anthropology, such work has always been closely connected to theory: French Marxist anthropology is just one example.[3] Meanwhile, recognition of the historical embeddedness of ethnography has been growing in recent decades. This is associated with anthropology's recent bout of self-criticism and reflexivity, and with wider critiques of the way in which Western scholarship has presented timeless, ahistorical 'others' (ibid.: 78). Today, understanding cultural and social organisation as dynamic, rather than fixed or determined by 'set' essentials, is central to contemporary anthropology. It is widely appreciated that culture does not exist in a vacuum, but is determined by, and in turn determines, historically specific political and economic contexts.

In this short chapter we cannot begin to discuss the vast range of anthropological work which places change at the centre of the analysis. Even if we only included research which focuses directly on situations where capitalist forms of production, exchange or labour relations have recently been introduced, the potential range of material is huge. It is not our intention to produce a comprehensive survey of such work, nor do we intend to discuss the many non-anthropological studies of development. Instead, in what follows we provide a quick 'taste' of the ways in which anthropologists have tackled economic change and growth, whether this was deliberately planned or more spontaneous. As we shall see, while not all of this work explicitly questions or challenges the dominant development discourse, some of it does so implicitly.

In general, the anthropology of development (and by this we mean planned and unplanned social and economic change) can be loosely arranged around the following themes:

1. The social and cultural effects of economic change.
2. The social and cultural effects of development projects (and why they fail).
3. The internal workings and discourses of the 'aid industry'.

Some work covers all these themes; the first two, in particular, are closely interrelated. Clearly too, the potential applicability of the different analyses varies. Work which addresses the second issue, for example, often aims to affect policy as well as add to academic debate. It is generally sympathetic rather than completely condemnatory of development practice, assuming that the understandings which it provides are crucial tools in the struggle to improve development from within. In this sense it tends to blur the boundaries between academic and applied anthropology. In contrast, anthropologists interested in the last question are usually less interested in aiding development practitioners; while their insights may have policy implications, such work rarely ends with practical recommendations. Instead they hope to problematise the very nature of development. As we shall see, the three themes can also be linked, albeit very loosely, to historical changes within both development and anthropology.

The social and cultural effects of economic change

Although the study of economic change has not always been academically fashionable, individual anthropologists have long been grappling with it. As we saw in the last chapter, the relationship between anthropology, its practical application and questions of change were originally (in British social anthropology at least) entangled with colonial rule, especially in Africa. Malinowski was the first anthropologist to propose a new branch of the subject: 'the anthropology of the changing native' (1929: 36, and cited in Grillo, 1985: 9), sending students such as Lucy Mair to Africa to study social change, rather than more abstract theoretical principles. Even Evans-Pritchard – accused today of having remained silent in his famous ethnographic writings on the Nuer about the frequent aerial bombings of their herds as part of the colonial government's 'pacification' programme in the 1930s during his fieldwork – argued in earlier work that the Nuer were in a state of transition, their clans and lineages broken up by endless wars (discussed by Kuper, 1983: 94). Let us start, then, with some of the early work of British anthropologists working in colonial Africa.

Rural to urban migration and 'detribalisation'

One of the earliest collective efforts to make sense of economic and political change in Africa was embodied by the Rhodes-Livingstone Institute in 1937. While it was originally assumed that the Institute's research would concentrate upon 'traditional' African rural life, the director, Godfrey Wilson, made it clear that he was most interested in urbanisation and its influence on rural life (Hannerz, 1980 : 123). In the books which resulted from Wilson's research in Broken Hill (now Zambia) (Wilson, 1941; 1942), he argued that while Central African society was normally in a state of equilibrium, destabilising changes had been introduced which had led to disequilibrium. These changes were mostly the result of the increasing influence of capitalist production within the region: industrialisation, and growing rural-to-urban migration. As in Zambia's Copperbelt, Broken Hill was dominated by the European mining industry, which largely determined African migration to and settlement within it. Because colonial policy discouraged permanent settlement, most of the male migrants working for the mines moved between their villages and the town. Wilson suggested that destabilisation might be offset if this policy were reversed and proposed that eventually the changes would be incorporated by the social system, leading once more to equilibrium.

Urban migration in Rhodesia, as in other parts of Africa, had a dramatic effect on rural areas. Many villages lost a large proportion of their male labour force, and most migrants could not afford to send back enough remittances to compensate. The work of other anthropologists confirmed this gloomy view of labour migration, linking it with decreasing agricultural output (A. Richards, 1939) and cultural decay (Schapera, 1947). While this perspective was to change in later studies which suggested that rural-to-urban migration in Africa might be a force of modernisation (for a review, see Eades, 1987: 3), other, more contemporary work has taken up similar themes. Colin Murray's analysis of labour migration in Lesotho, for example, shows how rural life has been deeply structured by its dependence on the export of labour to South Africa. Oscillating male migration has generated economic insecurity, marital disharmony and the destruction of traditional kinship relations. In other words, capital accumulated at the urban core takes place at the expense of the rural periphery (Murray, 1981).

While this body of work raises questions about the relationship of societies on the 'periphery' to the global political economy, research based in the Copperbelt towns has greatly contributed to anthropological understanding of ethnicity. The Rhodes-Livingstone Institute, and the continuation of its work under Max Gluckman at the University of Manchester, focused largely upon social and cultural forms within the mining towns. Central to much of this was the issue of 'detribalisation', the argument that once individuals moved to the towns their tribal bonds became less important, being superseded by class or workplace affiliations. Research showed that this was not necessarily the case. Rather, tribal identities and obligations changed, and were used in different ways in the urban setting. Mitchell's seminal analysis of the Kalela Dance (1956), Epstein's *Politics in an Urban African Community* (1958) and Cohen's slightly later analysis of Yoruba traders and the use of ethnicity for political and economic interests (1969) raised questions of identity, ethnic conflict and cultural diversity, which are of central interest to anthropologists today.

Agricultural change: polarisation

While the anthropology of urbanisation in Africa was rooted in pre-war colonial policy, studies of rural change in South and South East Asia were largely influenced by post-colonial states' efforts to modernise in the 1950s and 1960s. Much of this work indicated that the transition to cash-cropping, mechanisation and the growing importance of wage labour had a range of social effects, not least of which was increasing polarisation and the proletarianisation of the rural poor. It seemed that the 'Green Revolution' and other modernisation strategies were unlikely, at least in the forseeable future, to diminish poverty. These critiques contributed to growing scepticism about the 'trickle-down' effects of economic growth, and added to calls for a shift in policy towards 'basic needs' and the targeting of particularly vulnerable groups.

Let us start with Clifford Geertz's account of Indonesian agricultural change, *Agricultural Involution* (1963a). By providing an historical account of Indonesian agriculture, Geertz showed how colonial policies encouraged the development of a partial cash economy in which peasant farmers were forced to pay taxes to support plantation production for export. This, alongside the policies of the post-independence elite, contributed to growing dualism. The majority of farmers formed a labour-intensive sector in which they were unable to accumulate capital and produced mainly for subsistence, while another sector grew capital-intensive and technologically advanced under colonial management. Economic stagnation in Indonesia has therefore been deeply structured not only by history and ecology, but also by social and cultural factors (Geertz, 1963a: 154).

In contrast to Geertz's adventurous multidisciplinary approach, other anthropologists, in a more traditional mode, have focused upon the effects of economic change at the micro level. In South Asia, two of the most famous of these are Bailey's *Caste and the Economic Frontier* (1958) and Scarlett Epstein's *Economic Development and Social Change in South India* (1962). In a later work, *South India: Yesterday, Today and Tomorrow* (1973), Epstein discusses the effects of the introduction of new irrigation techniques and the growing importance of cash-cropping to two villages in south India. In the village of Wangala, where farmers were increasingly producing for and profiting from a local sugar refinery, the changes had not led to major social readjustment. The village continued to have few links with the external economy and the social structure remained largely unaltered, due to both the flexibility of the local political system and the fact that the economy was still wholly based upon agriculture. In contrast, in the second village, Dalena, which had remained a dry land enclave in the midst of an irrigated belt, male farmers were encouraged to move away from their relatively unprofitable agricultural pursuits and participate in other ways in the burgeoning economy which surrounded them. Some became traders, or worked in white-collar jobs in the local town. These multiple economic changes led to the breakdown of the hereditary political, social and ritual obligations, the changing status of local caste groups and the rise of new forms of hierarchy.

The different changes in each community indicate that processes of capitalist transformation are far from homogeneous, even within the same region. Instead, economic and technological changes inter-relate with pre-existing social and cultural forms in a variety of ways, and have diverse consequences. Epstein's work also shows that in both villages social differentiation was increasing. In Wangala, despite the government's abolition of 'untouchability' in 1949, those lowest in the caste hierachy remained in the same position. The gap between the poorest and the richest was, however, growing. Likewise, traditional bonds between employers and labourers were largely intact. In Dalena there had been some com-promises over 'untouchability', but at the same time the security of labourers had diminished; the poorest were becoming increasingly temporary and wholly dependent upon their small wages rather than the traditional patronage of their employers.

A wide literature supports Epstein's view that the modernisation of agriculture (the introduction of new technologies, cash-cropping, wage labour) in South Asia has contributed to growing rural polari-sation. Much of this constitutes a critique of the Green Revolution, correcting initial claims that the 'package' of agricultural innova-tions would cure all hunger. Again, the effects of the innovations depend partly upon pre-existing social relations. Harriss' study of social changes in North Arcot, south India, for example, shows that while farmers are increasingly linked to external markets and government institutions, traditional patron clientage is reinforced (J. Harriss, 1977). Meanwhile, the poorest are worse off, for alongside the new technology has come increasing competition over scarce resources, together in some cases with displacement of labour by the new technology (Farmer, 1977). These effects, added to the non-adoption of many parts of the package, have been noted across the world (Pearse, 1980).

Modernisation is thus not nearly so simple as many theorists during the 1950s and 1960s had assumed. While writers such as Epstein were not engaged in the critical deconstruction of 'develop-ment' which was to emerge several decades later in the work of post-modernist anthropologists, their ethnography vividly demon-strated the flaws in the conventional developmental thinking of the time. They also contributed to wider debates within anthropology;

for example, Bailey and Epstein were just two of many anthropologists working in South Asia on the changing nature of caste and kinship institutions during this period [4]

Capitalism and the 'world system'

As notions of modernisation and the 'trickle-down' effects of economic growth were being increasingly questioned by both anthropological findings and the evident failure of many development policies, other researchers were turning their attention to the relationship of local communities and cultures to the global political economy. This can be linked to the growing dominance during the 1970s of theories of dependency, and especially to Wallerstein's world system theory (Wallerstein, 1974), as well as the use of Marxism in the 1970s and 1980s by some anthropologists (for example, Bloch, 1983). Rather than analysing development in terms of the transformation of otherwise untouched or 'traditional' communities by economic or technological innovations, the emphasis here was more upon the ways in which societies on the 'periphery' had long been integrated into capitalism, and on the cultural expressions of economic and political dependency and/or resistance. Such work places indigenous experiences and expressions of history at the centre of the analysis; colonialism and neo-colonialism are often key to this.[5] It is worth noting that much of this research was carried out in Latin America, where dependency theory originated. Like dependency theory, the questions raised by this approach are less easily translated into national or regional policy. It critiques the basis of development discourse, rather than attempting to work within it.

A classic attempt to fuse neo-Marxist political economy with anthropological perspectives is Eric Wolf's *Europe and the People without History* (1982). This is an ambitious attempt to place the history of the world's peoples within the context of global capitalism, showing how the history of capitalism has tied even the most apparently remote areas and social groups into the system. In it, Wolf argues that concepts such as the mode of production involve social and cultural, as well as technical, aspects. Since he concentrates on the macro-level his analysis of culture is rather limited, however (Marcus and Fisher, 1986: 85). As others have pointed out too, the spread of European capitalism is far from being the only history to be told of the 'people without history' (Asad, 1987). Similar themes are taken up in Worsley's *The Three Worlds: Culture and World Development* (1984), which provides further analysis of the relationship between local cultural expressions and the exploitative workings of global capitalism.

The integration of political economy and history into ethnographic analysis opened important doors in anthropology during the 1980s, contributing to some of the most exciting work to be produced in recent decades. In this, the mediation between structure and experienced practice is central, indicating the diverse ways in which people struggle to construct meaning and act upon the forces which often subjugate and engulf them. Comaroff's *Body of Power, Spirit of Resistance* (1985), an analysis of the interrelationship between history and culture among the Baralong boo Ratshidi, a people on the margins of the South African state, is a classic example of such an approach. David Lan's *Guns and Rain* (1985), an ethnography of rural revolution in Zimbabwe, is another example.

Drawing more directly from neo-Marxist theories of dependency, two important studies by anthropologists working in Latin America indicate both the extent to which groups are linked into global capitalism, and the ways in which this is interpreted and culturally resisted. Michael Taussig's *The Devil and Commodity Fetishism in South America* (1980) is an account of the cultural as well as economic integration of Columbian peasants and of Bolivian tin miners into the money economy and proletarian wage labour. The Columbian peasants who seasonally sell their labour to plantations present the plantation economy and profits made from it as tied to the capitalist system, and thus to the devil. Plantations are conceptualised as quite separate from the peasants' own land; in the former, profit-making requires deals to be made with the devil, whereas in the latter it does not. In the Bolivian tin mines, workers worship Tio (the devil), who Taussig argues is a spiritual embodiment of capitalism and a way of mediating pre-capitalist beliefs with the introduction of wage labour and industrialisation. Similar themes are explored in June Nash's *We Eat the Mines and the Mines Eat Us* (1979). Again drawing on Latin American dependency theory and on Marxist analysis of ideology and class consciousness, Nash explores the cultural and social meanings given to capitalist exploitation at the periphery.

Taussig's and Nash's work concentrates largely upon local ideologies of capitalist integration, without directly questioning models of dependency and global exploitation. Other anthropologists, however, have added to the growing critique of dependency theory and its eventual fall from grace during the 1980s. In Norman Long's research in the Mantaro Valley of central Peru, for example, he found that neo-Marxism only offered limited insights (Long, 1977). Instead, his findings challenged dependency theorists' assumptions that integration into global capitalism could only lead to stagnation on the periphery. In his research he found both growth and diversification in the Mantaro Valley. Indeed, some groups had been highly entrepreneurial, generating considerable small-scale capital accumulation. Local producers had also developed a complex system of economic linkages, which was far from simply determined by the 'centre'. Contrary to the assumptions made by dependency theory, there were no obvious chains of hierarchy linking them to the metropolis, or to the mining corporation. Through anthropological methods (interviews, situational analysis, life history studies, social network methods and so on), Long's research therefore allowed him to indicate the different responses to change of the actors themselves, revealing a far more complex and dynamic situation than structuralist analysis of the macro level could ever allow.

Most important, perhaps, is Long's use of the notion of human agency; the recognition that people actively engage in shaping their own worlds, rather than their actions being wholly pre-ordained by capital or the intervention of the state (Long and Long, 1992: 33). Similar conclusions had been made by researchers working in squatter settlements in Latin America. Prompted in part by the findings of Mangin, a sociologist, and Turner,[6] an architect, various writers argued during the 1960s and 1970s that rather than being 'slums of despair' the settlements were in fact 'slums of hope' (Lloyd, 1979). Invasions of land were carefully planned and people worked together to obtain water, electricity and roads for their settlements, forming committees and gaining a voice through electing local politicians to state and metropolitan bodies. Rather than being passive 'victims' of international and national structures of exploitation, the squatters were active agents, working hard to transform their economic and social standing. Whether or not they were always successful depended to a large degree upon state policies towards squatting. They were not, however, 'marginal'; instead, they were marginalised by wider contexts, even while striving to improve themselves (Perlman, 1976).

While stress on the perspectives of actors, rather than the 'systems' of which they are a part, has always been central to anthropology, such ideas have been widely taken up within development studies in recent decades, partly perhaps both because they point to constructive changes which can be made into policy, and because the 'developmental' message is essentially optimistic: people are not wholly constrained by exploitative superstructures or the 'world system'; they are active agents and, if there is to be intervention, merely need to be 'helped to help themselves' (the motto of the British Overseas Development Administration). During the 1980s growing emphasis was put upon the subjects of development projects as 'actors', adding to ideas about participatory development, the 'farmer first' movement and the importance of 'indigenous knowledge', all of which will be discussed in later chapters. For now, however, let us turn to another major contribution of anthropology to the understanding of social and economic change: the analysis of gender relations.

The gendered effects of economic change

Alongside the first stirrings of feminist anthropology in the early 1970s came the growing recognition that economic development has differing effects on men and women. Increasing interest in the relationship between gender and development was precipitated largely by the publication of Ester Boserup's ground-breaking *Woman's Role in Economic Development* (1970). In this, Boserup pointed out that the sexual division of labour varies throughout the world and that, contrary to Western stereotypes, women often play a central role in economic production. Nowhere is this more true than in Africa, which Boserup contrasts with 'plough economies' where, she asserts, women are secluded and play a diminished role in production (an assumption which in fact is largely unfounded). Women's varied productive roles, she argues, are due to population pressure, land tenure and technology. As economies become more technologically developed, women are increasingly withdrawn from production or forced into the subsistence sector, while men take centre stage in the production of cash crops. These changes are not automatic, but have been influenced by ethnocentric colonial policies which assumed that women were not involved in agricultural production and thus bypassed female farmers in favour of men.

Boserup's work was an important catalyst for an enormous literature on the effects of development on gender relations. Much of this focuses on particular projects and policies, which we shall discuss in the next section of this chapter. Other researchers looked at the wider relationship between capitalist change and gender. This was not a new debate: as early as 1884 Engels had discussed the relationship between the subordination of women and the development of class relations alongside the privatisation of property, in *The Origin of the Family: Private Property and the State*. While lying largely dormant in anthropology up until the 1960s, such concepts were eagerly taken up and reworked by a new generation of feminist anthropologists during the 1970s (for example, Leacock, 1972; Sachs, 1975). While not all academics working on what became known as 'GAD' (gender and development) were anthropologists, much of their work drew heavily on the field of feminist anthropology, which during the 1970s was growing in intellectual credibility and theoretical rigour.[7] Not all of this work was directly concerned with economic 'development'; some feminist anthropology, for example, involved the restudy of the subjects of ethnographic classics from a feminist perspective,[8] while other work focused on women's supposed universal subordination and its cultural expressions.[9]

The capitalist transformation of subsistence economies is generally acknowledged as having a negative effect on women.[10] Change in land tenure, labour migration and a growing market in land and labour have all contributed to the marginalisation of women from processes of change, relegating them to subsistence production. The 'feminisation of subsistence' thesis is explained in two ways (Moore, 1988: 75). First, since women have reproductive as well as productive duties (they must feed, clothe, shelter and emotionally support their families), they are less free to spend time producing cash crops. Thus while men may be able to experiment with new technologies and production for exchange, women must first and foremost produce the subsistence foods on which their households depend. Second, male labour migration leaves women behind to carry the burden of supporting the subsistence sector.

While the 'feminisation of subsistence thesis' is in many ways problematic (for example, in many parts of Asia men still play a dominant role in subsistence agriculture), it raises similar issues to that of research on the Green Revolution: economic change has differential social effects. But rather than these differential effects being experienced *between* households, feminist anthropology indicates that they exist *within* them. Equality cannot be taken for granted at any level of social organisation (Folbre, 1986).

Ann Whitehead's research on the Kusasi in Ghana is an excellent example of these points, demonstrating that we need to deconstruct concepts of both the household and the sexual division of labour, which involves not just different tasks but also different access to resources (Whitehead, 1981). Among the Kusai there are two types of farm, private and household, and men and women have different access to resources, which they do not pool. The main constraint on productivity is access to labour rather than to land. Productivity depends to a large extent on the degree to which social networks – and thus labour – can be mobilised. Men are better able to do this than women: while they can call upon the labour of their wives, women can only use male household labour by paying for it with drink and food. Meanwhile men are often able to commandeer community-wide work parties. As this and other research clearly indicates, projects aimed at increasing productivity thus often have to negotiate complex economic and social relations which are embedded in the local cultural context. Assumptions cannot be made about the nature of households, the distribution of resources within them, or the social relations of production.

The work of feminist anthropologists in analysing the gendered effects of economic change has made a substantial contribution both to development studies and to anthropology. We shall discuss the former in the next section. Within academic anthropology, during the 1970s and 1980s feminists pushed a whole new domain of study onto the anthropological agenda: the cultural, political and economic construction of relations between men and women. This involved radically unpicking various anthropological concepts which had formerly been treated as unproblematic: the household, the 'domestic mode of production' and the division of labour were all deconstructed and reconstituted in far more incisive terms (see, for example, O. Harris, 1981). Feminist anthropology also sounded the final death knell for structural-functionalism: given what it told us about power, resistance and the cultural hegemony of patriarchy, the notion that societies are functionally integrated and in equilibrium was clearly no longer credible. The pressure from feminist anthropology to deconstruct androcentric categories and assumptions can also be seen as the precursor to the increasingly reflexive nature of anthroplogy in the 1980s and into the 1990s.

The social and cultural effects of development projects (and why they fail)

Clearly, many of the texts discussed above have been concerned with the issue of social and cultural impacts. Here, however, we shall consider work which focuses specifically upon development projects. Rather than treating them as external forces which affect the social group or community being studied, this may involve studying the internal workings of the projects themselves, an issue we shall return to in the next section. Much (but not all) of this work is largely sympathetic to the developmental effort (Ferguson, 1990: 9), presenting it as a collective effort to fight poverty, rather than a form of imperialism or dependency. The research agenda thus tends to be dominated by pragmatic assessments of what goes wrong with development projects, and how they could be improved. Within the anthropology of development, this body of work is thus the most easy to apply practically, and texts often end with lists of concrete recommendations. As we shall see, anthropologists tend to call for the same solutions: local participation, awareness of social and cultural complexities, and the use of ethnographic knowledge at the planning stage.

One of the most common criticisms made by anthropologists of development planning is that it is done in a 'top-down' manner: plans are made by distant officials who have little idea what the conditions, capabilities or needs are in the area or community which has been earmarked for developmental interventions. By imposing such plans on people, rather than allowing them to participate in the decision-making process, it is argued, interventions are doomed to failure, for development can only ever be sustainable if it is from the 'grassroots'. Criticisms are thus aimed not at development per se, but at the way in which it is carried out. Changes in policy and practice, it is optimistically assumed, will mean that development projects are increasingly successful in helping the poor.

Robert Chambers's *Rural Development: Putting the Last First* is a seminal statement of this position and draws heavily upon the insights of anthropology (Chambers, 1983). In this and subsequent publications, Chambers attacks the biased preconceptions of development planners, most of whom have only a very shaky understanding of rural life in so-called developing societies (Chambers, 1983; 1993). Their urban bias, the use of misinformed research and statistics, and their neglect of local solutions and knowledge means that development policies and projects can never succeed, for they do not understand the hidden nature of rural poverty. The only solution, Chambers argues, is to 'put the poor first' and, most importantly, enable them to participate in projects of their own design and appraisal.

Tony Barnett's *The Gezira Scheme: An Illusion of Development* is a classic critique of 'top-down' development (T. Barnett, 1977). The Gezira Scheme was a colonial economic development project begun during the 1920s which was intended to introduce intensive irrigated cotton production in Sudan. Despite the apparent well-being of the Gezira peasants, Barnett suggests that the project led to stagnation and dependency. The scheme was huge, involving 12 per cent of the total cultivated area in Sudan and the leasing of government land to over 80,000 tenants. These cultivated cotton for export, and were allowed neither to have more land than they could cultivate, nor to sell it. Barnett argues that the relationship between the cultivators and the Sudan Gezira board was paternalistic and authoritarian, based on British efforts to control 'black' labour. This meant that cultivators had few incentives to be innovative, and Sudan remained largely dependent upon foreign markets for its cotton. In such a context, aid is more to do with 'neo-colonialism' than even attempting to help the poor. To this extent Barnett's work has theoretically more in common with neo-Marxist analyses of the role of aid in reproducing the dependency of the periphery than with the more positive approach of writers such as Chambers.

Most anthropological critiques of development projects criticise planning which is insensitive to the cultural and social complexity of local conditions and thus to the diverse effects of externally induced change. Let us turn to work which examines the effects of this on gender relations within development projects.

As we have seen, anthropological research has had a major impact on understandings of the effect of economic change on gender relations. Not only have feminist anthropologists provided ethnographic accounts of this, they have also developed various analytic tools (the division of labour, production and reproduction, the household) to illuminate why development tends to have such different effects on men and women. Much of this work focuses on the effects of specific development projects. There is a vast literature on this; here, we intend only to give a brief introduction to some of the main issues and texts.

By misunderstanding the sexual division of labour, access to resources in the household and women's double burden of productive and reproductive work, development planning and projects frequently lead to the marginalisation of women. This is because of both pre-existing gender relations (which mean that men are better placed to appropriate new economic opportunities) and the patriarchal assumptions of planners. This process began with colonial adminstrators, who imported ethnocentric notions of 'the place of women', and continues today through the work of Western development planners. In *The Domestication of Women* Barbara Rogers argues that Western development planners make a range of Western, and thus patriarchal, assumptions about gender relations in developing countries (Rogers, 1980). It is often assumed, for example, that farmers are male, that women do not do heavy productive work and that nuclear families are the norm. Through androcentric and biased research, such as the use of national accounting procedures and surveys which assume that men are household heads, women become invisible. Women are thus systematically discriminated against, not least because there is discrimination within the development agencies themselves. Again, this process began with the 'men's club' (ibid.: 48) of colonial administration, but is continued today in organisations such as the FAO and World Bank.

The answer, Rogers argues, is not simply more projects for women, for these often produce a 'new segregation' in which women are simply trained in domestic science or given sewing machines for income generation. Instead, gender awareness must be built into planning procedures, a process which will necessarily involve reform of the development institutions involved. Similar conclusions are made by other, policy-oriented writers, such as Staudt (Staudt, 1990; 1991) and the contributors to Ostergaard's *Gender and Development: A Practical Guide* (Ostergaard, 1992).

While Rogers takes a more general view of the discriminatory effects of planned development, other writers concentrate on particular projects. Dey's account of irrigation projects in the Gambia shows that by assuming that men controlled land, labour and income, the projects failed to increase national rice production and increased women's dependency on men (Dey, 1981). Within the farming system of the Mandinka, crop production is traditionally dominated by collective production for household consumption (*maruo*), but also involves separate cultivation by men and women on land they are allocated by the household head in return for their *maruo* labour (*kamanyango*). Crops from this land are the property of the male or female cultivators. However, under rice irrigation projects sponsored by Taiwan (1966–74), the World Bank (1973–76) and China (1975–79), only men were given *kamanyango* rights to irrigated land; in other irrigated plots designated as *maruo*, men increasingly used women's skilled collective labour, but were able to pay them low wages because of the lack of other income-generating opportunities available to women. Women's traditional economic rights were thus systematically undermined by the projects, a process which had started during the colonial period, when once more the reciprocal rights and duties of farming were undermined by policies which encouraged male farmers to produce cash crops and failed to recognise the central role of female producers. By ignoring the complexities of the farming system and concentrating on male farmers, the projects thus not only disadvantaged women, but lost out on their valuable expertise.

Because gender relations are culturally specific, development projects have different effects according to where they are carried out and the ways in which they are implemented. Data from Asia, for example, shows that whereas farm mechanisation led to declining female labour in rice-farming villages in the Philippines, in Japan female participation has remained relatively high (Ng, 1991: 188). In her case study of the introduction of advanced mechanisation in a rice-growing village in West Malaysia, Ng shows how women's participation in the labour force has declined (Ng, 1991). The Northwest Selangor Integrated Agricultural Development Project, launched in 1978, aimed to increase yields, maximise income and thus alleviate rural poverty by the introduction of Green Revolution-type technologies. While this has indeed led to higher yields, the division of labour by gender has been transformed, significantly reducing women's contribution to farming and thus leading to a reduction in their productive skills. With their displacement from rice production, their domestic role is increasingly important to women, due to the prevailing gender ideology which places priority on women's reproductive work; this is encouraged by both the state and rural patriarchy. Class is an important factor too. While women from rich and middle-income households have increasingly (and apparently happily) retreated to the domestic arena, women from poor households need to work to raise the cash for the new inputs necessary for increased productivity. There are thus two broad trends: patriarchal households among the rich and middle-income households, and female-headed households among the poor.

The analyses of development projects by feminist anthropologists have had important implications for policy-makers.[11] There is not space here for a comprehensive review of the effects of women in development (WID) and gender and development (GAD) on development policy.[12] Suffice it to say that since 1975, with the start of the first UN Development Decade for Women, gender has been increasingly acknowledged as an important issue within development circles. Many agencies now have explicit policies on gender, employing 'experts' to ensure that their projects give sufficient consideration to the interests of women. The World Bank, for example, has a WID unit, while UNIFEM (United Nations Development Fund for Women) has been a United Nations agency since 1985 (Madeley, 1991: 29). Gender training has also taken off since the 1980s, with agencies funding the training of both their own staff and that of local governments and other institutions in recipient countries.[13] Whether or not these efforts have had any real impact on improving the detrimental effects of development on women is, however, debatable. Indeed, some argue that WID policies and training reproduce ethnocentric assumptions about the nature of gender and women's subordination; that they coopt radical feminist critiques into the development discourse, thus neutralising them. We shall return to these issues later.

Closely related to anthropological critiques of 'top-down' planning is the criticism that planners fail to acknowledge adequately the importance, and potential, of local knowledge. Instead, projects often involve the assumption that Western or urban knowledge is superior to the knowledge of the people 'to be developed'; they are regarded as ignorant although, as anthropologists have repeatedly shown, they have their own areas of appropriate expertise. This is tied to the 'farmer first' movement (Chambers et al., 1989). It also raises interesting questions about the interrelationship of different forms of knowledge, which we shall return to in the next section. For now, however, let us consider cases where 'top-down' planning means that not enough is known about the culture or conditions of an area or target group before a project is embarked upon.

Development projects often fail because of the ignorance of planners rather than the ignorance of the beneficiaries. This might involve a range of factors, such as local ecological conditions, the availability of particular resources, physical and climatic conditions and so on. The result is inappropriate intervention, which may end in disaster. (An example is the infamous Groundnut Scheme in Tanzania; see Wood, 1950.) The success of all projects depends upon whether or not they are socially and culturally appropriate, yet it is ironically these factors which tend to be least considered. Much literature therefore focuses upon the need for ethnographic knowledge at the planning stage of project design (for example, Mair, 1984; Hill, 1986; Pottier, 1993). Again, this perspective is ultimately optimistic: with better planning (and the use of ethnography), it is assumed, development projects will succeed in helping the poor.

Mamdani's classic analysis of the failure of the Khanna study, an attempt to introduce birth control to the Indian village of Manupur, is a fascinating account of developmental top-downism and ignorance (Mamdani, 1972). Because of the cultural and economic value of having as many children as possible, Mamdani argues that population programmes are unlikely to have much success in rural India. Programme planners in the Khanna study, however, assumed that villagers' rejection of contraception was due to 'ignorance', thus completely ignoring the social and economic realities of the village. Once again, anthropological methods and questions, rather than bureaucratic planning, reveal the true constraints on 'successful' development. While Mamdani is to be congratulated for powerfully illustrating the cultural and economic influences on family planning uptake, he can also be criticised for assuming that local attitudes to family planning are homogeneous. Other work questions this, indicating that men and women often have very different views and that it is men who usually control eventual fertility decisions. This is an area where feminist researchers clearly have much to contribute (for further discussion, see Kabeer, 1994: 187–222).

Pottier's edited collection, *Practising Development*, takes these issues substantially further. It also clearly reflects changes within developmental practice, wherein notions of participation and 'farmer first' have gained increasing currency in recent years (Pottier, 1993). While all contributions take for granted the need for anthropological insights at the planning stage and show how this is already a common practice for some organisations – for example, the International Fund for Agricultural Development (IFAD) (Seddon, 1993) and Band Aid (Garber and Jenden, 1993) – most examine how social science perspectives can be effectively incorporated into development programmes. This is not simply a matter of becoming literate in the local culture, as if it were composed of essential and accessible elements. A critical perspective here is that 'the social worlds within which development efforts take shape are essentially fluid' (Pottier, 1993: 7). Gatter's Zambian case study, for example, demonstrates how farming practices tend to be systematised by development workers, who thus misunderstand their complexity and fluidity (Gatter, 1993). To avoid such misrepresentations, and make ethnographic knowledge meaningful, there must therefore be a continual collection of ethnographic data. This research need not necessarily be carried out by expatriate consultants but can be done by trained field staff, especially those in NGOs. Crucially, Pottier's collection adopts an approach increasingly emerging in the anthropology of development: that of studying development bureaucracies and institutions in themselves, as well as the discourses which they produce. Let us turn to our third theme.

The internal workings and discourses of the 'aid industry'

Rather than simply viewing development as an external force, which acts upon the 'real' subjects of anthropological enquiry (the 'people'), anthropological accounts of development are increasingly treating its institutions, political processes and ideologies as valid sites of ethnographic enquiry in themselves. While this approach is not solely confined to the late 1980s and 1990s, its increasing dominance reflects contemporary trends in anthropology. Before turning to this, let us start with the anthropology of development planning.

Development anthropologists have been aware of the need to study the internal working of development institutions for some time, although studies of administration are usually focused far more on the recipients of planned change than on the 'developers'. Early work in the applied anthropology tradition such as H.G. Barnett's *Anthropology in Administration* (1956) deals mainly with the practical uses to which anthropological knowledge could be put by administrators, using examples drawn from the author's experience of working in the Trust Territory of the Pacific Islands, and only occasionally turns its gaze upon the system itself. Cochrane's *Development Anthropology* (1971) emphasises the need for administrators, under the guidance of anthropologists, to recognise the cultural issues surrounding development in addition to the more familiar economic and technological aspects in which they are trained. Belshaw's *The Sorceror's Apprentice* (1976) seeks to draw anthropological concerns away from the 'exotic' towards real policy issues in the dominant culture and to counter the tendencies of administrators only to 'know and control'.

More recently, and more ambitiously, Robertson's *People and the State* (1984) attempts to analyse planned development as a political encounter between the people and the state. Development agencies, he argues, are premissed on the need to turn an unreliable citizenry into a structured public; development interventions are thus the site of contest between the people and bureaucracy (1984: 4). Much of the book recounts the history of planning, from post-revolutionary Russia and colonial planning to the economic planning of contemporary Third World states. Robertson also makes a plea for anthropology to become more centrally involved in development. Although historically anthropology has been weak on state theory, he suggests that it can potentially offer an overview of the whole planning process, thus making a vital contribution to wider understandings of development. Like Cochrane, Robertson is interested in the practical uses of anthropology and appears to be optimistic about the potential of planned change. As he concludes: 'anthropology may ultimately prove its worth by helping to explain a confused and lethally divided world to itself, and to indicate humane and realistic prospects for progress' (Robertson, 1984: 306).

Project and planning ethnography is linked to shifting paradigms within development studies. Here too, there is increasing recognition that the realities within which people act and make decisions are multiple and changing. This is closely related to actor-oriented research, in which the world views of individual actors (rather than passive target groups or beneficiaries), and the interfaces between them and bureaucratic institutions, are the focus of study (Long and Long, 1992). Notions of 'farmer first' development, and participation, are influential here. On a slightly different level, recognition of the need to understand (and then change) the workings of bureaucracy (in, for example, recent writings on gender and development: Staudt, 1990; 1991) is also important.

The authors discussed above present planning as a relevant and important area of anthropological research. All share – in different degrees – a practical agenda: to improve the planning process, usually with help from anthropological inputs. In contrast to this, more recent work deconstructs and problematises the very notion of development by analysing it as a form of discourse. This work is not intended to be instrumental for policy-makers, as it critiques the epistemological assumptions within which they work. Instead, it has far-reaching implications for the way in which 'development' is conceptualised, pointing to a radical reappraisal of the ways in which global poverty and inequality are conceptualised and tackled. As we shall see, such work has been strongly influenced by post-modern understanding of culture as negotiated, contested and processual. Social realities in these accounts are multiple, and change according to context. To this extent writers do not search for objective 'truths' about development or its effects, but seek to understand the ways in which it is socially constructed and in turn constructs its subjects. Much of this has been influenced by Foucault's work on discourse, knowledge and power, which we discuss below.

The new foci in the anthropology of development on discourse are linked to the recent debates within anthropology which we discussed in Chapter 1. These question the discipline's portrayal of an ahistorical, exotic 'other' which exists in opposition to the Western self. In contrast, within 'post-modern' anthropology all domains are seen as valid subjects for research; institutions and discourses from the anthropologist's own society become relevant areas of study (Marcus and Fischer, 1986: 111–13); To redress the balance of previous orientalism, it is suggested, anthropologists should deconstruct cultural assumptions of the North as well as the South, or what Rabinow terms 'anthropologising the West' (1986: 241). Such work can also indicate how power is gained, and reproduced, at local, national and global levels. While there are many potential fieldwork sites for this, 'development' is an obvious candidate. This might involve studying aid agencies, the categories, knowledges and culture of development, or conducting fieldwork among expatriate groups.

The study of development institutions and ideologies also contributes to recent debates on 'globalisation'. This refers to the increasingly interconnected nature of the world through international travel, labour migration and technology such as telephones, computer networks and TVs which have spread across the world and created global links. Elements of globalisation, it is suggested, link previously isolated cultures and produce new transnational cultures, which transcend national boundaries (Featherstone, 1990: 6). By researching international agencies, the ideas which they produce and how these are disseminated and made meaningful at different levels, the lives and culture of development consultants, or social movements such as NGOs or environmental pressure groups which cross-cut geographical boundaries, anthropologists are ideally placed to study the processes of 'globalisation' which are supposedly becoming so important as we approach the twenty-first century.

To understand what is meant by 'development discourse', we should start with the work of Foucault, arguably the most important thinker of the late twentieth century. In *The Order of Things* (1970), Foucault focuses upon 'fields' of knowledge, such as economics or natural history, and the conventions according to which they were classified and represented in particular periods. While they are represented as objective and politically neutral, he thus shows how areas of knowledge are socially, historically and politically constructed. Discourses of power, while presented as objective and 'natural', actually construct their subjects in particular ways and exercise power over them. Malinowski's 'scientific ethnography', for example, claimed to generate objective and scientific accounts of native 'others', which presented them in a particular light and so justified their subordination. Knowledge is thus inherently political. As Foucault put it: 'the criteria of what constitutes knowledge, what is to be excluded, and who is qualified to know involves acts of power' (1971; cited in Scoones and Thompson, 1993: 12). Discourses thus subsume practices and structures, with very real effects.

From this, areas of developmental knowledge or expertise can be deconstructed as historically and politically specific constructions of reality, which are more to do with the exercise of power in particular historical contexts than presenting 'objective' realities. The notion of discourse 'gives us the possibility of singling out "development" as an encompassing social space and at the same time of separating ourselves from it by perceiving it in a totally new form' (Escobar, 1995: 6). How such discourses interrelate with other structures, the ways in which they are contested and the interface between developmental and other forms of knowledge are just a few important questions generated by this approach. This is an area where the study of development has a major role to play in wider theoretical debates in anthropology, for development projects provide an opportunity for examining the dynamic interplay of different discourses and forms of knowledge (Worby, 1984).

Arturo Escobar, whom we have already cited several times, is a key figure in the growing trend of deconstructing developmental discourse. In a paper published in 1988, for example, he examines the history of development studies and its production and circulation of certain discourses, seeing these as integral to the exercise of power; what he calls the 'politics of truth' (Escobar, 1988: 431). Development practice, he argues, uses a specific corpus of techniques which organise a type of knowledge and a type of power. The expertise of development specialists transcends the social realities of the 'clients' of development, who are labelled and thus structured in particular ways ('women-headed households'/ 'small farmers,' etc.). Clients are thus controlled by development and can only manoeuvre within the limits set by it. As he puts it in *Encountering Development*, 'Development had achieved the status of a certainty in the social imaginary' (Escobar, 1995: 5).

In *The Anti-Politics Machine* (1990) James Ferguson takes a similar approach by analysing the Thaba-Tseka project in Lesotho. The resulting text demonstrates exciting possibilities for project ethnography. Rather than being concerned with whether development is 'good' or 'bad', or how it could be improved, Ferguson argues that we should analyse the relationship between development projects, social control and the reproduction of relations of inequality. This cannot be simply explained by models of dependency; structures do not directly answer the 'needs' of capitalism, but reproduce themselves through a variety of processes and struggles (ibid.: 13). By analysing the conceptual apparatus of planned development in Lesotho and juxtaposing this with ethnographic material from a project's 'target area', he shows how while development projects usually fail in their explicit objectives, they have another often unrealised function: that of furthering the state's power.

The Anti-Politics Machine opens with the deconstruction of a World Bank report on Lesotho. Ferguson shows how its amazing inaccuracies and mistakes are not the result of bad scholarship, but of the need to present the country in a particular way. Lesotho is frequently referred to in the report as 'traditional' and isolated, with aboriginal agriculture and a stagnant economy. In reality this is far from the truth, for the country has long been economically and politically intertwined with South Africa. In addition, the report only considers Lesotho at a national level. The implications are thus, first, that development interventions will transform and modernise the country; and, second, that change is entirely a function of the action or inaction of the government.

Ferguson argues that discourses are attached to and support particular institutions (ibid.: 68). Only statements which are useful to the development institutions concerned are therefore included in their reports; radical or pessimistic analyses are banished. The discourse is thus dynamically interrelated with development practice, affecting the actual design and implementation of projects. In its definition of all problems as 'technical' the discourse ignores social conditions, a central reason why the project fails. Crucially too, development is presented as politically neutral. Instrumentally, however, the project unintentionally enables the state to further its power over the mountain areas which it targeted. Rather than this being a hidden aim of developmental practice, and the discourse a form of mystification, Ferguson argues that development planning is a small cog in a larger machine; discourse and practice are articulated in this, but they do not determine it. Plans fail, but while their objectives are not met, they still have instrumental effects, for they are part of a larger machinery of power and control.

Considering development as discourse raises important questions about the nature of developmental knowledge and its interface with other representations of reality. Anthropology can have an important role here, first in demonstrating that there are many other ways of knowing (thus undermining development's hegemonic status), and second in showing what happens when different knowledges meet. In another contribution to the growing 'post-modern' anthropology of development, for example, the relationship between scientific and local knowledge within development practice is explored. As the articles in *An Anthropological Critique of Development* (Hobart, 1993) indicate, claims to knowledge and the attribution of ignorance are central themes in development discourse. The scientific and 'rational' knowledge favoured by development constructs foreign 'experts' as agents, and local people as passive and ignorant.

Rather than presenting local knowledge as homogeneous and systematic, these accounts show that it is diverse and fluid. These multiple epistemologies are produced in particular social, political and economic contexts; instead of being bodies of facts, what is important is how, rather than what, things are known. This is a different approach from much of mainstream development discourse, where knowledge is only mentioned as an abstract noun, and those that know are thus stripped of their agency (Hobart, 1993: 21). It is also tied to a growing critique of the 'farmer first' movement, which while providing a necessary corrective to modernisation theory's assumption that traditional beliefs and practice are an obstacle to progress, tends to simplify and essentialise local knowledge, or assume that, like scientific knowledge, it can be understood as a 'system' (Gatter, 1993; Scoones and Thompson, 1993; 1994).

Within these accounts people appear as agents, whose knowledge interacts in a variety of ways with that of development agencies. Richards, for example, shows how rather than being free-standing, indigenous knowledge can be understood as improvised performance. West African cultivators possess performance skills as well as technical and ecological knowledge, mixing their crops in a certain way, providing food and drumming for their labourers, and so forth. This has been missed by most agricultural research and its ensuing 'scientific' expertise, which carries out agricultural experiments in 'set' conditions, ignoring the vital fact that farmers use their creativity and performance skills in cultivation (P. Richards, 1993).

In other words, people do not passively receive knowledge or directions from the outside, but dynamically interact with it. Another example of this is provided by Burghart (1993), who set out to study local knowledge of health and hygiene in a Hindu cobblers' village in Nepal. Although Burghart assumed that there would be a symmetrical exchange of knowlege (his technical knowledge versus their views on hygiene) and that he could construct an objective model of their knowledge, this was not to be the case. Instead, the cobblers refused to accept his role, constructing him instead as a Hindu lord, who was seen as benevolent when the well-cleaning he had initiated went well, and then as malevolent when the water became bitter.

As this body of work indicates, anthropologists need to examine the ways in which people and the discourses which they produce interact according to their different cultural, economic and historical contexts. Research must be actor-oriented, not only through studying those to 'be developed', but in terms of how individual and group agencies cross-cut, reproduce or resist the power relations of state and international development interventions. Through these and similar insights, the anthropology of development opens up and becomes something infinitely more interesting than simply the study of the 'problems' of development.

Conclusion

If development is to be understood as a hegemonic discourse in which Third World peoples are objectified, ordered and controlled, how can anthropological involvement in it be justified? Surely the only ethical response is to vehemently reject it and walk away? While accepting that development is indeed politically highly problematic, we do not believe that non-involvement is the only possible response. Instead, there are various important ways in which anthropologists, the methods they use and the insights they have can help subvert and reorient development, contributing to its eventual demise and transformation into post-development discourse.

Throughout this chapter we have indicated various ways in which this might be done. By analysing the social effects of development, anthropological accounts undermine its central assumptions. Clearly, local societies do not necessarily strive towards scientific 'progress'; they also have multiple responses to global capitalism and economic growth, which have very definitely not had the positive effects which developers assumed. As anthropologists have shown again and again, the world is not divisible into neat categories which can be targeted and acted upon, nor can universalising laws be applied or predictions made; human life is far too complicated and diverse for that. By deconstructing development, its subjective and culturally produced nature is revealed. Development is no more 'true' than any other way of understanding and acting upon the world. It is just that as an organising discourse it is often more powerful.

Anthropologists can therefore critique and undermine development through ethnography and analysis. But this is not all. Rather than accepting that development discourse is unchangeable, we suggest that anthropologists can also help change development discourse from within. Rather than being monolithic and static, development discourse is more fluid and liable to change than many analyses allow. This is acknowledged in part by Escobar, who accepts that the discourse can be modified by the introduction of new objects and variables, but who at the same time insists that ultimately the system of relations which holds its different elements together remains the same (1995: 42). Need this necessarily be the case? In the following chapters we shall suggest that the discourse can be changed: new practices and knowledges can be and are introduced, reorienting some aspects of development away from its earlier positions. The discourse is also far more diverse and contested than many accounts suggest. There are development agencies other than the World Bank,[14] for example, and report writing is often a highly contested business, having as much to do with internal power relations (which, again, are as yet barely touched upon by discourse analysts) as a hegemonic representation of the Third World 'other'.

In the next chapters we shall indicate ways in which the discourse might be challenged from within through the application of anthropological insights by applied anthropologists and development workers alike. As we shall see, anthropologists are increasingly picking away at development agencies, infiltrating their decision-making bodies, lobbying them from the inside and contributing to their reports. The World Bank report analysed by Ferguson (1990) is not necessarily representative; many reports now include sections written by anthropologists which use different images and realities.

As Ferguson implies, however, the extent to which these are allowed to diverge from the institutional line is often limited – an important issue for applied anthropologists, which we shall return to in Chapter 6. There are very real dangers of the dominant discourse coopting anthropological concepts by translating them into simplified and homogenising categories: 'women-headed households', 'indigenous knowledge' and 'community development' are all examples of how important insights have been incorporated into development discourse, made 'policy-friendly' and in some cases distorted. 'Women in development' is another.[15] This is an important insight, which we discuss further later in the book.

Combined with the important task of deconstruction, anthropologists 'in' and 'of' development can therefore also help change the representations that development institutions produce. Development anthropology is at an exciting juncture. While post-modernism has caused a degree of crisis for both development studies and anthropology, we suggest that by combining the two domains, important steps forward can be taken. We are not suggesting that anthropologists should become developers, nor that we should necessarily strive to mould our concepts around the rigid jargon of donors. Instead, anthropological perspectives can be adopted by various actors, including local community organisations and NGOs. They can also help shift discussions away from 'development' and towards a focus upon social relations of poverty and inequality.

4 SUBVERTING THE DISCOURSE – KNOWLEDGE AND PRACTICE

As we suggested in the last chapter, one of the most important functions of the anthropology of development is its ability to deconstruct the assumptions and power relations of development, a task which has been gathering in momentum over the last decade or so. While these debates have been mostly carried out within academic domains, other anthropologists have been working hard with and within developmental institutions to alter policy. Such anthropologists may perform a variety of roles: they may be employed as independent consultants, or as salaried staff; others may be involved with pressure groups which lobby agencies or produce alternative visions of change. Anthropological perspectives and methods which help subvert and transform the dominant discourses of development may also be used by a range of non-specialists.

Such work is not easy. Indeed, Escobar (1991) has argued that anthropological involvement in development is inherently compromising: applied anthropologists 'buy in' to the discourse, reproducing and benefiting from its power relations. The path they tread is indeed fraught with difficulty. Since donors and development agencies work within a particular discourse, anthropological insights may easily become distorted and 'hardened' into policies which are then applied unilaterally to recipient societies. Once again, the world is packaged and controlled in a particular way.[1] Anthropologists may also face dire contradictions, for their premises are in many ways inherently different from those of developers. While anthropologists are trained to be cultural relativists, development agencies are usually committed to universal principles of progress. This often involves ethnocentric assumptions about what constitutes desirable social change. Strategies of 'social development' and 'women in development', for example, all involve changing society in ways which may not be 'culturally appropriate'.

We shall continue to discuss these contradictions throughout this book. This chapter, however, outlines the main ways in which anthropological insights can be applied to planned change and policy in order to change the dominant discourse from within. Rather than being wholly monolithic, static and encompassing, we suggest that development work actually comprises a variety of countervailing perspectives and practices, as well as a multiplicity of voices. Developmental decision-making and policy are therefore less simple or homogeneous than one might assume. Anthropologists, along with others, can help to unpick oppressive representations and practices, put different questions on the agenda and form new, alternative discourses.

Most of the insights which anthropologists provide are rooted first and foremost in common sense. We are not claiming that they have 'exclusive' expertise which others cannot gain access to. One possibility which we will be exploring later in this book is that local development workers might collect their own ethnography and develop their own anthropological intuitions. What we do suggest, however, is that the anthropological eye, trained as it is to focus on particular issues, is invaluable in the planning, execution and assessment of positive, non-oppressive developmental interventions. This is not so much because anthropologists have access to a body of objective 'facts' about any given society, but more that they know what questions to ask and how to ask them. While, in retrospect at least, such questions may appear to be obvious, time and time again, as the failure of so many development interventions testifies, they are forgotten.

Below are some of the main issues addressed by applied anthropologists. As we shall see, these are deeply informed by the findings of non-applied anthropology, some of which were reviewed in the last chapter. Again, knowledge for understanding and knowledge for action are inseparable. While these questions are often first raised by anthropologists, we suggest that, ideally at least, development anthropologists should not be in the business of predicting what is 'best' for the poor (although, as some of the case studies in Chapter 6 indicate, bureaucratic and political factors mean that this is often precisely what they end up doing). In contrast, anthropologists working in development can help facilitate ways for the 'victims' or 'recipients' (depending on one's perspective) to have a voice in the development process, so that ultimately it is they who dictate their interests and the most appropriate form of developmental interventions. The rest of the chapter will be organised around the following themes:

1. Access.
2. Effects.
3. Control.

Access

As anthropological research indicates, economic growth can exacerbate rather than eradicate poverty and exploitation. Colonialism and neo-colonialism have meant that the rewards of capitalist growth are spread very unevenly between different parts of the world. This means that policies which promote economic growth, or are presupposed on the notion of 'trickle-down', are unlikely to benefit everyone equally, for by definition capitalism promotes accumulation for some at the expense of others. This inequality exists at international and national levels, both of which anthropologists may wish to analyse and comment upon. Access may depend on inequality both within communities, between local groups and the state, or at an international level. It should, however, be noted that although some anthropologists have attempted to analyse the relationship between world capitalism and global exploitation,[2] the majority are more accustomed to investigating social relations at the micro level.

Although unequal distribution may appear to be an obvious and crucial issue, planners often forget that in the communities where they are working people's access to resources and decision-making power is rarely equal. This may be due to political naivety, but is also because those who plan from the outside tend to assume that 'the poor' are all the same and thus have the same interests. As all anthropologists are aware, however, most communities are highly heterogeneous. There are also many different forms of inequality: those depending upon constructions of race, gender, class and age are just some of the most basic. Each of these in turn is structured and experienced according to the particular cultural, economic and political context. We cannot therefore declare that particular groups are always more disadvantaged than others and must thus be the 'targets' of aid. 'Women-headed households', for example, are indeed often disadvantaged. But they are also not all the same, even within the same cultural context, let alone in different societies (Lewis, 1993).

Inequality, and differential access to and control over resources, also exists at many levels within communities. This may involve inequality between different households, whether structured through caste, ethnicity, social status or economic class. All of these factors may also cross-cut, or coincide with each other. Inequality may exist between different kinship groups, thus transcending the boundaries of individual households, or it may exist within households, whether this is in terms of gender, age or particular kinship relations. Combined with this, the exercise of power involves various types of relationship, interaction and social action. If power is defined, after Weber, as the ability to influence events, then clearly it may come through a variety of sources. It may be legitimate ('authority') or unofficial (the ability to influence events informally, perhaps through personal relationships, covert strategising and so on).

In considering who gets what, we must therefore be aware of several key issues. First, while inequality exists in all societies, it is structured in particular ways according to its cultural and historical context. Second, power over resources and decision-making is not always explicit. Even while officially there are equal rights for all citizens, in reality this may be far from the case. It is thus hardly surprising that development interventions so often benefit only particular groups, or end up disadvantaging those it was assumed they would help. To illustrate this, let us consider some case studies which illustrate various levels and forms of inequality, and the ways in which this affects people's access to the 'benefits' of developmental resources.

Case 1. Albania: differential access to rural resources in the post-communist era[3]

We begin with a short case study of Albania, the poorest country in Europe, in which a strictly isolationist and totalitarian communist regime did its best to eliminate economic inequalities in the countryside in the 40 years before 1990 through the imposition of a system of collective farming.

The Stalinist government of Enver Hoxha was repressive and inefficient, but it did meet people's basic material needs and included a comprehensive welfare system which provided reasonable health-care and education facilities for the majority of the population. In agriculture, despite low levels of production and a serious disregard for long-term environmental issues, farming inputs such as tractor ploughing services and fertilisers were available and agronomists were on hand to advise the cooperatives. In 1990, after the upheavals in the rest of Eastern Europe, the government was finally brought down through largely peaceful protest. The political system collapsed, ushering in a new era of social democracy and tentative capitalist development. During the downfall of the government there was a spontaneous and violent uprising by the people, not against the communists themselves but against all the physical trappings of the old regime. Village schools, health centres and other elements of infrastructure were destroyed by angry villagers.

A long period of structural adjustment began, managed by the World Bank and including a privatisation drive, a land reform process and the opening of the country for the first time to foreign investment. But during this period of transition, which like in most of the former communist countries of Eastern Europe remains in its infancy, most of the services of the former state were in rapid decline or collapsed completely. Today, the country is dependent on food aid. The social safety net, which had included a system of old age pensions, sickness benefits and food subsidies, barely exists. Completely unprepared for these new realities, most farmers have been thrown back on to their own resources and many have retreated into subsistence agriculture. Many villagers are returning to pre-communist traditional systems of village government through elders. Local mosques and churches, which had been closed or destroyed under communism, have become the community focus for survival and welfare.

A small number of rural people have, however, benefited from the collapse of communism, by holding on to important cooperative assets at the moment of their dissolution. In one village, the goatherd was able to sell most of the community's cooperative's herd for private gain. In another, a farmer ended up with a tractor which he was able to rent out in a private ploughing service, making enough profit to buy another tractor a year later. Almost overnight, new layers of rural inequality have been created; the survival strategies of different households now depend on their level of access to a range of material, social and cultural resources.

Case 2. Mali Sud Rural Development Project: inequality between communities[1]

The Mali Sud Project was launched in 1977 to develop the southern region of Mali – a landlocked country in the Western Sahel. It was extended for a further five years in 1983, funded largely by foreign aid: US$61 million out of a total of US$84 million. The project's objective was to increase agricultural potential in the area, by boosting the output of key crops such as maize and sorghum, to promote village development associations and to improve standards of living within rural areas through basic health services and water supplies. The project area spanned some 3500 villages, covering a range of ecological conditions, from arid (having only around 400mm of rain a year) to the relatively fertile (further south, some areas enjoy 1400mm of rain annually).

In the first eight years the project did indeed increase the output of many of these crops. Output of the staple foods sorghum and millet increased by 10 per cent, and the area given over to maize saw a 60 per cent increase. But it was only some villages which benefited. In areas where there was inadequate rainfall, maize was ecologically inappropriate. Following the encouragement of the project, however, people had planted maize extensively. In many cases they lost the whole crop.

The main problem with the Mali Sud Project was that it did not help the poorest, many of whom were vulnerable to famine.[5] The project only offered credit and technical advice to farmers who wanted to develop new land and buy new seeds, fertiliser and technology. These were distributed through officially recognised village committees, which not all villages had. Indeed, the committees tended only to exist in wealthier villages, where there was more motivation and organisational skills. Those villages which received help have clearly enjoyed a rise in their standard of living, yet those living in the poorer villages, without a committee, received nothing.

By 1985, some of the poorest villages in the arid areas of Mali which were excluded from the project were on the brink of famine. They desperately needed seeds, especially high-yield varieties to increase their food output, yet were not eligible for help from the project. This was due to two reasons. First, they were not part of a village committee; and second, they had insufficient credit to qualify for a loan with which to buy seeds from the project: all farmers given credit needed at least some capital as a guarantee before being funded. Those most in need of assistance were therefore excluded.

The Mali Sud Project excluded those living in the poorest communities because of pre-determined project criteria. But as Madeley points out, projects in other parts of the world have demonstrated that the very poor can be successfully given loans without providing material guarantees. The next case study demonstrates that particular groups can be excluded from project benefits not because of pre-existing criteria, but because insufficient attention has been given to the dynamics of resource allocation in the settlements targeted for 'development'. Rather than simply excluding the most vulnerable groups, this seems to have made their circumstances even more difficult.

Case 3. Land rights in Calcutta: inequality between households[6]

A recent study of the effects of physically upgrading 'bustees' (slums) in Calcutta demonstrates how the original, and poorest, inhabitants have tended to be disadvantaged, rather than benefiting from the improvements (M. Foster, 1989). Slum improvement, which superficially is a physical rather than a social or political process (the provision of sanitation, paved roads, the construction of new houses and so on), thus has variable effects on different groups according to where they are placed on existing socioeconomic hierarchies within the same urban communty. Without taking these differences into consideration in the planning stage, and by treating all slum-dwellers as if they have equal access to their homes, Foster argues that such projects have damaging effects on the most vulnerable. As they lead to an unforeseen rise in rents, many of the poorest bustee inhabitants are ultimately forced to move to increasingly marginal areas of the city. The upgrading of legal bustees has thus been accompanied by a growth in illegal squatter settlements, which are untouched by slum-improvement programmes.

The Indian government has been involved in slum upgrading since the 1970s. In Calcutta, a fund of US$80 million was made available in 1971 to improve environmental and health conditions in the city, and in 1971–81 1.7 million slum-dwellers were affected by the programme. Important differences in their relative access to property and economic status were, however, largely ignored, as were the needs of the poorest of Calcutta's poor, the pavement dwellers. Foster's research into different bustees shows a wide range of settlement histories and different types of tenancy among inhabitants. While the earliest settlers often built their own homes, many houses are now owned by landlords who can illegally raise rents through informal *salaam* (gratuity) and key payments, even though officially rents are controlled. Tenants who have moved in more recently tend to pay higher rents; many of these already have jobs in the centre of the city, and some have commissioned space to be reserved for them as their households in other areas expand.

Bustees are thus being 'gentrified' as these richer dwellers move in. Meanwhile landlords are illegally extracting higher rents in a variety of hidden ways. Slum upgrading adds momentum to this process, attracting wealthier inhabitants and enabling landlords to charge more and more. The poorest households, and especially those headed by women, who are particularly vulnerable to landlords' coercive techniques, are thus being forced out.

Foster argues that the key to identifying the beneficiaries of urban environmental upgrading lies in understanding existing patterns of land control. By failing to consider these factors and treating slum-dwellers as all the same, it seems that once again development aids the richest while disadvantaging the poorest. These effects could only have been avoided by understanding the complex nature of tenancy and property ownership in Calcutta bustees at the planning stage, rather than assuming that bustees are homogeneous communities, with shared interests.

The negative side effects of slum improvement cannot of course be entirely blamed on bustee upgrading. Given the pressure on urban land, such processes are also likely to occur without physical improvements. Avoiding such negative effects is also difficult, for clearly the legal changes necessary for this are beyond the power of urban development authorities or aid agencies. More recent projects funded by foreign donors have not been permitted by local government to work with the poorest pavement dwellers, because they are regarded as illegal squatters. Here, then, constraints imposed by the recipient government have prevented aid from being as 'poverty-focused' as the donors might have wished.

As we know, unequal access occurs within households, as well as between them. In the next case, we shall see how the construction of gender relations in Bangladesh means that even if projects are specifically aimed at women, they do not necessarily benefit from them.

Case 4. Women's credit groups in Bangladesh: inequality within households[7]

In 1975 the Bangladeshi government introduced a programme of rural women's cooperatives in 19 selected administrative districts controlled by the Integrated Rural Development Programme. These women's cooperatives were village-based and structured on the model of pre-existing men's peasant committees. Each cooperative was run by a management committee, elected by members. These represented the cooperative at fortnightly training sessions in health, nutrition, family planning, literacy, vegetable gardening, livestock and poultry rearing and food processing, sharing their knowledge with other members back in their village. Their primary focus was, however, the granting of small loans, which in conjunction with the training was supposed to increase members' income-earning capacity.

In a village studied by Rozario (1992) these loans seemed to be the main reason why women joined the cooperatives. At an interest rate of 12.5 per cent, a woman could apply for 500 taka[8] if she had at least 50 taka worth of shares. Since the interest rates charged by private moneylenders are extortionate in Bangladesh (sometimes running at 100 per cent), and banks are unlikely to give credit to small landowners and the landless, obtaining these loans was obviously highly desirable.

Rozario's research indicates that loans intended to be used by women for their own income generation were either going towards joint household expenses, or being coopted by men. Loans taken out by the poorest women were often spent on basic household items, such as food, clothing and medicine. These women, however, were the ones most likely to invest their loans in growing vegetables, or poultry raising. In contrast, wealthier women told Rozario that they did not know how their husbands spent the loans, which they had passed directly to them. They simply signed the forms to collect the loan. Since so many loans were not repaid, with women claiming that they could not control their husbands' decisions or ability to repay, eventually husbands' signatures were required before a loan was made. Men were thus officially given greater control over women's credit.

Evidence from elsewhere in Bangladesh suggests similar processes are common to credit programmes which give loans to women (Goetz, 1994). Because women and men do not have equal access to resources within households, time and time again loans which are given to women are passed by the recipients to their husbands. Combined with this, because it is women's responsibility to feed and clothe their families, money earmarked for income generation is spent on a household's reproductive needs. Class is clearly an important factor too. Women from richer households, who are more strictly secluded, seem to have the least control over the credit. This may be because ideologies of purdah (female seclusion) prevent such women from entering markets and other public and male domains. The buying and selling of vegetables or poultry may therefore be seen as 'unrespectable' for them, while for poorer women social prestige is not something they can afford. All women, however, shoulder the burden of repayment if and when their husbands default.

By disregarding the ways in which resources are allocated within Bangladeshi households, the cultural construction of women's work and their access to markets, credit programmes in Bangladesh are likely to be controlled by men, even if they are originally intended for women. A key factor here might be that it is cash, rather than other resources, which is loaned. Cash is traditionally associated with male domains, whereas other commodities (poultry, grain, household goods) are traditionally within the female domain. If project planners had located gender relations and inequality within the specific cultural context of Bangladesh, the results reported by Rozario might therefore have been avoided.

To summarise, anthropological study of development helps generate a range of questions which focus on people's access to resources provided by planned change. These may be answered

---

Access: Key Questions

What are the most important resources within society?
How is access to resources organised?
Are key resources equally shared, or do some groups have more control than others?
Are there obvious economic differences within communities?

Do some groups have more decision-making power than others?
Are some groups denied a voice?
Are some people incited to speak?
Is access to resources equal within households?
Do some groups have particular interests/needs?

Are there project criteria which constrain some people's access?
Is a certain level of capital necessary ?
Does the project only apply to preconceived categories, e.g. landowners, male farmers or household heads?

Are these factors adequately considered in the development plan/policy?

through the anthropological methods outlined in Chapter 2, or through more participatory methods (see Chapter 5). Conventionally in development practice such questions are posed by 'expert' consultants, but this need not necessarily be the case: local participants, activists, non-governmental workers and so on may all contribute. Most important is that the answers are fed back effectively into planning and policy.

Gathering such information is not of course unproblematic; whether or not the objective 'truth' of sociopolitical relations can ever be reached is a moot point, not only because outsiders tend to find it extremely difficult to find such things out, but also because the 'truth' tends to vary according to the positioning and perspectives of different actors: it is unfixed and variable. We shall return to these problems at the end of this chapter.

Effects

What are the social and cultural effects of development? This question is clearly closely linked to relative access. Rather than focusing on the distribution of benefits, however, it teases out different questions. By asking about the social effects of development, we are forced to consider the often complex social repercussions which may spill over into quite unexpected domains. Such questions are also vital in assessing projects or programmes which planners lacking in anthropological insight may not have orginally considered to have any particular social implications, since these projects were primarily conceived of in technical terms.

Focusing upon social effects also demonstrates the highly complex nature of social change. People are embedded in a range of social, economic and political relationships which affect their access to property and labour, their decision-making power within their communities and households, their position in the division of labour and so on. Although anthropologists may not be able to predict exactly what the social effects of development will be, from what they may already know, and by asking the right questions, they are often far better equipped than most to make informed guesses. While the social effects of development must clearly be investigated during and after projects, through procedures of evaluation and appraisal, such questions also need to be posed at their inception. As we see below, the failure to do this has led to many grave mistakes.

Case 5. The Kariba Dam: the effects of resettlement[9]

Many large-scale projects which are designed to improve national infrastructure, and which are perceived as being solely technical, require the resettlement of large numbers of people. The building of roads, air-strips and dams to generate hydroelectric power provides classic examples. The social implications of these projects are often not fully comprehended until after they are underway, and key questions which might at least have limited the damage done to the groups that are forced to move are not asked. The Kariba Dam is a classic example (see Scudder, 1980).

As Mair points out, when hydroelectric dams are built the displaced population is unlikely to benefit directly, for the electricity is usually intended for the inhabitants of distant cities (Mair, 1984: 110). The hardships caused for those who are forced to move can, however, be reduced if their social, economic and cultural circumstances are considered by administrators. In the Gwembe country (Zambia and Zimbabwe) where the Kariba Dam was built, there was insufficient consideration of these factors, even though many officials were deeply concerned for the people's welfare. In addition, a series of organisational mistakes were made. The worst of these was that although the population was originally allowed to choose where they would relocate, a technical decision was taken to raise the level of the lake, resulting in the flooding of the area proposed for resettlement. This effectively destroyed any goodwill or confidence in the administrators that the relocatees might have had. While some villagers did move to sites they had chosen, at least 6000 were sent to the Lusitu Plateau, 160 kilometres away. Although the government had promised that water would be supplied, not only was the drilling machinery provided inadequate, but the water proved to be undrinkable, so that pipelines eventually had to bring water from the Zambezi River. In the time it took for these to be built, many people suffered from dysentry.

The people were moved to the area by truck. They were not allowed to return to Gwembe country. Since the administrators assumed they had no property, many valuable possessions were left behind or broken. The scheme also totally ignored the local organisation of work. Men were sent ahead to Lusitu to prepare the land and build houses in the very season when they would normally have been earning cash and clearing fields. Women were thus left behind to do all the agricultural work, while their men did tasks in Lusitu which traditionally women would have contributed to. On top of all this, compensation payments were inappropriate to customary property rights. Household heads were compensated for all the huts in their homestead, even though these were often built and owned by younger male relatives. A fixed sum of compensation was awarded to each individual, including children, but paid to the household head. Most of these shared out the money, but none shared equally; some young men claimed that they had to earn their share from their fathers by working for them first.

Although the problem of water supply in Lusitu was technical, most of the other problems relate directly to issues of an anthropological nature. Had key questions been asked before planning the move

---

The Effects of Resettlement: Key Questions

What is the nature of local power and hierarchy?
How is difference and inequality structured?
Are particular groups marginalised?
Do some groups monopolise political power and resources?

What is the nature of the household?
How is the household organised?
Who lives where?
How is decision-making power allocated within households?
How do these factors customarily change over time?

How are local property relations organised?
What goods are highly valued?
What access do different social groups or household members have to property or other resources?
What are the usual patterns of inheritance?
How do these factors relate to the household development cycle?

How is work organised?
What are the main tasks done in the community, and during what seasons?
Who does what work?
What is the importance of kinship roles or relations in the allocation of labour?

How suitable is the proposed relocation site, given the above economic, social, and cultural factors?

and the payment of compensation, many of the negative effects might have been avoided.

The list of questions in the box is not of course comprehensive. It is also specific to Gwembe country. In different contexts, other issues may be important. For example, when squatter settlements are cleared, perhaps because a road is planned or simply because they are an 'eyesore', detailed questions must be asked regarding people's relationship to the homes they live in, tenancy arrangements and so on. There must also be safeguards to ensure that opportunists do not claim property which less powerful individuals occupy, or that 'household heads' are not given lump sums which may be withheld from other members. It is vital that these questions are asked at the planning stage, not after the project has already started.

Case 6. The Maasai Housing Project: technological change[10]

Since technology is usually produced, distributed, used and controlled by different groups of people, changes in any of these areas are likely to have knock-on effects on a range of social and economic relations. Different activities also involve varying amounts of power and status, according to each cultural context. Simply because some people produce a certain type of goods, for example, it cannot be assumed that they enjoy economic power, for they do not necessarily control its distribution and use. Likewise, people using a technology do not necessarily also control it. What implications does this have for projects involving technological change? The following example demonstrates that technological innovations and training in a housing project in Kenya have had various repercussions on local gender relations. These effects are by no means universal; rather, they depend upon the specific cultural context in which the project is taking place.

A recent report indicates that while some technological innovations in Kenya have had largely positive effects on women, for others the effects have been more mixed (ITDG, 1992). The Maasai Housing Project is a good example. Maasai women traditionally play a central role in the innovation, production, use and control of housing materials, but since the inception of the project their role in innovating new technologies has been reduced. In their place, men are becoming increasingly involved. Ironically, however, women's workload has increased.

The effects of the Maasai Housing Project must be understood in the wider context of Maasai life in Kajiado, Kenya. Although customarily associated with pastoralism, local Maasai have become increasingly settled. Alongside this more sedentary way of life, evidence indicates that women now shoulder greater burdens of work. For example, while men were traditionally responsible for livestock herding, women have now started herding, even though men still buy, sell and control the livestock. Most women work around 15 hours a day; lack of time is thus one of their largest problems. Other factors which prevent a greater share of decision-making power and access to resources for women are their lack of access to training and business opportunities, their underconfidence, the threat of male violence, and their exclusion from decision-making and ownership.

The Maasai Housing Project was introduced to Kajiado District by the Arid and Semi-Arid Lands Programme (ASAL) in conjunction with a partner NGO. It started work in 1990, with the identification of eleven women's groups and the construction of a demonstration 'modern', three-roomed house. In 1991 women were invited to a workshop in which they expressed their own preferences regarding shape, size and interior of their ideal houses. The project then supervised the construction of five houses, three for rental and two for private use. A Maasai woman was employed as an extension worker, but the technical specialist and programme managers were men. A 1992 report suggested that women should be more central to the project: training courses should suit their time constraints, and housing designs should encompass their needs.

One problem was that the project's 'improved' houses took longer to build and thus added to women's work burden. While one woman reported that having a modern house gave her more status, most claimed that the greatest benefits were derived from technological improvements, rather than any social or political changes. Although it was hoped that one women's group would rent their house out while running a shop nearby in order to raise the money to provide it with better facilities, the group reported that this was not possible since they did not have the time or the money to run a shop. The house was thus left unoccupied.

Before the changes were introduced women were the main innovators and producers of housing; centrally, they also controlled the finished products. After the project, however, men were increasingly involved in innovation through their participation in training courses and in some aspects of construction (for example, carpentry). While women were still the main producers of housing, men had also started to distribute it. Combined with this, the values and statuses of each activity have also begun to change. Since modernity is highly valued in Kajiado, the distribution and control of modern houses leads to more status than that of traditional houses. This may be another reason why men are becoming increasingly involved. There is therefore a very real danger that men may increasingly control housing, while women will continue to do the bulk of the work and be the main users of the completed houses. Changes in the gender relations of house production may also therefore lead to to changes in the gender relations of house design and control. Rather than benefiting from the project, women will be disempowered by it.

One way that these negative effects may be avoided is by ensuring that men are paid by women for their labour, thus giving them few rights over the finished product. Likewise, by improving traditional housing designs which are associated with female knowledge, male control of innovation might be reduced. It should also be remembered that the social relations of technology are not only culturally specific, they are also technologically specific. Housing among the Maasai is not an exclusively female domain. This means that men may choose to become involved in housing projects if they perceive that they will benefit from them. In contrast, other technologies are locally constructed as being exclusively female. For example, the production of stoves is seen by the Maasai

---

Technological Change: Key Questions

How is local knowledge used, produced, distributed and controlled?
Who does what, and how is the work organised?
What is the relationship between these activities and decision-making power and status?

What are the constraints facing women?
How can project activities (training, group meetings and so on) fit most appropriately into women's tight work schedules?

How might the new houses be more appropriately designed?
Could the new designs be less, rather than more, labour-intensive?

What is the relationship between production, distribution and control?
Does the building and distribution of houses automatically lead to their control?
Would paying male house-builders wages reduce the danger that they will control the finished product?

as 'women's work'. Improved stove technology is therefore offered only to women by projects, without apparently discriminating against men. In this case, the new technology saves women time, rather than increasing their workload.

The Maasai Housing Project has not had wholly negative effects on local women. Indeed, great efforts have been made to recognise their productive role in house building and to enable them to participate in the design of new houses. The accompanying questions (see box) might, however, help 'fine tune' it.

Control

As the above case studies indicate, it is crucial to understand the dynamics of local societies if particular groups are not to be marginalised or further disadvantaged through development interventions. It would, however, be misleading to indicate that these issues are resolved solely through top-down planning. Indeed, this replicates dominant development discourses which presuppose that planning and policy-making simply need to be tweaked in particular directions to 'solve' the problems of development. Top-down planning is far from being the only solution. However well thought out development plans are, if they are designed and implemented by outsiders they are in continual danger of being unsustainable in the long term and of contributing to dependency; when funding ends, so does the project.

Unless people can take control of their own resources and agendas, development is thus caught in a vicious circle; by 'providing' for others, projects inherently encourage the dependency of recipients on outside funds and workers. Development discourses must therefore be challenged until they recognise that local people are active agents, and by changing their practices enable them to participate[11] in project planning and implementation. In this section we indicate how development practice prevents people from taking control and how it might be changed from within. As in the rest of this chapter, we are confining our attention to planned change and assuming that, at some level, external donors are involved.

Working with local groups and institutions

Development plans often assume that the implementing agencies of a project or programme will come from outside the local community: there is a clear distinction between the 'givers' of a service or resource (development workers) and the 'receivers' (local people). Since developers are primarily interested in problems and solutions which are perceived in technological terms, local social structures tend to be seen as at best irrelevant and at worst an 'obstacle'. Indeed, outsiders often fail to recognise the degree to which communities have their own internal forms of organisation, decision-making and lobbying.

Unsurprisingly, however, projects are often most successful when they work through pre-existing social structures and institutions. There may, for example, be pre-existing groups which are working to bring resources or services to their communities. These may take many different forms. For example, as we saw in Chapter 3, Latin American squatter settlements are often carefully planned by inhabitants, with local neighbourhood committees formed to develop the settlement. In other communities the group may have formed for a single purpose: gathering together to raise money for a school, a clinic or a place of worship, for example. Sports clubs are common forms of community-based groups, as are political parties. All of these vary from place to place; their suitablity as implementors or partners for development work will depend on both their particular characteristics and those of the development plan.

Anthropologically-minded advisors have an important role to play in contesting dominant discourses which ignore such groups. By finding out about them, representing their interests to planners, or enabling them to speak for themselves (for example, by arranging meetings or workshops), anthropologists in development can demonstrate a community's or group's potential for participation. Anthropological research and representation can also show that people are not passive 'recipients', but are accustomed to taking matters into their own hands.

Whether or not these groups become the basis for participation in a project is of course dependent upon a range of factors. The most important of these is probably the development agency's commitment to participation. It should also not be assumed that local groups wish to participate. As we shall see in the next chapter, much may depend upon the various meanings of participation being used. What is most important, however, is that such groups are asked what their interests are. They might decide that they need advice, training or extra resources. But they might just as easily wish to be left alone.

If there is a traditional system of communal decision-making, it may be easier and more expedient to use this as a participatory channel rather than creating new committees or institutions. If these institutions are dominated by a powerful elite, or particular groups are excluded, this may of course create problems, but simply to bypass local power-holders may cause greater difficulties in the long run. The work of Proshika, a Bangladeshi NGO, provides an example. While its projects were ultimately aimed at the local landless, organising them into groups and helping to raise their political consciousness in order to gain greater control of their situation, fieldworkers often found it expedient to gain the trust of local elites and work through existing political structures. Where this was not done in the initial stages, the projects often met with fierce opposition.[12] In other cases existing committees or decision-makers might be linked to a new structure. In contexts where community decision-making is dominated by men, for instance, a separate woman's committee could be set up, feeding into the existing male-dominated one. If women are unused to being on committees or having a political voice, they may need particular support or training. Such projects cannot achieve miracles. Men may continue to dominate and women to have an unequal say in what takes place. But at least an opportunity for them to redefine their political roles has been provided.

Often there are non-governmental organisations already working within an area.[13] Because these are smaller in scale than governmental agencies and are locally based, these often work far more successfully at the grassroots than bilateral aid projects,[14] and are more experienced in participatory development. Increasingly, projects which aim to give beneficiaries greater control are attempting to work through NGOs already involved at the grassroots. Applied anthropologists may be asked to identify which local NGOs have the most participatory methodologies and which might be most able to carry out such work. This involves various ideological and practical problems, which we shall discuss further in Chapters 5 and 6.

The following case study is an example of how project planning can build upon and strengthen pre-existing local groups and institutions in order to enable people to participate more fully in processes of change. As it indicates, development discourses are not homogeneously 'top-down'; they are both highly contested from within and liable to change over time.

Case 7. Labour welfare in tea plantations: enabling control[15]

A project to improve the quality of tea production in South Asia had been funded for several decades by a bilateral donor. Originally the project had been almost wholly technical, focusing on upgrading the quality of tea plants and productive techniques. While there was a labour welfare component, this concentrated on providing services for labourers within the plantations: improving their housing; providing tube-wells and health services.

By the late 1980s the labour welfare component began to be re-appraised, not least because of ideological changes within the donor agency. Rather than simply providing services for labourers, policy-makers decided that the project should enable them to take greater control of resources; as much as possible, the project should provide a framework for the labourers to run their own project. This was politically highly controversial, for the plantations were owned by private individuals and companies, who wanted their labourers to be as passive as possible.

An anthropological consultant was hired to assess the viability of such plans by researching social structure and organisation among the labourers. What she found were high levels of pre-existing 'indigenous' organisation. Labourers lived in 'lines' of housing, within which foremen were appointed to oversee the maintenance of resources (such as tube-wells) and report problems to the estate management. Locally formed committees took responsibility for other decisions; for instance, those involving internal social affairs. Where resources (such as housing) had been provided by the plantation, there was a tendency to rely on the management of the estates to maintain them. Where labourers had built their own houses, however, they maintained them. Combined with this, in some estates female labourers were involved in managing credit and savings groups, an activity which appeared to have been initiated by the women themselves, rather than any outside agency. They also had their own indigenous healers and birth attendants, as well as the health services provided by the plantations.

Lastly, registered labourers were all members of the national trade union for tea workers. This had a long history of militancy. Local level action – strikes, demonstrations and the garroting of managers – regularly brought production to a halt in some estates. Each plantation therefore included union leaders, who had substantial experience in political organisation, lobbying and action. Many of the most forthright of these were women.

Thus while in some ways they had been forced into a passive role by the non-participatory allocation of services within the project, in other domains labourers were already actively taking control of affairs. Building upon this knowledge, project workers planned a new phase in the labour welfare component of the project. Local committees, based on the pre-existing organisation of the 'lines', would be set up. These would involve equal numbers of women and men; given the activism of some female labourers, it was reasonable to assume that this would not be too difficult. The committees would be based around the management and allocation of a 'social fund', to be provided through the project. It would be up to them how these funds were used. If they wanted to spend them on training, primary education or improved health services, they would decide.

Appropriate organisational structures

People are often excluded from participating in and ultimately controlling planned development because the organisational form it takes is inappropriate. Indeed, bureaucratic planning and administration are in many ways inherently anti-participatory, for they are deeply intolerant of alternative ways of perceiving and organising activities, time and information. Institutional procedures are therefore central ways in which development practices exclude supposed beneficiaries, even if superficially policy aims at 'participation'. These problems are not by definition insurmountable, but most bureaucracies will have to undergo major reorientations if their procedures are to be more open and flexible. Understanding the ways in which people are excluded by organisational structures and procedures means taking a step towards achieving this.

An example of the exclusive nature of planning procedures is the project framework, which some donors now insist upon before providing funds. This involves an organisational chart in which planners specify project objectives, inputs, timings and the criteria they will use to measure successful output.[16] While this is undoubtedly a useful way of clarifying plans, the production of such a framework is also clearly much easier for administrators accustomed to particular ways of thinking and planning, and may require time-consuming training.

Project reports are another way in which administration and decision-making remain 'top-down'. Reports and other forms of documentation tend to be key to the formulation of policy within aid agencies, yet they are also often highly exclusive to anyone from outside the institution. Reports are usually produced in very particular ways (for example, conventions such as listing recommendations at the beginning of the report, summarising information in appendices, keeping the text to a certain length, using particular bureaucratic phrasings and jargon). Those from outside the organisation who are not familiar with such conventions are thus effectively excluded from effective communication.

Projects which supposedly allow for local 'participation' are often planned in a way which makes such participation impossible. This is especially the case with projects which involve large-scale technical components, such as building. This tends to be planned around a rigid timetable and can usually be implemented relatively quickly. To set up the mechanisms for local participation in planning, however, usually takes far longer. Meanwhile those responsible for building are keen to progress as quickly as possible. These types of contradiction are extremely common, pointing to a larger problem in donor-led development: working with large budgets, which they are anxious to spend, donors and recipient governments are often reluctant to spend time 'fiddling around' with the complexities of setting up local committees and consulting communities about their plans. Instead, projects which absorb funds efficiently and are administratively relatively simple (building roads or dams) are preferred.

The timing of project activities may also be inappropriate. Again, this is the result of not consulting local people first. Meetings, for example, may be held at inconvenient times. Women may not be able to attend meetings or classes held at night. In other contexts women and men may not be able to attend those held in the day because of work demands. Once more these are issues which are best decided by the people involved. Anthropologists working in development should not take these decisions on behalf of beneficiaries, but wherever possible should ensure, at the very least, that plans involve careful consultation with them.

The location of project activities should also be considered, for they might be held in a place from which some people are excluded. In many Muslim societies women do not usually go into public places where there are many men. They may also be unable to travel to nearby towns to be trained, receive credit and so on, both for reasons of modesty and family honour but also because they have domestic responsibilities throughout the day. Each context is of course different, but project activities are usually more accessible when they are decentralised.

Lastly, planners need to consider whether they are making appropriate demands on participants. As we know, men, and especially women, have to meet huge work demands in much of the world, yet this is often ill considered in the plans of outsiders. Projects which do not take these into consideration are therefore unlikely to gain much local support. A good example of this is income-generation projects which are highly labour-intensive. In the tea plantation project described above, an earlier plan in the labour welfare component of the project had been for income-generation activities for unregistered labourers, who often receive only very small incomes and, as a labour reserve, are not always in full employment. The problem, however, was that the plantations needed to have a continual supply of labour for times of high demand; if the unregistered labourers had an alternative source of income, the plantations would not have been so easily able to demand their work. The proposals were therefore blocked by the management.

Appropriate communication

People are often prevented from taking a more active role in development because it is conducted in cultural codes and languages which are alien to them. As we saw in Chapter 3, recent anthropological analyses of development discourse suggest that by its very nature it excludes people, disregards their knowledge and portrays them as 'ignorant', by upholding Western scientific rationality as the only paradigm for understanding and communication (Hobart, 1993).

While in the majority of cases this scientific rationality may provide solutions, it need not necessarily be the case. Again, the discourse is more heterogeneous and open to change than many commentators suggest. As we shall see in the next chapter, there have already been significant advances in the understanding of what are termed 'indigenous knowledge systems'[17] by developers. Anthropological knowledge has had an important role in promoting such concerns. It can also help to suggest more appropriate ways of getting messages across and enabling people to participate by using their own cultural idioms rather than those imposed from the outside. Again, this is not necessarily because anthropologists in development have 'expert' knowledge of a particular culture, but because they can insist at the planning stage that the advice of local people is sought.

Communication must be both appropriate and effective. The notion of appropriate communication may appear to be obvious, but it is extraordinary how often the local cultural and linguistic context is not considered in project planning. For example, in the early 1990s Katy Gardner sat in on a UNICEF training session for midwives in Orissa in east India, in which they were shown a training video made in the Punjab, several thousand kilometres away. The video was in Punjabi, and used traditional Punjabi implements and methods. Moreover, women sitting at the back of the small room could hardly see the video screen. However, there are many other examples where great efforts have been taken to ensure that developmental messages are appropriate. Literacy materials, for example, as pioneered by Paulo Friere and developed by NGOs throughout the world, take care to teach literacy using culturally appropriate idioms and contexts. We shall discuss functional education further in Chapter 5.

One simple way to communicate effectively is to use pre-existing cultural forms. Community education projects often use traditional forms of entertainment to great effect. Jatra, or traditional travelling theatre in India, for example, has been used by community health projects to get across family planning messages. And in places where there is no, or very limited, electricity, communities may gather together to watch televisions powered by batteries. Again, this may provide a useful forum for showing films on public health, or other forms of community education.

But perhaps most importantly, planners must consider whether the message itself is appropriate. As anthropological analyses indicate, local knowledge is often based on assumptions that are quite different from those of 'rational' developmental knowledge (Pottier, 1993; Hobart, 1993). Training or education which disregards the ways in which people understand the world, and simply assumes that scientific or rational knowledge is accessible and useful, is therefore unlikely to be successful.

As we saw in Chapter 3, Richards argues that farming practices in West Africa can be understood as involving performance skills as well as detailed ecological and technical knowledge. Rather than skills being learned and 'set', farmers improvise their agricultural skills (P. Richards, 1993). Persuading farmers to adopt new seed varieties which have been developed in laboratory conditions because they are scientifically more advanced, or attempting to 'train' them in practices based on scientific understandings of agriculture, therefore disregards the very nature of such farmers' knowledge and is unlikely to meet with much success. People understand events and ideas on their own terms. As long as development work involves the imposition of ideas and knowledge rather than being a dialogue, people are unlikely to be able to gain greater control of it, or voluntarily participate in it.

Conclusion

As the case studies cited in this chapter show, the more that is known about the dynamics and organisation of societies, at all levels, the more it is possible to ensure that particular groups are not excluded from or disadvantaged by planned change. Although one does not need to be an academic anthropologist to obtain this information, we suggest that understanding what questions to ask is primarily an anthropological skill. We are not suggesting that the insights and strategies discussed in this chapter should be confined to an elite of international anthropological consultants or 'experts'. Rather than certain individuals being the repositories of such knowledge, it is particular insights and methods which are important, and these are potentially accessible to everybody. Indeed, anthropological perspectives already inform much work being carried out by NGOs, and form the basis of various new research methodologies (such as participatory action research and participatory rural appraisal) which are currently gaining widespread acceptance in some developmental domains. We shall discuss these in the next chapter.

There is also no single way of gaining the sort of knowledge we have been discussing here. While traditional participant observation is certainly a possibility, such in-depth and time-consuming research is often not possible within the context of development work. The use of local consultants is nearly always preferable to hiring expatriates; local participants can also become 'indigenous anthropologists' – setting their own research agendas and answering questions on their own terms. Likewise, locally based NGOs often have extensive knowledge of local culture and social organisation (although this is not always the case).

The ease with which such information can be obtained should not be overestimated, however. Questions can be asked in any number of ways but there are no guarantees that the correct answers will be given, or even that there are 'correct' answers. To a certain extent social realities always depend upon the subjective perspectives of those viewing the situation. Reality is also often highly contested; different interest groups will represent it in different ways (landlords and tenants, for example, are unlikely to agree about what the 'correct' level of rents should be). The ways in which outsiders are perceived may also influence how reality is represented to them. Researchers associated with aid agencies, for instance, may be seen as potential 'providers'. In these contexts it may be actively in people's interest to represent themselves more in terms of 'needs' than of self-sufficiency. In other contexts (for example, where researchers are associated with the government), local people may be extremely reticent to share information about landholdings, income and so forth.

Lastly, while new methodologies such as participatory rural appraisal offer interesting alternatives to more top-down research, the danger is that they may easily be reduced to mechanistic gestures, a series of pre-specified activities which development workers carry out as quickly as possible with little understanding of the rationale behind them, before getting started on the 'real' business of the project. Such dangers are exacerbated when projects are hemmed in by time-frameworks and targets.

There are no easy answers to the problems posed by 'finding out'. The first step towards more effective and empowering forms of planned change is, however, to get the right questions on the agenda. A variety of formal and informal methods can be used to find out the answers, but those involved must also accept that there are few 'objective' social truths, that cultures cannot be reduced to a few bare essentials which can be used to predict a particular result. Human life does not take place in a laboratory, and its study cannot be approached like a science. Rather, developers must understand that the societies with whom they work are highly dynamic, variable and likely to have a range of strong opinions about the directions of change which they wish to see.

Questions and their answers are not of course the same as actual policies and strategies. In Chapter 5 we therefore turn to particular practices within development which seem to offer viable alternatives to the dominant discourse, and which can be directly related to the anthropological insights outlined in this and the previous chapter. Some of these ideas are already current in certain areas of practice. As we shall see, these take us far beyond the conventional concerns of economic growth and 'development'.

5 NEW DIRECTIONS – PRACTICE AND CHANGE

As we saw in Chapter 2, the project of 'applied anthropology', which was begun in the colonial period, was only occasionally successful in its attempts to influence mainstream development practice. However, more recently ideas which have been generated by the anthropology of development (which we discussed in Chapter 3) have combined with the efforts of those anthropologists working critically within development frameworks (Chapter 4) to influence, challenge and subvert the dominant development discourse so that they have begun ultimately to influence actual development practice.

In this chapter we shall argue that the prevailing 'mainstream' discourse of development is far from monolithic. Although structured by relations of power in which particular countries, institutions and groups dominate, development practice and policy are increasingly heterogeneous, and are constantly challenged from more 'radical' positions by people working both within and outside mainstream development institutions. In what follows we shall outline some of these new directions. As we shall suggest, however, while these often generate promising new and alternative approaches to long-standing development perspectives, many also provide only tantalising glimpses into what might be possible rather than fully fledged changes in development thinking and practice. The risks of cooption and dilution within the still powerful logic of the top-down development paradigm remain ever present. Thus, although challenged by alternative perspectives, the extent to which the discourse has so far been significantly transformed is open to question. Indeed, some would argue that essentially nothing has changed. As Escobar puts it: 'Although the discourse has gone through a series of structural changes, the architecture of the

103

discursive formation laid down in the period 1945–55 has remained unchanged, allowing the discourse to adapt to new conditions' (1995: 42).

To what extent is this in fact the case? In this and the next chapter we hope to indicate that the evidence is mixed: while Escobar's conclusions may be too pessimistic, ideas which start their life as radical alternatives all too often become a neutralised and non-threatening part of the mainstream. Let us start with a policy response to critiques of development which indicate that it does not benefit the poorest sections of society: income generation and the notion of 'targeting'.

Poverty focused aid and 'income generation'

During the mid-1970s the apparent failure of many modernisation policies led to a new emphasis on the importance of 'basic needs' and 'poverty-focused aid'. Expensive attempts to promote industrialisation and cash-cropping had left the poorest groups still unfed, unhoused and uneducated. Chenery et al.'s *Redistribution with Growth* (1974) was a key text in this reassessment, as was Brandt et al.'s *North and South: A Programme for Survival* (1980). Chenery et al.'s work stressed the need to improve distribution of the benefits of development without sacrificing overall growth (see Robertson, 1984: 59). They argued that particular groups, assumed to have more or less homogeneous needs, should be identified as 'target groups': a concept we discuss in the next section.

This shift during the 1970s came at the same time as a growing focus on structural issues of class and gender, which were associated with the anthropological critique of modernisation. Now there was an increasing recognition of the need to mobilise people who had been bypassed by or written out of the development process and to encourage their participation in project planning and implementation. Such ideas brought with them a new attention to issues such as intrahousehold inequality, equitable income distribution, a recognition of the value of indigenous in addition to external or 'expert' knowledge, the importance of local-level organisation and the need to mobilise underprivileged and neglected groups of people to access resources, rights and services.

Some foreign donors began to pay attention to these issues. For example, the Swedish International Development Authority (SIDA) made the reduction of economic and social inequality a specific goal of its development assistance in 1978. Within the British aid budget an explicit policy decision was taken during the 1980s to make aid 'poverty-focused' and to target women as beneficiaries. Some projects are still basically concerned with the provision of services, but others seek a more active role from their beneficiaries.

Income generation is one example. Here, individuals or groups of poor people are enabled through contact with a government agency or NGO to generate more income for themselves, through credit, marketing advice, skills training or a combination of all three. These strategies for building what is sometimes termed 'micro-entrepreneurship' can provide important new survival routes for the poor, while they are particularly attractive to some development agencies because they fit well with neo-liberal ideas about enterprise culture, markets and privatisation.

Closely linked with the income-generation approach are savings groups, which help people to save for themselves and provide access to credit without interest. The pioneering work of Bangladesh's Grameen Bank, which has been supported by foreign donors such as SIDA, is a famous example of this type of project which has now been replicated in many other parts of the world, including the US (Madeley, 1991: 87–97; Holcombe, 1995). The bank has found that by lending relatively small amounts of money to the very poorest rural people (and particularly to women), even at market rates of interest, those taking out loans can identify small-scale investment opportunities – typically rearing farm animals or husking rice for others on a contract basis – and repay their loans on time. By stressing group identity and by building group solidarity among its members, the bank has found it possible to motivate people to repay the loan far more effectively than conventional banks (which in any case normally lend only to richer people) have done. By freeing people from their dependence upon the local moneylenders, who charge enormous levels of interest, the bank may also have a wider development impact. However, as we saw in Chapter 4, there are also problems with the approach.

'Target groups'

In Chapters 3 and 4 we saw how anthropologists have challenged the bland view of many developers that everybody in 'the community' will necessarily benefit from the introduction of new resources or services, by drawing attention to the local power structure and the ability of the better-off to capture benefits. This 'relational' view of social and economic life, which stresses the interdependent but conflictual sets of relations which make up communities, has contributed within development to an increased awareness of the need to ensure that newly provided resources flow to those who need them most. This change in emphasis is also of course associated with the critique of modernisation theory and 'trickle down' which gathered force throughout the 1970s.

Awareness has grown of the need for specific sections of a population, sometimes known in a rather ominous military metaphor as 'target groups', to be singled out for special attention. In their literature and statements of intent most development agencies these days highlight the particular groups of people whom they wish to assist, often terming them 'the beneficiaries', reflecting worrying assumptions about their passivity in the process. These groups obviously vary contextually. There is considerable difference across communities as to the types of people who fall into such target groups: landless men and women, indigenous minorities, urban squatters, female-headed households or farmers who farm ecologically fragile lands. What holds the targeting idea together is the objective of including people who have been 'left out' of the development process.

There are, however, inherent dangers in this approach, which all too easily feeds back into 'top-down' discourses and reflects the unequal power of those involved. For example, the pitfalls of outsider 'labelling', in which complex realities are forced into simple, easily digestible categories, have been discussed by Wood (1985). The end result may be the further marginalisation of 'targets', along with a reluctance to acknowledge the structural relationships which perpetuate differential access to opportunities. The notion of the target group is closely related to the controlling urge embodied in the idea of 'projectised' development, in which the socioeconomic categories of beneficiaries simply become another variable which can be defined and adjusted by project staff.

A good example of this problem can be found in discussions around the female-headed household, which has become a prominent feature of development discourse in many countries. For example, although female-headed households in Bangladesh are often represented within development agency discourse as having uniform needs, the category is in fact a varied one, cutting across both rich and poor social groups. These households are also sometimes transitory, located within sets of wider social relationships (which crucially affects their access to resources) and geographically scattered, which makes neat 'targeting' by outside agencies impossible (Lewis, 1993).

Non-governmental organisations (NGOs)

As the limitations of state-sponsored, project-based, top-down development became apparent, the 1980s and the 1990s saw increasing attention focused on private, professional development organisations and the voluntary sector by development agencies. This so-called third sector is now widely seen as containing potentially viable alternatives to conventional approaches to development and relief work.

At one level the changing level of support given to NGOs suggests a significant shift in development practice, for funds are increasingly being channelled to organisations on the outside of the 'mainstream' which often offer radical new approaches to how the work of 'development' is carried out. This, together with the diversity of approaches within the NGO sector, illustrates once more that development discourse is far from homogeneous or rigidly fixed. At the same time, however, some critics argue that rather than enabling NGOs to change the agenda, the increased funding of NGOs by Northern aid agencies has simply brought a potential threat to them under control. Let us examine some of the evidence.

In both North and South, the influence of NGOs is increasing as privatisation agendas reduce the role of the state in the delivery of services. Many development agencies now promote the belief that NGOs have special strengths because of the flexibility derived from the small scale of their operations, the degree of participation of their 'clients' and the replicability of their initiatives. Many donor agencies now direct more and more of their budgets towards NGOs in preference to government agencies. For example, SIDA's disbursements to NGOs increased from 13 per cent of total funds in 1983 to close to 30 per cent in 1994 (Riddell and Bebbington, 1995).

Figures quoted by Edwards and Hulme (1992) indicate that the number of development NGOs registered in the OECD countries has risen from 1600 in 1980 to 2970 in 1993 and that their spending has increased from US$2.8 billion to US$5.8 billion. There have been similar increases in the numbers and scale of NGOs in many Southern countries, where NGOs often constitute a response by alienated middle-class groups within civil society to a weak or resource-poor state's inability to deliver services and resources (Farrington and Lewis, 1993). In Bangladesh, admittedly an extreme example in that national NGOs supported by foreign funds have expanded dramatically to fill gaps in service provision left by the weak and under-resourced state, larger NGOs such as the Bangladesh Rural Advancement Committee (BRAC) and Proshika are beginning to count their landless group members in terms of millions rather than thousands.

As we have seen, NGOs are believed to be able to allocate resources and services more efficiently and to reach people more effectively than state institutions (Paul, 1991). NGOs themselves have claimed that their comparative advantage is derived from a stronger commitment and motivation, coupled with a better ability to form good-quality relationships with people, compared with government agencies. For example, as Bebbington (1991: 24) points out in the context of agricultural development work, NGOs 'are more willing to ask farmers what they think, to take their farming practices seriously, and consequently to orient technology adaptation and transfer towards real concerns'.

The origins, activities and performance of NGOs have varied dramatically between and within different country contexts, where particular state histories have permitted varying levels of 'space' within which NGOs can exist and work. In countries where a politically repressive regime has prevented local levels of organisation, many NGOs have existed as radical, underground organisations, as in the case of the Philippines under President Ferdinand Marcos (1965–86). Where the state has sought assistance with service delivery or project implementation, frequently with donor agency support, NGOs have often merged seamlessly with mainstream government structures. In communist Albania, the notion of a civil society with its arena for organisation outside the state hardly existed at all and NGOs were unknown.

NGOs themselves are a diverse set of actors, with origins in both North and South. There are important differences in scale and between local, national and international spheres of activity.[1] Some NGOs carry out their own project-based development activities, which can range from the direct provision of services (credit, agricultural inputs, health-care and education) to group formation and consciousness-raising, both of which aim to make people aware of new possibilities for self-determined change. Others do not work directly with beneficiaries but instead fund, train or otherwise support partner organisations at the grassroots. There is also an increasing number of activist NGOs who see their work in terms of lobbying, information exchange or advocacy aimed at changing the wider policy environment. NGOs are becoming important not just in terms of their ability to work directly with people, but also in terms of their potential contribution to the strengthening of civil society – democracy, legal rights and access to information (Clark, 1990).

NGOs have claimed, with some justification, that they can work more closely with poor people than similar government agencies can (Edwards and Hulme, 1992; Bebbington and Farrington, 1993; Clark, 1990). Critics, however, have drawn attention to the prevalence of a number of 'NGO myths' and show, with some success, that these supposed advantages are in fact largely unsubstantiated (Tendler, 1982). Furthermore, there is a growing radical critique of NGOs which argues that, rather than promoting deep-rooted change, they actually preserve the status quo by setting up a system of patronage based on the flow of development assistance, which undermines and depoliticises local grassroots organisation (Hashemi, 1989; Arellano-Lopez and Petras, 1994; Tvedt, 1995).

Despite these qualifications, many NGOs working directly with the poor have taken what might be described as an 'anthropological approach' to their field activities. Rather than working from the top downwards, many of the more effective NGOs have evolved from local communities and draw their field staff from the areas where they are working. Unlike many government or donor projects, they spend time discussing local interests with different sections of the community in order to build up a picture of the dynamic relationships which exist among different groups and classes. For example, this is the approach of Proshika, the Bangladeshi NGO (Khan et al., 1993; Kramsjo and Wood, 1992). A distinctive NGO organisational style has emerged: field staff are encouraged to spend time with local people and pass information about their needs and interests to the NGO in order to inform and shape future policy; in addition, less rigid boundaries are visible between junior and senior staff. This contrasts with the more rigid, directive roles usually taken by government in development activities, in which officials often subordinate development agendas to the more pressing demands of control and authority (Fowler, 1990).

This responsiveness to local needs can go beyond mere service delivery. In agriculture, NGOs have sometimes been able to undertake client-oriented research which has been based on agendas set by local group members and to promote technologies which meet locally generated needs, especially among the low-income sections of the population which are frequently passed over by formal government agricultural efforts. The use of local institutions and practices as the starting point has often proved a fruitful basis for innovation.[2]

Some NGO work also resembles the old dream of 'advocacy anthropology' in which outsiders try to promote the rights of the communities with which they work either during local conflicts (for example, with local elites) or in the wider state context (such as land rights or the legal rights of women). NGOs find that if they wish to influence the 'big picture', they cannot ignore what the government is doing. At the same time, government agencies increasingly see NGOs as a source of dynamism and innovation and are seeking to draw upon their services, either by forming partnerships or, in less satisfactory cases, by cooption. But in some countries (such as the Philippines and Bangladesh) there are tentative signs that prevailing government administrative culture and procedure are being slowly questioned and reformed.

Just as the role of anthropologists as development participants raises a number of uncomfortable questions, there are similar dilemmas to be faced by those who argue that NGOs constitute an all-purpose solution to the problems of development practice. How accountable are these NGOs to the people whom they claim to represent? How efficient are NGOs in reality, and do they merely perform better than government agencies because they receive pro-portionately more resources for the tasks which they undertake? Do NGOs simply reproduce patronage relations at the local level by becoming the new purveyors of state resources in the countryside? Are NGOs therefore weakening the state further and perpetuating this weakness by drawing scarce staff and other resources away from it?

What is particularly interesting about NGOs is that many have radical origins and are engaging critically with the prevailing devel-opment discourse, occasionally influencing donor and government attitudes and practices along the way. While the work of some NGOs provides fascinating windows into alternative development paradigms, the large numbers of opportunistic or coopted organi-sations, which also form part of the category 'NGO', serve to remind us that real challenges to the existing order are all too easily neutralised.

'Participation'

Participation is another term which, although derived from radical ideas challenging developmental orthodoxy, is now to be found in the development plans and policy statements of the most mainstream institutions. Again, whether this represents a significant change in the discourse, or the cooption of challenges to it, is open to debate.

Like many of the currently fashionable development 'buzz words', the precise meaning of participation is elusive. Adnan et al. (1992) argue that meanings of participation can be broken down into three broad categories. First, participation can simply refer to a process in which information about a planned project is made available to the public. This may involve listening to local people's views about the plans, a more structured survey, or a formal dialogue regarding project options. This type of participation often only involves community leaders. It also leaves most decision-making power in the hands of the planners.

Second, participation might include project-related activities rather than mere information flows. This might involve using labour from the community, or a longer-term commitment by local groups to maintain services or facilities or even to plan for their future use (for instance, committees set up to manage sanitation facilities in an upgraded slum). Again, the initiative has come from the outside. People are involved, but are not directly in control.

Lastly, there are people's own initiatives. These fall outside the scope of the project agenda; they are therefore, some argue, the only true form of participation, for they are not imposed from the outside. If mobilisation comes from the poorer sections of the community, it also truly empowering. A famous example of this is the Chipko movement in the Himalayas that began in the 1970s, in which women mobilised themselves to protect the trees that were so vital for their economy from commercial loggers (Shiva, 1988).

The idea of participation is drawn from radical roots, but in practice has now become so ever-present in development jargon as to be often virtually without meaning. Many critics of development therefore view participation as a degraded term, which has served only to 'soften' top-downism and has been successfully stripped of its previous radical connotations (Rahnema, 1992). It can allow ideas to be imported into communities and then attributed to them: a token agenda of involvement at one level of the project (usually at the implementation rather than the planning stage) can then be used to legitimise decisions which have already been taken by powerful outsiders. Even when participatory research methods are deployed by development agencies, while people might be able to influence events by providing information or knowledge which may eventually feed into policy or project design, they are not actually taking the key decisions.

Nevertheless, the concept of participation strikes at the heart of previous developmental paradigms by suggesting that development should come from the bottom-up instead of through top-down policies and the agency of the state. Only when the supposed beneficiaries of development interventions participate in the planning and implementation of the projects which are intended to benefit them will they have any real interest in making development projects succeed. Participation is therefore a key prerequisite for sustainability.

Some agencies, such as the UK's Overseas Development Administration, thus now talk of local people as being 'stake-holders' in development, seeing this as a way of forming a stronger basis for their involvement. If people know that they stand to benefit from a particular intervention, the reasoning goes, they will work to ensure that the project suceeds and will contribute ideas for improvement. Not only will this lead to better projects, it will form an important goal of development in the context of the 'good government' aims of many donors, since it strengthens local accountability and democracy (Eyben, 1994).

However, as anthropologists will already be aware, the notion of 'participation' is itself problematic. For a start, it masks differences between people: local heterogeneity is dissolved into vague notions of 'community'. This may disregard important cross-cutting divisions of class, gender and age, which may lead to substantial differences in local views and interests. Notions of effective participation therefore involve having to disentangle conflicting interests within local communities and building support for the interests of particular, identifiable groupings of people. Participation, if it is handled properly, can create an opening for more vulnerable sections of the community to determine the form and outcome of development initiatives which are being undertaken in their name. This is undoubtedly a difficult, time-consuming and complicated process.

In practice, the rhetoric of participation can easily be misused while real power remains in the hands of outsiders:

1. It can legitimise a project by gaining the sanction or formal approval of key people in the community, which then feeds back into project appraisal criteria and helps to make the project a 'success'.
2. 'Participatory discussion' can provide an opportunity for local people to 'understand' what it is that the development agency seeks from them. Certain people can then, in return for the

promise of a supply of resources to the community, tell developers what they want to hear.

3. It can open up an opportunity for certain interests within the community to be 'written in' to the project design, or to gain control of its implementation, which tends to skew benefits towards better-off sections of the population.

Just as some government agencies are now seeking to establish greater credibility for their still essentially 'top-down' programmes by enlisting the services of locally based NGOs, participation is often desired by development agencies for the ideological legitimacy it brings. Yet is is also feared for its practical implications. Planners usually do not wish to involve local communities; they have institutional deadlines and a predetermined agenda, which by the time it reaches the community cannot be changed. These contradictions show how easily an objective of participation can feed effortlessly back into existing models of 'top-down' development and become neutralised by the dominant discourse.

Participatory research methodologies

With the increasing acceptance of participation as a desirable goal in development practice have come other important changes in research and project methodologies, particularly within agricultural work. This is closely related to the anthropological perspectives on local knowledge and human agency, outlined in previous chapters, as well as anthropological methodologies. Increasingly, considerable attention is now being paid to changing the ways in which local knowledge and information are elicited, understood and built upon by those engaged in development activities.

The work of Robert Chambers has been extremely influential in this regard, in its attempts to counter excessively formalistic approaches to 'data collection' by development workers and professionals. Participatory rural appraisal (PRA) and its variants aim to enable rural people to plan and enact solutions to problems by analysing their own knowledge of local conditions, facilitated by outsiders. This approach (Chambers, 1992: 5) has drawn upon insights borrowed from social anthropology, such as:

1. The idea of learning in the field as 'flexible art rather than rigid science'.
2. The need to learn in the field, informally, through conversations and relaxed observation.

3. The importance of the researcher's attitudes, behaviour and rapport with local people.
4. The emic/etic distinction, an anthropological concept drawn from linguistics, which contrasts the 'indigenous' reality of social actors with the observer's perception of that reality.
5. The validity and potential value of indigenous knowledge.

PRA therefore involves training researchers to go to villages and spend time talking to groups of people 'in situ', encouraging them to express local problems and potential solutions in their own terms. Care is taken to represent as many different sets of interests as possible, and the focus is on mutual learning between researcher and informant.

While such ideas are familiar to anthropologists, one has to remember that engineers, economists and agriculturalists receive little or no training in such matters. The research and administrative culture of many development agencies and government departments places scant value on direct communication with their constituencies, in environments where people have usually been seen as the 'objects' rather than the 'subjects' of the development process. PRA has therefore begun to challenge the assumptions of development practitioners trained within bureaucratic, status-conscious and quantitative research-based institutional cultures.

The growth of PRA, and the quite surprising amount of attention it currently receives, provides an opportunity to examine whether anthropology can really be used as a 'quick fix' by development practitioners in this way. If PRA seeks to do more or less what anthropologists do, how realistic is it to attempt to do justice to participant observation in a few days or weeks when anthropologists have usually taken far longer periods of time to try to get beneath the surface of a community?

PRA has become a tool which is now included in many projects, but it can easily be used within existing top-down frameworks if it is misapplied. It can sometimes be used to legitimise certain approaches and ideas and, if it is carried out cynically, can be employed to show support for pre-existing viewpoints. There is a temptation for those utilising PRA less scrupulously to enact what might be termed a 'participatory ritual', either because they are cynical about the whole process in the first place or because it has become just another part of their job. While such people might be sympathetic to the aims of PRA, they may balk at the levels of complexity (and resulting frustration) which arise from taking participation too seriously. For example, villagers can be routinely

---

Participatory action research[3]

Participatory action research is a loose group of methodologies undertaken by agencies – such as NGOs – in areas of Asia and Africa. It assumes that the main objective of development is the fulfilment of the human urge for creative engagement, and does not therefore focus on poverty alleviation, 'basic needs' or structural change as the immediate goals to be tackled.

In this way, PAR seeks to avoid the dependence which results from many external interventions in communities by stressing the outsider as animator, facilitating the promotion of people's self-development. The influence of the radical Brazilian educator Paulo Freire can be seen in this line of thinking. Typically, catalytic initiatives are brought about by educated outsiders, free of party political allegiances, who encourage groups of people to get together to discuss the reason for their poverty and engage in their own social investigation.

Group building follows, combined with discussion of prioritised actions which can be undertaken to address the principal causes of their poverty. External resources can be provided for support, but are not regarded as a precondition for problem-solving. The aim is to generate a 'progressive action-reflection rhythm' or 'people's praxis'. As the groups form links with other similar groups and encourage new ones, the dependence on the initial external stimulus is then supposed to fall away, though contact may be maintained.

---

consulted, maps and charts can be drawn, games can be played to reveal local realities, but experts may well go off and implement their project much as planned. Like 'participation', PRA is easily abused in practice.[4]

But even if PRA *is* carried out properly, can workable compromises be reached between the interests of the rich and the poor members of communities through such open discussion? Who speaks and who remains silent in these encounters? If an anthropologist needs at least a year to start understanding how a village community actually works (as anthropological tradition tells us), how can PRA achieve genuine community-based insights in such a short period of time, even if a more participatory methodology than usual is adopted? What are the dangers of 'quick and dirty' anthropology, and can it be justified in certain situations? All these questions need to be examined further. While PRA in many ways provides an easy target for the critiques of anthropologists, it is probably the case that the methodology is only rarely carried out in the ways and to the lengths which were originally intended.

Some NGOs have developed similar forms of research which are geared towards a more responsive approach to local problems, much of which can be undertaken by people themselves. The concept of 'action research' attempts to combine learning and doing. Proshika, for example, has developed a reflexive research method-ology which the NGO terms 'participatory action research' (Wood and Palmer-Jones, 1990: 25):

> While projects are designed between groups and the field staff with as much forethought as possible, new forms of social action obviously generate unforeseen processes and problems, which have to be studied by those involved as part of the social action itself.

A link between research and action has a two-fold purpose. It prevents the emergence of discrete elements within the NGO whose research and evaluatory functions 'constitute judgements' on the work of others. It provides constructive opportunities for the 'subjects' of the research to tie the research agenda to their needs. Action research becomes a process in which research is combined with practical problem-solving, with the participation of those who have identified and need to overcome a problem. This brings us full circle back to Chapter 2: reflexive action research has long been one of the aims of the more radical proponents of 'applied anthropol-ogy'. It may be that the NGO context forms one of the most fruitful arenas for work of this kind.

'Empowerment'

The shift in development thought during the 1980s away from the assumptions of top-down change towards alternative development models has, at its root, a conception of empowerment as a form of developmental change brought about by local problem-solving efforts and techniques. Empowerment has been described as being 'nurturing, liberating, even energising to the unaffluent and the unpowerful' (Black, 1991: 21). This concept of empowerment is in part drawn from the ideas of the Brazilian educationalist Paulo Freire, based on the need to stimulate and support people's abilities to understand, question and resist the structural reasons for their poverty through learning, organisation and action (see box on 'Development and literacy'). For many radical development theorists and practitioners, particularly in the NGO sector, the aim of promoting participation should be empowerment (Carroll, 1992).

Development and literacy[5]

Considerable attention has been given to the issue of literacy in developing countries. In Bangladesh, where the literacy level is around 35 per cent, illiteracy has been correctly identified as one of the country's most pressing development problems. It has been a prevailing myth of development that literacy can be seen as an independent variable in the development process which can be measured by a universal yardstick. Anthropologists and sociologists have shown it is important to recognise that literacy has to be viewed in the context of other variables and should therefore form part of an integrated approach to development.

For example, people use the skill of literacy for their own and perceived interests, which are not always 'development-oriented': in rural Bangladesh, such skills can sometimes be used to further the interests of the literate at the expense of the illiterate. Literacy programmes therefore have to be based on a firm understanding of the uses to which literacy can be put – literacy is an 'ambivalent servant'.

The NGO Friends in Village Development Bangladesh (FIVDB) has developed a functional literacy programme for landless men and women, who organise themselves into groups. Literacy training is combined with organisation support, savings and credit, technical assistance for income-generating activities and the gradual building of self-respect and self-confidence. Literacy is therefore linked to generating local group structures and capacity-building. Basic aspects of health and nutrition are taught alongside literacy.

A useful discussion of empowerment emerges from John Friedmann's analysis of the politics of alternative development. Friedmann develops a theory of poverty which views it not simply as the absence of material or other resources, but as a form of social, political and psychological disempowerment which must be challenged. In this view, whole sections of the population – landless rural workers, subsistence peasants and shanty town inhabitants, for example – have been systematically excluded from participation in the development process. Friedmann (1992: vii) therefore makes empowerment the central aim in his discussion of the politics of 'alternative development':

The empowerment approach, which is fundamental to an alternative development, places the emphasis on autonomy in the decision-making of territorially organized communities, local self-reliance (but not autarky), direct (participatory) democracy, and experiential social learning. Its starting point is the locality, because civil society is most readily mobilized around local issues.

Friedmann sees the need for alternative development models to acknowledge the rights and established needs of citizen households and individuals, which involves a political struggle for empowerment and against structural constraints. For example, the NGO Proshika's work has included group formation in which landless people take action in pursuit of their rights against locally powerful individuals.

The local power structure in countries such as Bangladesh is a crucial barrier to more equitable forms of change: it siphons off externally supplied resources intended for the poor, impedes the rule of law by substituting formal justice by de facto rules of force to settle disputes, and contributes to growing impoverishment by supporting moneylending with exploitative rates of interest (see BRAC, 1979). In one example documented in a recent collection of case studies from Bangladesh, groups of landless people in Gazipur district successfully organised a public boycott of a local landowner who was engaged in stealing public agricultural land by securing false land-title documents. The landowner had no access to public transport or hired labour and suffered public humiliation, and the group members who had lost rightful access to the land won the legal case against him in the courts (Kramsjo and Wood, 1992: 63).

There are of course contradictions within the current discourse of empowerment. Like participation, empowerment has become a frequently degraded term in mainstream development. Rahnema (1992: 123) sees the term simply as providing development discourse with a new form of legitimation and convincing people 'not only that economic and state authorities are the real power, but that they are within everyone's reach, provided everyone is ready to participate fully in the development design'.

In some countries, governments now talk glibly of empowerment of the poor in their development plans, having stripped the term of any real meaning. In other planning documents there is an assumption that empowerment can be achieved simply by providing credit to low-income people. As Korten (1990) notes, it is not really possible for one person to 'empower' another: people can only empower themselves. Korten argues that this requires a process of 'mutual empowerment' in a group setting, often with outsiders as facilitators. The danger of creating dependent groups, well-versed in the rhetoric of consciousness-raising but remaining essentially unchanged by the experience, has been observed in Bangladesh (Hashemi, 1989).

On a more practical level, outsiders need to think very carefully about their responsibilities in encouraging potentially violent confrontations between vulnerable groups and well-organised and powerful elites backed by the state (Bebbington, 1991). This might be an approach favoured by those who see much of the mainstream or 'alternative' discussions of empowerment within the development discourse as inadequate or compromised. For example, the Naxalite Maoists in India in the 1960s demonstrated, at an extreme level, the futility of such confrontation in terms of securing long-term change in rural areas (Cassen et al., 1978). Many of the rural people were left even more vulnerable to violent reprisal during the repression which followed the uprisings.

Farming systems research

As we have seen, top-down development has tended to apply Western high-technology solutions to problems of poverty while undervaluing or disregarding local forms of knowledge: an area in which anthropologists are often very interested. Local knowledge, it has been argued, is often situated in practice and in real situations (P. Richards, 1993). For example, whereas in Bangladesh small-scale fish-fry traders are encouraged by 'expert' outsiders to transport their fish over long distances using expensive and cumbersome oxygen cylinders and plastic bags, one recent anthropological study found that there was little reason why they could not continue to rely on a far more practical, local low-cost solution developed locally over generations, which uses clay or aluminium cooking pots and involves the oxygenation of the water by hand 'splashing' (Lewis et al., 1993).

The emergence of farming systems research (FSR) in the late 1970s reflected many of these concerns. FSR focuses on the small farm as a basic system for research and development and attempts to bring about the strong involvement of farmers themselves in every stage of the research and development process (Conway, 1986: 18). The farmer's decision-making is treated as being rational rather than guided, as was often supposed, by ignorance or conservatism. The objective is to improve the relevance and appropriateness of research, and this includes the participation of social scientists alongside biological scientists. FSR is also emphatically holistic, treating decisions and procedures for one crop within the wider farming system and its economic, social and environmental components. FSR therefore draws upon a number of anthropological insights in the way it attempts to minimise outsider ethnocentric assumptions and to understand the complex interconnectedness of social, economic and natural phenomena.

The new emphasis on indigenous knowledge (what might be termed the 'farmer first' approach: Chambers et al., 1989) has also encouraged some organisations to attempt to work with local or 'traditional' institutions instead of creating new ones. Some NGOs have been able to link up with existing people's organisations, with which they can then work in a servicing and advocacy role, strengthening and supporting the development and adaptation of local organisational forms. For example, the Mag-uumad Foundation Inc. (MFI), which works in Cebu in the Philippines, has worked with upland farmers to develop soil and water conservation technologies. Although the approach is relatively labour-intensive in the first few seasons of operation and could therefore be prohibitively costly for farmers, it has been found that work can be undertaken by farmers within the existing framework of *alayon* reciprocal village work groups. This age-old system has now successfully adapted itself to accommodate this newer form of community labouring (Cerna and Miclat-Teves, 1993).

While some NGOs and government agencies have turned FSR into a progressive tool, its terms and concepts have now entered the mainstream, so that it is common to hear many agricultural extension workers and researchers talk of 'farmer participatory research' while retaining essentially top-down approaches. Likewise, there is a tendency for local knowledge to become overly systematised, and reduced to a quasi-scientific schema which ignores its wider epistemological base. Local knowledges cannot always be simply reduced to a blueprint, ready to be inserted into a development plan, especially when they spring from quite different cultural contexts from those of the developers. These problems have been raised in a number of critques of the 'farmer first' movement (in particular, see Scoones and Thompson, 1993; 1994). Like many of the new ideas we have discussed, FSR has found favour in some areas of the development mainstream, but usually in a form which conforms to existing paradigms and practices without challenging the wider assumptions and objectives of development. Whether or not this continues to be the case remains to be seen.

Community development

Anthropologists and sociologists have long argued that life is not divided neatly into compartments and that the workings of a local economy are inseparable from wider social, political and cultural processes. The concept of community development is central to this integrated approach. Without strengthening local communities, and encouraging them to take a more active role in the planning and maintenance of their facilities, the argument goes, strategies for improvement are doomed to fail. Many projects therefore now involve a 'community development' component. One example is recent slum improvement projects in India. Here, slum 'upgrading' (the provision of improved sanitation and housing) is being increasingly integrated with social strategies. Setting up local committees that are responsible for maintaining the improved facilities and planning the future development of their community, the provision of halls or libraries, or the establishment of savings groups to encourage a sense of community are all strategies in recent British projects aimed at integrated slum improvement projects which have a strong community development component.

Community development has a tendency to become largely cosmetic unless it involves the active participation of the community in the planning stages of the project. One very real area of difficulty is that these approaches rest on a notion of 'community' which any anthropologist knows is by definition very shaky ground. Who or what constitutes the community? There are bound to be different sets of interests with a range of different needs, different types of power and varying degrees of visibility. Furthermore, its origins can be traced back to colonial social welfare policies in Africa in the 1940s (Midgley, 1995), and the notion of 'social development' as deployed by development agencies can at times be dangerously close to modernisation-type thought in which communities are judged, by a variety of ill-defined criteria, to be either more or less developed.

Women in Development (WID) and Gender and Development (GAD)

Debates surrounding empowerment share some of their origins with the recognition of the importance of gender issues in development. As we have seen, during the 1970s and into the 1980s gender relations were increasingly recognised as central in determining people's access to resources and the ways in which they experience development. In this section, we shall consider how some of these debates have been translated into policy within development agencies.

A major step towards official acceptance of the need to consider more carefully the relationship between development and gender came in the guise of the UN Decade for Women (1975–85). During this period there were important changes in the ways both policy-makers and academics approached gender. Whereas previously both groups had tended to concentrate on 'women' and their domestic reproductive roles, by the mid-1980s policy increasingly emphasised women's employment, income-generation capacities and so on, rather than the provision of welfare services for them. We shall outline these different policy approaches and their relationship to different theoretical positions within development shortly.

The UN Decade marked what appeared at first to be a growing institutional commitment to women's issues, although the rationale behind this varied. Prompted partly by the work of writers such as Boserup, and also as a reflection of the successes of feminism in the North, which had enabled a few women to reach managerial positions within aid agencies and had pushed feminist issues on to the political agenda, many development agencies by the early 1980s had determined to 'do something' for women. For example, in Sweden parliament was subject in the 1970s and 1980s to successful lobbying pressure by Swedish women's organisations for official aid to address specifically women's needs and this became reflected in SIDA's programmes. The United States Agency for International Aid (USAID) also rapidly adopted the new phrase 'women in development', with the establishment of an Office of Women in Development. Although the meanings of WID are far from fixed, USAID seemed to use it in terms of the potential contribution women could make to the development effort, as a so far untapped resource. Many other institutions followed suit, setting up WID offices or, like the British ODA, building a commitment to women into official policy. Indeed, it is now commonplace for government ministries, NGOs and multilateral agencies to pay lip-service (if nothing else) to the aims of WID, and some donors insist on a WID component in project proposals before they consider funding.

The WID approach, however, tends to focus only on women in isolation, rather than the social, cultural and political relations of which they are a part. As feminist anthropologists have frequently pointed out, it is gender and not sex which is at issue. This has led to a shift towards 'gender and development' (GAD), which turns attention away from women as an isolated category to the wider relations of which they are a part. It should, however, be noted that the terms are often used interchangeably, and policies all too frequently focus attention only on women. Indeed, despite the energy and resources directed at gender issues, WID/GAD still frequently remain an 'add-on' to mainstream policy (Moser, 1993: 4).

WID/GAD approaches are far from homogeneous. In her account of WID projects, Caroline Moser outlines five main approaches, each associated with a distinct developmental philosophy (1989: 1799–825). While we must beware of over-schematising affairs (for example, policies and projects often involve a variety of assumptions and approaches), this clearly indicates the range of responses to gender issues within development practice. A 'welfare' type project, for example, is linked to charitable notions of 'doing good' for women and children and involves the top-down provision of services and goods for beneficiaries, without demanding any return on their behalf. While this approach was common in the 1960s and early 1970s, with the growing influence of feminism as the 1970s unfolded, notions of 'equity' increasingly gained sway in some development circles. These aimed at boosting the rights and power of women within developing countries, again usually through top-down changes in governmental policy, state intervention and so on.

Another approach which gained popularity in the 1970s and 1980s is 'anti-poverty', in which poverty is recognised as women's main problem. This was closely allied to the 'basic needs' movement, which had taken off during the 1970s. Solutions include income-generation projects, skill generation and so on. These strategies are often identical to those advocated by the 'efficiency approach', but their underlying philosophy is fundamentally different. Efficiency was central to much developmental philosophy during the 1980s, in line with the dominant political ideologies of the time. Accordingly, women were targets of development projects only because the centrality of their productive contribution was recognised. If projects aimed to improve recipients' well-being, rather than being based in notions of welfare or universal human rights, the underlying philosophy was that this would, in turn, increase their efficiency in the productive process and thus add to capitalist growth.

All of these approaches assume that change is initiated first and foremost from the outside, through donor-led policies and planning. As well as being fundamentally 'top-down', they have also been accused of ethnocentrism. Many of their fiercest critics are

Southern women, who argue that discourses of WID/GAD reflect the preoccupations and assumptions of Western feminists rather than the women they purport to be representing and assisting. Indeed, by homogenising all 'Third World' women (in concepts such as 'female-headed households', or in policies which treat the interests of women in vastly different cultural, economic and political contexts as the same) and treating them as victims in dire need of policies which alter their status, these approaches feed into colonial stereotypes and categories (see, in particular, Mohanty, 1988). Indeed, by treating them as 'victims' of their culture, they negate and undermine the *agency* of Southern women (White, 1992: 15–22).

Another criticism made of WID/GAD approaches is that they make ethnocentric assumptions regarding the content of relations between men and women in different societies, seeing only exploitation, subordination and conflict, whereas the women concerned might put more stress on cooperation and the importance of familial bonds (Barrios de la Chungara, 1983). Lastly, WID/GAD is accused of ignoring the true underlying causes of Southern women's subordination and poverty, which are more to do with colonial and post-colonial exploitation and inequality than the cultural construction of gender within their particular societies (Sen and Grown, 1987). This returns us to the concept of 'empowerment'.

Many of the institutional and policy changes regarding gender and development are to be welcomed. However, they also illustrate the capacity of radical concepts to be neutralised within development discourse. There is still a very great deal of work to be done, and this should not simply extend pre-existing WID/GAD programmes which are themselves often deeply problematic. At worst, the effect of WID/GAD approaches in development has been to transform what are in reality complex and nuanced conceptual tools and insights into overly simplified categories and phrases, which nonetheless are made central to policy (such as 'women-headed households') but effectively stripped of their radical implications.

Furthermore, since the techniques and jargon of many developers is comparatively rigid, with their insistence on frameworks, outputs and so on, the task of translating the work of feminist anthropologists into policy statements or a list of recommendations is far from easy. There is also a danger of gender policies collapsing into a new form of social engineering, whereby the object of the exercise is to 'raise women's status', regardless of the wider cultural context. We shall be exploring these points further in our concluding chapter.

Conclusion

This chapter has indicated various ways in which, far from being monolithic, development discourse is heterogeneous, contested and constantly changing. As we have seen, there is considerable evidence that many development practitioners are gradually becoming aware of concepts such as participation and empowerment, are considering participatory methodologies, realising that local knowledge should be valued and taking gender issues more seriously. This shifting awareness is doubtless influenced by wider changes unrelated to anthropology, such as the failure of economic models of development to deliver better living standards to the poor, but is also due in part to the anthropological perspectives detailed in previous chapters.

Such shifts in the awareness of developers have also led to changes in actual policies and practice. Gender training, as practised today by many Northern agencies involving both their own employees and those of recipient organisations, is one example (for a wider discussion, see Kabeer, 1994: 264–305). Another is the increased funding of NGOs by agencies, or the commitment (on paper at least) to participatory methodologies.

These changes have not, however, been achieved without a struggle. It is important to remember that just as 'development' does not involve a unitary body of ideas and practices, 'developers' are not a unitary body of people. The discourse is contested by different interest groups and individuals within agencies, as well as between them. A development policy or resulting project may be the result of considerable struggle by different actors to promote what they believe development should involve. For example, while 'WID' objectives may be widely accepted by many agencies in the 1990s (or at least, while many pay lip-service to them), this has often involved many years of lobbying by feminists working to change the patriarchal nature of development discourse. Meanwhile, what 'gender and development' should involve, both practically and theoretically, remains hotly debated.

It would, however, be misleading to give the impression that development discourse in the 1990s is a 'free for all' in which opponents of equal strength contest the policy agenda. The fact remains that some actors – and institutions – are more powerful than others. The new ideas and practices discussed here are also by no means all of equal political weight. Within the discourse, some concepts are dominant and pervasive while others remain subordinate. As we have indicated, this often means that more radical ideas become coopted and neutralised, leading to contradictions between official policy and practice. 'Participation', for example, might be heavily emphasised in an agency's planning documents, but hardly take place at all 'on the ground'. Likewise, 'empowerment' is a concept intended to imply an alternative development agenda based on local grassroots action and power, but the term is also increasingly part of the language of governments and of mainstream management theory in the private sector.

Need this always be the case? Is Escobar correct in arguing that the 'architecture of the discursive formation' remains essentially the same? The answers are clearly highly complex, depending both on what arenas of practice and types of relations one is examining, and on what criteria one takes as indicating significant change. For example, do staffing levels within agencies indicate a shift in development practice? Within some agencies, social anthropologists are being increasingly employed as top-level policy advisors, as are feminists committed to WID or GAD. Does this mean that the ideas which such groups embody are being actively taken on board, or are such groups being coopted by more dominant and powerful interests? Likewise, while lobbyists within and outside agencies may be successful in changing official policy (a commitment in agency documents to 'women' or 'poverty alleviation', for example), this is not necessarily the same as changing actual practice.

Another arena one might examine is that of changing relations between NGOs and bilateral or multilateral donors. Increased levels of funding given to some of the more radical NGOs could be evidence that the balance of power within development is indeed changing. However, it could also be a case of 'old wine in new bottles', especially if those running NGOs are members of the most privileged groups who are merely taking over the functions of the state.

To argue effectively for or against Escobar's point one therefore needs to examine what happens 'on the ground', over many years. In whose hands does power remain? As anthropologists will be aware, this is not an easy question to answer; it requires considerably more research and is an area in which anthropologists of development potentially have much to contribute. The outcome of developmental work is also affected by factors outside the control of developers. It is thus too simple always to argue that the 'dominant' development discourse has once again succeeded in neutralising radical alternatives. For example, Southern governments may act to curtail the activities of NGOs funded by Northern aid agencies if their work is too threatening to local power relations. Likewise, projects which attempt to increase the status of women may be unintentionally scuppered by inattention to the complexities of local gender relations. This may be the result of misinformation and bad practice, but does not necessarily indicate an international conspiracy of patriarchy.

In this chapter we have therefore suggested that processes are working in several directions at once – both towards and against change. At times and in some ways the dominant discourse and the power relations it involves are maintained; at other times, in other ways, they are challenged and slowly transformed. In the next chapter we examine in more detail the actual processes which take place in the machinery of development both to repress and neutralise challenges and – slowly – to adapt to new ideas and alternatives.

6 ANTHROPOLOGISTS WITHIN DEVELOPMENT

So far we have discussed conceptual issues and drawn upon the anthropological and development literature for illustrations of most of our points. In what follows, we discuss some of our own experiences as anthropologists working in what might be termed the 'aid industry', in development agencies such as international donors, private consultancy firms and non-governmental organisations. We will provide some examples of the different forms which this type of applied work can take through personal case studies.

These case studies, as well as documenting some of the practical realities faced by anthropologists in the development context, serve to reinforce an important theme which runs through much of this book: that contrary to the impression given in much contemporary analysis, discourses of development are not all the same; nor indeed are they fixed. Instead, they are constantly being contested and are therefore open to change. Many of the issues we have raised in this book place anthropologists in a potentially strong position to contribute to and influence such change. How this might be done from within the aid industry is the subject of this chapter.

Anthropologists as consultants

In Chapters 2 and 4 we discussed the history of applied anthropology and considered some of the roles played by applied anthropologists in development. In what follows we continue to discuss the activities of professional anthropologists, working largely outside academia, within the development industry. Anthropologists are now employed in growing numbers by development agencies, organisations and private consultancy firms. A discussion of applied anthropology does not therefore simply raise questions of what a professional anthropologist might do, but also includes an analysis of the framework in which he or she operates.

The role of anthropologist as consultant originated in the practice of government agencies referring issues of fact or policy to independent authorities. Examples of this are the links established between the United States Trust Territory administration and ethnologists at the University of Hawaii, and those between the government of India and the director of its new Department of Anthropology during the 1940s (H.G. Barnett, 1956: 28). Recent years have seen the development of the anthropologist as 'policy professional', alongside other professionals with development-related expertise such as engineers and economists. In the UK, this role has been expanded upon in detail by Alan Rew (1985), an anthropologist who has consistently prioritised this kind of work while maintaining a base within academia. In the US, Allen Hoben (1982) has written on a similar theme. There are an increasing number of professional posts for applied anthropologists outside academia, for example in the UK's Overseas Development Administration (whose newly expanded 'social development advisor' positions, discussed in more detail later in this chapter, are frequently filled by anthropologists), or in actual development projects which may run for periods of several years.

The types of work which professional anthropologists are asked to undertake can vary considerably. They may include applied research to produce supporting data for planned interventions; contributions to the appraisal and evaluation planning of development projects; or attempting to build local participation into the project. Assignments can vary from a short consultancy job lasting a few weeks, to a placement on a project for several years as one of the full-time staff. The anthropologist is usually made a specialist member of a team which may include people from other disciplines, such as engineering, management or economics.

There may be, understandably, an assumption that the anthropologist can bring to bear a distinctive set of insights and skills to a given series of problems or issues. Anthropologists have sometimes been portrayed as bringing a special, almost magical, ingredient seen as hitherto missing in development.[1] Even some anthropologists themselves have been prone to get carried away by this line of thinking, and Cochrane (1976) was moved to write in a moment of great optimism: 'The third world badly needs the kind of expertise that only anthropologists have to offer.' No doubt this reflected the mood of the time, when anthropology seemed to offer quite straightforward possibilities of contributing to the changing development paradigm. But as we shall see, it is extremely difficult to identify specifically what it is, in practical terms, that professional anthropologists do have to offer development.[2]

One good starting point here is to consider the anthropological approach to collecting information and ideas, which is usually based upon face-to-face contact with people. As we argued in the last chapter, there can be no doubt that anthropological methodologies are receiving more and more attention in development and policy circles. One well-known example of this is the growth of participatory rural appraisal (PRA), which draws on some of anthropology's methodological insights; another is farming systems research (FSR), which seeks to combine the indigenous knowledge and practice of farmers with specialised outsider knowledge in order to improve support for the poor and marginal farmers who usually find their needs ignored by conventional agricultural extension approaches.

But how do professional anthropologists work when they find themselves under the practical constraints of the development workplace? Within the framework of consultancy there is a tremendous pressure on the anthropologist to contribute constructively to interdisciplinary teams and to try to provide realistic solutions to problems. Some anthropologists find applied work difficult because they are used to a solitary, self-regulating work regimen. Others, their interest in anthropology motivated by left-leaning, anarchist or rejectionist positions, can find themselves reluctant to compromise within mainstream contexts. Aside from the personal feelings of the anthropologist, there are certain methodological compromises which may have to be made by the consultant. The main one is time: whereas most people who have completed a doctoral degree will have spent between one and two years doing their fieldwork, work in the development context may be allotted a few months or even only weeks by the employing agency. While it may be possible to do meaningful work by returning to communities already well-known from previous work, this is less than ideal for an anthropologist asked to work in a completely new context. Such assignments can offer an exciting challenge, but it may prove professionally frustrating and may generate research findings which lack theoretical strength or methodological rigour.

Working within agencies

While some anthropologists work as freelance consultants, others are employed as salaried staff by government or non-governmental agencies. In the case of these anthropologists, much of the day-to-day work they have to undertake is administrative. Rather than being hired for their knowledge of any particular society or for their potential as fieldworkers, such anthropologists must bring to their work a set of insights and questions which enable them to critique and advise on existing projects and policy, as well as to help formulate new ideas and strategy within the agency.

Social development advisors (SDAs) employed by the ODA provide a good example of this type of work (for a longer discussion of the role of SDAs within the ODA during the 1980s, see Conlin, 1985). As we shall see, their changing profile within the organisation over recent years also demonstrates how development agendas and practices can change over time.

Like other professional advisors (e.g. economists, engineers and ecologists), SDAs offer advice to desk officers responsible for particular geographical regions and the projects within them. Since they control regional budgets, these adminstrators have considerable power. The SDA remit is to comment on any 'social' issue. How this is defined does of course depend upon one's perspective. One immediate problem is that desk and regional officers without social science training might not recognise a project or policy as having social implications when to the SDAs it clearly does. Part of their work is therefore political: to get the administrators on their side.

The work of SDAs might involve, among other things, commenting upon project proposals, producing statements on policy-related issues and participating in missions to projects 'in the field'[3] as part of teams of advisors and administrators. As employees of the government they may also end up offering advice on the Overseas Development Minister's speeches!

In many ways SDAs are forced to conform to the dominant discourse of the ODA. In 1990 this was heavily biased towards economics and to notions of growth and efficiency. Many employees, especially those involved in more technical activities, clearly believed strongly in modernity and the benefits of technological progress. To question these explicitly or to refuse to comply to established practices (particular bureaucratic procedures and assumptions, e.g. the production of a specific style of report and use of a specific language) would, given the balance of power within the ODA, not have much advanced the SDAs' cause. Instead, SDAs worked over the period stealthily to put social issues on the agenda.

To an extent they have been successful. In 1990 the three SDAs employed by the ODA did not have their own separate department, and were headed by an economist. In 1995, however, the number of

SDAs employed by the ODA more than trebled, and they now have their own separate Social Development Department. Increasingly social issues are reflected in policy and form part of project appraisals and evaluations. Slowly the balance of power within the organisation is beginning to change. The discourses it produces through its reports, its policy statements and the actual content of meetings is also shifting, albeit only slightly, to more anthropologically informed ways of seeing and doing. This does not necessarily mean that ODA-style development is more empowering and participatory on the ground. The bureaucratic and political constraints are huge. SDAs remain only one small part of a much larger machinery. They too are not completely free of 'top-downism'. What it does indicate, however, is that development is contested and fought over within aid agencies. Consequently it is continually in a state of flux and change.

The compromise between pure and applied

The official origins of applied anthropology led some anthropologists such as Brokensha (1966) to reserve the term only for work undertaken on behalf of governments in an official capacity. However, this reflects only part of the picture; applied anthropology has always been rather more than this definition allows. In the US, for example, as we saw in Chapter 2, the private sector as well as government has made use of anthropologists; this trend is growing as anthropologists are increasingly employed by private consultancy companies and hired by many different types of agency. The growing importance of local, national or international NGOs in development also renders such a definition of applied anthropology obselete. There are a range of agencies active in agriculture, health, education and infrastructure work with whom anthropologists now come into contact and with whom they may wish to collaborate.

But what is really meant by 'applied' work? Applied anthropology has previously tended to be used only in the case of a specific, formal application of anthropological work to solving particular problems. But it might be argued that all anthropology is in a sense applied since it is concerned – usually – with field level research with communities of real people and tries to reflect the views of those people. At the same time, many anthropologists who do not themselves have any direct involvement in development issues have nevertheless contributed theoretical ideas which inform the ways in which we think about development. Anthropological investigation does not therefore need to be undertaken with a specific purpose in mind for it to be objectively useful. Even if the original intention behind a piece of research was not an applied one, it can be drawn upon subsequently (and used or misused) by practitioners. In the context of development, the distinction between pure and applied all too easily begins to dissolve.

Non-commissioned research may be of practical value to a range of other people beyond academia, including governments, donor agencies or NGOs, regardless of whether or not the work was motivated by practical problem-solving.[4] It is also important to distinguish clearly between the 'means' and the 'ends' of applied anthropology. What kinds of outcomes are applied anthropologists trying to achieve in their work, and what control do they have over these outcomes? These questions have led to some interesting theoretical areas of debate. Bastide (1973: 6) argues that the subject contains a paradox which is implicit in any 'liberal' science: applied anthropology implies the means for controlled change, but does not necessarily contain clear ideas about exactly 'what' these means can contribute towards. The way out of this dilemma, he suggests, is that research can be linked to action. Marx's concept of 'praxis' provides an alternative in which it is recognised that value judgements cannot be separated from conceptions of reality. This insight can therefore generate a form of research which is linked to action:

theoretical knowledge develops at the same time as practical knowledge, in and of the same movement of praxis. Human intervention in social reality is both action and science at once, since it permits us at the same time to change the world, and in changing it, to discover it. (Bastide, 1973: 6)

While there is a sense in which applied anthropology is about 'changing the world', it is unlikely that the anthropologist will have a better idea of how to change it than anyone else, but he or she may bring a certain kind of perspective to the problem, one which involves, and seeks to represent, the outlooks and views of all those involved.

Achieving influence

Applied anthropological work, even when it is of a very high standard, is only as good as its ability to influence, directly or indirectly, those who hold or seek to hold power. An important set of questions surrounds the need for anthropologists to reach the people who make policy decisions. While there are institutions in the UK which undertake policy-related research in development issues (such as the Overseas Development Institute and the Institute of Development Studies), these have usually concentrated more on economic than on anthropological matters.

It is well known that anthropologists have not always communicated well with interdisciplinary colleagues or administrators. Strathern (1993: 10) outlines a number of common pitfalls in the Papua New Guinea context which have made the anthropologist's work less relevant and accessible to policy-makers than it should have been. For many years anthropologists used a research methodology which portrayed communities in static terms. The use of the 'ethnographic present' drew anthropological attention away from examining issues which arise from social change. Another problem is the fieldwork 'rite of passage' of the anthropology postgraduate who tends to head for isolated areas of the country where detailed ethnographic material can be collected away from the more visible and uncertain complexities of areas experiencing rapid change. This has led to an incompleteness in ethnographic coverage. Added to these factors is the age-old complaint of the time-lag between the completion of fieldwork and writing up the work, which can in any case arrive in a form which is inaccessible to administrators with limited time. Furthermore, Strathern argues, anthropologists have tended to oppose, a priori, the Papua New Guinea government's approach to development policy, which was growth-oriented and sought to encourage foreign investment at almost any cost.

Recently there has been more discussion about the practical ways in which anthropologists can make their findings more useful to the agencies employing them, the need to write more accessible reports and how to work more effectively within an interdisciplinary team. (Rew, 1985; Epstein and Ahmed, 1984). There is clearly a long way to go before anthropologists and development practitioners, particularly those primarily concerned with technical or administrative priorities, can learn to communicate with each other easily.

On the other hand, for anthropologists interested in development issues there need be no fixed boundary between the academic and consultancy roles. Many applied anthropologists find that these two areas of work can be mutually reinforcing, since they provide the opportunity for creating links between research, applied work and teaching. For the consultant who remains linked to an academic institution, consultancy work can be strengthened by a periodic return to pure research, during which intellectual batteries can be recharged through less pressured periods of reflection on theoretical issues.

Perhaps the anthropologists who stand the best chance of doing worthwhile development work are those who combine long-term academic research with shorter, carefully selected forays into applied consultancy. During the consultancy assignments, ideas can be reformulated into forms which are more readily accessible to policy-makers – short reports, workshop presentations and training sessions. But there often remains a significant gulf between the 'applied' and the 'academic' types of information and understanding. Furthermore, many policy-makers simply do not have time to take on lengthy theoretical works and respond far more readily to face-to-face discussions or short briefing documents.

The question of ethics

A discussion of applied anthropology brings into focus some difficult ethical questions. The first of these is the joint issue of accountability and responsibility: for whom is the work being undertaken and to whom are the findings provided? Information is a source of power in the interactions and conflicts between rich and poor, and as such quickly becomes highly sensitive. The applied work context illustrates the dangers which can arise, in terms of accountability and quality, if anthropological skills are placed formally at the service of administrators and policy-makers. Unless anthropologists' involvement provides openings for the weaker sections of a local community to increase their influence over the possible outcomes of a development project, he or she may have only contributed to a development project's control over people as the objects rather than the subjects of the 'development process'.

A second question is the issue of quality. The constraints placed on the work of the applied anthropologist, such as a short time-scale or the need for a clear set of user-friendly conclusions, has tended to lead to methodological or theoretical short-cuts being taken. Among some anthropologists there has been a tendency to view applied work as being of second-rate quality. While such criticisms are sometimes valid (and there is no doubt that poor-quality work can emerge under time-bound, subject-specific conditions), the tendency of 'pure' anthropologists to write off work undertaken by their applied colleagues is often unjustified. In the end, the quality of work will vary according to the commitment and ability of the researcher, and whether it is produced under academic research conditions or commissioned by an agency.

From this more general discussion let us now turn to some specific examples of how anthropologists might work within the world of development. These involve important questions about whether or not anthropologists are compromising themselves by 'buying in' to the whole development discourse, as Escobar has forcefully argued in recent years, or whether the discourse itself can be changed. The case studies which follow explore the room for manoeuvre which may exist. From these we will try to draw general lessons from our experiences working in the 'aid industry', without going into too much detail concerning the specific country or organisational contexts. This has been necessary partly because we are dealing – we hope frankly – with issues which may be seen as sensitive by those involved. We have followed the tradition in ethnographic writing of preserving anonymity so that the identities of informants can be safeguarded. In consultancy work, there may be a further restriction on work undertaken which means that copyright of the material generated remains with the employing agency. This rule can become a serious barrier to information diffusion, and is frequently used to withhold material which relates to failures or difficult themes which may show organisations of individuals in a bad light. For example, while undertaking a literature review recently on the issue of corruption for the Swedish International Development Authority (SIDA), it became clear that a vast amount of data and documentation resided in a largely unaccessible form as restricted reports carried out by consultants working for donors, governments and international organisations (Lewis, 1992). Nevertheless, we hope that the material presented does not lose its meaning through being unspecific on geographical, cultural or organisational details. We have sought to retain as much of the relevant narrative as possible. Our approach parallels that traditionally adopted by anthropologists writing ethnography: these cases studies represent personal, ethnographic and often subjective accounts of experience.

Case 1. Evaluating rural cooperative training

The first case study illustrates the difficulty of communicating with often defensive and potentially hostile informants in the project setting. This involves complex questions of ethics and power which may require careful negotiation. This case study also illustrates how projects can become dysfunctional and take on a logic of their own, growing increasingly out of touch with their 'clients'. The outsider perspective provided by the short-term consultant can be of great value in bringing a sense of proportion and balance, and the sceptical instincts of the anthropologist in particular can be useful in seeing through some of the problems.

A consultancy assignment was undertaken by an anthropologist for a European agency to evaluate a cooperative training programme for farmers. This was being carried out in association with an Asian government's Rural Cooperatives Board (RCB). The study was apparently triggered by a growing realisation on behalf of the foreign donor that no-one who was responsible at any of the different administrative levels of the agency really knew about the progress of the project any more. The foreign consultant who had designed and taken the initial interest in the work had left. No-one had subsequently managed to understand the project in its entirety, especially as it had changed in both personnel and emphases over the years.

Indeed, it almost seemed that staff at both the main and the regional offices were secretly counting on the fact that someone else within the administration had more of a grasp of what had become a very complicated project than they did. A chain of mutually supportive relationships had resulted, although it was becoming apparent that such a fragile project 'status quo' could not be sustained for long. In the end, it was acknowledged by the donor agency that something had to be done. This absence of knowledge about the project was mirrored by a lack of information about the impact of the training on the farmers themselves, and the way in which cooperatives worked (or didn't work) on the ground.

The story of the project is as follows. The RCB is responsible for forming thousands of farmers' cooperatives in villages across the country, a process which has been in motion since the 1960s. A rural cooperative model had been developed using relatively innovative ideas and became, for a brief period, an international development success story. Groups of village farmers were encouraged to pool their resources, learn cooperative management skills, define their particular needs (production, processing, marketing, etc.) and thereby gain access to subsidised government credit and agricultural inputs, while at the same time learning to solve their economic problems collectively. The government had then taken the basic model and 'scaled it up', with the assistance of foreign donors, so that it covered the whole country. However, the country-wide replication of the project had weakened its effectiveness during the 1970s, since it had been stretched beyond the control of its founders and their constant care, inspiration and attention.

Several academic studies over the years had indicated the weaknesses of the cooperative system, which tended to be dominated by richer farmers and viewed instrumentally as a means of securing subsidised inputs rather than as a system of mutual economic advancement. Combined with this, a burgeoning NGO sector had evolved which was successfully developing alternative models of rural development that implicitly highlighted the RCB's weaknesses. Nevertheless, the government had now developed a national framework for strengthening farmers' activities, and most of the main bilateral aid agencies had judged support to the RCB, with its mandate for rural cooperatives, as a priority.

For several years, the donor agency had been funding a team of expatriate cooperative specialists to strengthen the RCB's staff training capability, by training the training staff and developing appropriate training materials. The aim was to promote a more participatory training ethos than the 'top-down' tradition embodied in traditional government approaches. This training was to begin at the managerial level of the RCB's administrative hierarchy, the objective being to assist the training message to spread through regional and local level administrative structures.

The project had been functioning for six years by the time this particular review was commissioned. There had been reviews of some of the other aspects over the years, and although the anthropologist attempted to track some of them down, none were initially made available to him. It seemed that the various actors involved had managed to build up relationships of mutual interdependence based on a common interest in seeing the project continue, while objective information about the project's progress was juggled between them so that no single group in the end took responsibility for the deficiencies which were becoming apparent to many associated with the project.

The anthropologist's job ultimately involved trying to assess the impact of the training at the village level by talking to farmers about the usefulness of the training they had received. But before this was possible, it was necessary to make sense of the project's history, personnel changes and shifts in emphasis through the various phases of its existence. The experience of walking into the project office was not unlike other anthropological encounters, in which one is faced simultaneously with the dual tasks of explaining or justifying one's presence and trying to make sense of alien language, locations, codes of behaviour and power structures. The project staff had not requested that the study take place and remained unsure, even suspicious, of its objectives and justification.

Spatially, the city-based office illustrated the boundaries of a hierarchy with clearly marked distinctions in status between different project staff. Each expatriate consultant sat at a desk in a large open-plan office, around which clustered, on drawn-up chairs, people known as 'local consultants', whom it quickly turned out acted in most cases more as personal assistants to the foreigners, or as go-betweens between them and the government. There were also differences among the expatriates, based on length of service to the project. One of the longest serving team members had mysteriously moved his office and entourage across the hall to an entirely separate suite, where a new project title had been pasted on the door; little communication apparently took place between the new and old offices. The anthropologist was informed that this team member was no longer technically part of the project, although he seemed to be still working on the same set of problems. Was the anthropologist supposed to talk to him or not?

One of the first lessons the anthropologist learned was that while it is natural for everyone concerned to feel a little defensive when the evaluator arrives, several responsive strategies are open to project staff. Some are friendly and open from the start, while others adopt an aloof stance and treat initial tentative or necessarily ill-informed enquiries with ill-disguised disdain. Others patiently reply at length in terms designed to confuse rather than clarify. Some are openly hostile, while still others are never available for comment. Another approach is to fend off enquiries with piles of long, detailed and not necessarily relevant reports. Some behave towards outsiders very differently outside the office in a social context, where much of the interesting, complex or 'difficult' information can emerge. All of this behaviour was immediately recognisable from village fieldwork undertaken a few years earlier ...

During the next two months the anthropologist conducted research with the town-based consultants and other staff as informants and supervised a grassroots study with local farmers and cooperative staff. The results were very disturbing. The training activities seemed to have reached very few farmers. Moreover, many of the cooperatives which the project existed to service existed only in name. While some staff remained indifferent or hostile, nevertheless the anthropologist built up good relationships with others. Everyone had their own 'version' of the events and the facts of the project. Despite the emerging evidence of lack of impact, many could find it easy to ignore, avoid responsibility for or, more interestingly, explain this failure without necessarily questioning the project and its usefulness. One member of the team actually took it upon himself to 'wine and dine' the anthropologist one night and explain that it might be good for him (in terms of the anthropologist's career) if he wrote a positive report. When the anthropologist made it obvious that this would not be possible, relations became very bad with this particular (quite powerful) individual.

In the end the anthropologist discussed the report with project staff before leaving, and no serious factual objections were raised. The project was phased out soon afterwards, partly as a result of the report, but also due to growing evidence from other sources that all was not well. In the end the anthropologist heard informally that his report was apparently received quite well by the donor concerned, but he was never invited to give detailed feedback or to defend particular points against criticism, apart from a short debriefing on his way home. The ritual of undertaking the study seemed not to require it. It would be interesting to know how many people actually read the report.

There are difficult ethical choices in work of this kind. It is tempting for the anthropologist evaluator to attempt perfection in judging the realities of a poor project, forgetting that there are rules (the project objectives) against which a project should be judged, rather than judging it against 'pure' principles. Another temptation – especially if one is in need of work – is to be as positive as possible, which may, in the short term at least, be the path of least resistance.

Points for discussion

1. Power is hierarchical in development projects: between expatriate and local staff, external consultants and local personnel, project staff and local people or 'clients'.
2. Ethical questions arise continually during applied consultancy work. Does the anthropologist want to spoil the chances of another, similar job, by giving a project a negative write-up? Will it be a useful academic career move to publish a paper which 'rubbishes' a project even if it is slightly overstated? Or is it tempting to err on the side of caution, provide a clean bill of health for a project and hope for more work of this kind? There may be different objectives for consultancy reports and academic papers which lead to the taking of different positions with the same material according to context. This can sometimes appear to be hypocritical.
3. Projects can run for considerable periods of time without effective evaluation or objective assessment. Various interests (donors, implementors, staff factions) can combine to support continuation without due regard to results, or with an overoptimistic belief that, regardless of structural limitations, positive results will eventually be demonstrable.

4. The anthropologist's knowledge of the wider agrarian country context conflicted with the primarily desk-based outlook of the planners. The latter preferred to concentrate on the theoretical existence of farmers' cooperatives, and on the sets of interests whose well-being depended on an assumption that the cooperatives were in existence and functioning. Although by questioning this the anthropologist came into conflict with project staff (who sometimes said, 'You may be right, but it's not our job to question that side of things'), an overall perspective was provided which allowed a fuller investigation of the problems.

5. The skills needed for project-based work such as this generated many of the usual methodological problems in an anthropologist's relationship to different informants, their expectations and reasons for 'slanting' certain types of information.

Case 2. Disaster prevention – cyclone shelters, community participation and NGOs

Our second case study is an illuminating tale of good developmental intention and bad project design. It illustrates the need to consider social issues from the very beginning of a project's life-cycle; ensuring that 'community development' takes place is as complex and time-consuming as constructing buildings, perhaps even more so. It has to be carefully planned, rather than added on as a last minute appendage, as is so frequently the case in large-scale technical projects. This case study is, sadly, a lesson in 'how not to' run a project which supposedly involves 'community development'. It indicates not only the constraints experienced by developmental anthropologists, but also those facing the wider success of many large-scale projects.

Background

After a disastrous cyclone in the late 1980s in which many thousands of people were killed, donors rushed to provide aid for the construction of cyclone shelters in the coastal area of a small, highly populated and largely aid-dependent country in the tropics. As in so many natural disasters in the South, many lives might have been saved had appropriate preventative and rescue systems been in operation: better warning systems, infrastructure and, crucially in this case, cyclone shelters. While a substantial number of cyclone shelters existed when the cyclone struck, many people did not use them even though, in theory at least, they had been warned that a cyclone was likely (cyclones can usually be predicted several days in advance).

There were several reasons for this. First, many people had under-estimated the seriousness of the cyclone warning, living as they did in a climate where in particular seasons cyclones are a regular threat. Second, many others either chose not to use their local shelters, or were denied access to them. Some of the existing shelters were in very bad shape, shaking in the wind, with crumbling walls and broken stairways; in these cases, it seemed safer to stay away from the buildings rather than enter them. In other instances, people did not leave their houses for fear of looting. Many women stayed behind with their children, for the shelters were perceived as 'public' spaces where they might be harrassed by men. Within the context of local gender relations, in which purdah (veiling) is a cultural ideal, this was tragically common. Lastly, some of the shelters were either occupied by particularly powerful families (who denied access to others), locked, or being used for storing grain or cattle and thus impossible to use. Again, the local context of economic and social differentiation, factionalism and patron–clientage helps explain why some groups had earlier gained control of the shelters. Clearly, while cyclones are primarily climatic, social and cultural factors play a large role in determining what happens before, during and after them.

While there is little which development agencies can do to prevent cyclones from occurring, measures to limit their destruction are not simply technical. Cyclone-resistant shelters certainly have to be built, but various other steps need to be taken to ensure that people use them. These can be summarised as follows:

1. Shelters must be socially appropriate: their design must take into account cultural factors such as purdah by providing separate rooms and latrines for women.
2. Shelters must be sited appropriately, e.g.: close to settlements so that people do not have to walk long distances to reach them.
3. People must be aware of the existence and purpose of the shelter.
4. Shelters must be seen locally as shared community buildings, which everyone has access to. Perceived 'ownership' may vitally influence whether or not the shelters are used in an emergency.

One way of ensuring points 3 and 4 are achieved is to put the buildings to other uses when there is no emergency. Ideally, these should involve as many different groups as possible. Since socially marginalised groups (e.g. the landless, women, migrant labourers) are those most likely to be denied access during a cyclone, these activities might be best targeted at them.

5. The buildings must be regularly maintained. This should be done by the community, again in order to give people a sense of 'ownership', but also to achieve the long-term sustainability of maintenance activities.

The provision of cyclone shelters clearly involves a host of social issues. To ensure their use by all groups during a cyclone, the projects must also be as participatory as possible; ideally, the building of shelters should be integrated into wider, 'community development' type programmes.

The cyclone shelter cum primary school project

In the immediate aftermath of the cyclone, many donors and NGOs were keen to build cyclone shelters in the worst affected areas of the country. This programme, funded by a large multilateral donor, involved the construction of a proposed 200 shelters in specified regions of the coastal area. As agreed by the national government, the shelters would also double as government-run primary schools, many of which had been destroyed in the recent disaster. Combined with this, the financing memorandum signed by the donor and the government proposed that the buildings would be used by local NGOs to ensure wider community use of the buildings and participation in their maintenance. The NGOs, it was hoped, would also be involved in disaster preparedness training. While it was not specified how this would take place, it was assumed that the NGOs involved would promote schemes to generate income for building maintenance, and carry out appropriate training programmes. They would also share the building with the government-run primary school.

The implementation of the project was contracted out to a European engineering firm, which we shall call Smith and Company. It had local counterparts within the 'Project Implementation Unit', who were hired and employed by the national government. Although Smith and Company had long-term overseas experience, this was wholly in construction. None of its employees had background knowledge of the country concerned, of social development or of NGOs. This was not perceived by the company as a problem, for when the contracts it won from donors demanded social inputs, it simply hired short-term external consultants. In the firm's eyes, the project was primarily to do with building shelters. The subsequent use of these, their impact on local groups and issues of 'development' were not seen (at least by the team leader) as relevant. As the team leader ingenuously put it: 'We're here to make money, not for development.'

Smith and Company was, however, contractually obliged by the donor to carry out the 'social component' of the project. Within the project design, which had been written by the donor, two months were provided for an expatriate social consultant and four months for a local social consultant. The terms of reference for these were extremely vague, for the team leader lacked sufficient knowledge of 'social development' or NGOs to know what might be required. Indeed, as he later confided to the expatriate consultant, for the first six months of the project he was not even sure what an NGO was. Upon arriving to carry out the job, the expatriate social consultant was told: 'Do whatever you think is appropriate.' A de facto version of these invisible terms of reference was to:

- assess the viability of collaborating with local NGOs in the use of the cyclone shelters; and
- set up mechanisms for contracting social development activities to local NGOs.

This was an enormous task. Since the project involved 200 shelters, in theory this could have meant collaborating with 200 different NGOs. While in some coastal areas there were already several well-respected NGOs working within local communities, in others there were few, if any. Even if only the larger, national level NGOs with a greater geographical spread were involved, the logistics of assessing them and negotiating and coordinating their involvement were mind-boggling, especially in a context where there was little national coordination of NGOs and the spirit was more one of competition than cooperation.

NGOs could be invited to submit project proposals, but there was little to prevent these from being bogus. As one might expect, whenever donors are offering comparatively large sums of money, it is not uncommon for some organisations to overestimate their own capacity and capabilities in order to access funds. On top of this, the government had an ambivalent attitude towards NGOs, and for the first 18 months of the project the Ministry of Education, which first and foremost saw the buildings as primary schools rather than cyclone shelters, refused to cooperate.

Although the objectives of the project were laudable on a superficial level, in reality its design was therefore highly naive, reflecting the donor's ignorance of local conditions and of what collaborative work with NGOs might involve. Even if large numbers of NGOs were to be integrated into the project, there were no procedures in the design for monitoring and evaluating their work. Nor had the future sustainability of their programmes been considered. The project intended to fund them in their 'community development' activities for three years, after which time its work would be considered finished and Smith and Company would wind down its operations. Yet, unlike the construction of buildings, 'community development' cannot be carried out in a few brief months. Instead, the work of the best NGOs can never be short-term: simply setting up a savings group or providing functional education can take several years, especially if the organisation has no pre-existing contacts in the community concerned. Taking things further involves even more time.

Combined with this, the project objective of community 'participation' was preposterous. The selection of sites and shelter design was already nearing completion during the social consultant's first input. There was clearly no opportunity for local people to participate in these processes. Suggestions that they might be involved in the supervision of contractors' work, as had been the case in the cyclone-shelter building programmes of some of the more radical NGOs, were not taken seriously by the Project Implementation Unit. While included as a buzz word in the project design, participation was simply not possible given that project objectives and schedules had been prepared far in advance.

The social consultants had a total of six months to do their work. While the local sociologist might have been invaluable, he was unfortunately entirely unsuitable, having been recruited by engineers who had not known what qualities to look for. In effect, then, the bulk of the work was left to the expatriate consultant, who had two months to do a job which needed at least a year, should have been started before the building of the shelters and would certainly need to continue after the construction was completed.

After completing his first month's input, the expatriate consultant had compiled a list of suitable NGOs working in one area of the proposed project. He had visited as many of these as possible, but since the list only included seven shelter sites this was only the tip of the iceberg. Initial 'feelers' had been put out as to whether organisations might be interested in participating in the project. The least reputable or experienced had jumped at the chance of funding, while the best had indicated that they did not have the capacity to expand further, let alone for so many shelters. The Project Implementation Unit, however, was keen for NGOs to take on as many sites as possible, for this would make project administration far easier. It also insisted that it should dictate to the NGOs what activities they would carry out. The Smith and Company team leader, whose previous experience had been wholly in the commercial sector, saw them very much as potential employees contracted to do a specific job and was aghast that they did not necessarily 'jump' when called.

In his report to the project, the consultant recommended that the only way in which NGO involvement might be successfully implemented was to employ a full-time local consultant to assess NGO proposals, negotiate their involvement and help monitor work. Although the donor readily agreed to this suggestion, one year later this had been repeatedly refused by the Ministry of Education. After the consultant's input had ended, the team leader, left without advice, initiated discussions with a large, semi-governmental organisation with a presence in the coastal area and a national reputation for corruption. Since this was the only organisation which could deal with such a large-scale project, this appeared to be the only option left.

The Primary Schools cum Cyclone Shelters Project is a case *par excellence* of bad planning, assuming that the donors were sincere in their desire to integrate local communities in the use and maintenance of their shelters. It is an example of how in so many capital-intensive projects, social usage is perceived by the 'developers' as marginal. There was plenty of scope for creative anthropological input, but it should have been at the beginning of the project. Matters would also have been helped had the Project Implemention Unit not been composed entirely of expatriate engineers, with no local experience or knowledge of social issues. Much time was spent by the beleaguered team leader learning what NGOs were, and what they did. Like many of Smith and Company's employees, his commitment to their aims was minimal, for he saw his work in terms of profit and construction.

Points for discussion

1. Should anthropologists collaborate with private consultancy companies who quite openly admit that their presence in Southern countries is only for profit? While the obvious answer might be 'no', we should bear in mind that an anthropologist can play an educative role within such companies, helping to open colleagues' eyes to the social implications of their work.

2. Does an anthropological presence legitimise a project which in reality involves very little social development or participation? In this case, the answer is probably 'yes'. However, it would be too cynical to suggest that this was the original intention of the donors, who genuinely hoped that by including a paragraph in their project design they would have a 'community development' style project.

How might similar scenarios be avoided? Let us turn to our last case study, an example of the potentials unleashed by anthropological involvement from the outset.

Case 3. The fish farm – 'the tail wagging the dog'?

Our third case study highlights the tensions between the 'technical fix' aspects of many projects and the types of 'soft' information that are of interest to anthropologists. It concludes with an example of the productive 'fusing', after some initial difficulties, of these two sets of emphases.

In recent years the government, donors and NGOs in an Asian country discovered that while agriculture was nearing optimum conditions in terms of local resource utilisation and deployment, the inland fisheries sector appeared to offer considerable potential for improving resource utilisation, increasing production of scarce animal protein and improving food availability for the population. Increasing fish production through aquaculture (the culturing of fish in ponds) came to be seen as an important route for increasing food production and thereby addressing the issue of poverty.

Fish have long been an important part of the local diet, since the country contains a vast river delta and is water-logged for much of the year. Declining natural availability and increasing population pressure have, however, led to strains on the availability of wild fish and the prevailing 'extensive' system of farming. Aquaculture, which is just beginning to be practised intensively, is seen as a viable solution to this deficit. Fish can be spawned artificially in hatcheries, introduced into ponds in the form of small 'fingerlings' 5 or 8 centimetres long (sometimes known also as 'fry'), and then grown to food fish size for sale or consumption within about six months.

Since this more intensive approach to growing fish is still relatively new, the development agencies have worked to try to support its growth with technical advice and assistance. In particular, one European government agency developed a multi-million pound project based around the construction of a large, high-technology fish hatchery which it was hoped would provide a vast supply of hatchlings for local fish farmers and growers in an area with very limited natural supply. Although limited amounts of hatchlings had hitherto been available from the rivers, this level of availability had become plainly inadequate for present needs.

The idea quickly gained support and a project was planned with the participation of the government's Fisheries Department. An old and disused hatchery was located and a plan was developed to upgrade it into a large, multi-pond production unit offering many different species of fish to local farmers, coupled with advice on extension, help with gaining access to inputs and credit facilities. The design was drawn up rather quickly by the planners, without much reference to local people, and without sufficient understanding of either the constraints under which they were producing their fish or the potential value of local knowledge.

As work progressed, expatriate and local project staff began learning more about the local economy and ecology. Some of this 'on the job' learning began to contradict certain assumptions implicit in the project design. For example, the aquaculture which was being conducted locally (albeit on a fairly small scale) was supported by a complex network of relationships and transactions, involving both rich and poor people, who benefited disproportionately from the participation in the networks.

In order to explore further the issues which were coming to light, a series of social research studies were commissioned by the donor, involving researchers from a UK university working in collaboration with a local research organisation. A number of these studies were undertaken using an anthropological methodology based upon participant observation and semi-structured interviews. These began to reveal a range of 'hidden' issues which it became clear were of great importance to the success of the project.

In particular, while the planners had assumed that the benefits of increased fish production would 'trickle down' to those in the community with low incomes, such a view was hard to sustain. The complex network of producers, intermediaries and traders included both wealthy members of the local rural elites and landless people with few assets and low incomes. The local markets through which inputs for aquaculture were bought and sold were far from perfect. Instead, there were cartels controlling the movement of hatchlings and fingerlings around the country, and forms of 'tied' credit (e.g. in which an agreement bound the less powerful credit-taker to an obligation to sell produce back to the credit-giver at a disadvantageous price) which restricted the ability of buyers and sellers to shop around for the best prices.

Furthermore, the planners' assumptions about technical solutions to local problems had taken little account of local knowledge, which was found to be highly developed in certain rather surprising ways. For example, while the high-technology solution to fish seed transportation required the use of oxygen canisters and plastic bags, local traders had long been using an indigenous system involving aluminium or clay cooking pots and the maintenance of the required oxygen levels using a highly skilled – if tiring – hand splashing technique. Without the knowledge or help of Western 'experts', local fish seed traders were moving vast qualities of fingerlings around the country on trains, buses and rickshaws, sometimes over distances of more than 160 kilometres, using this sophisticated system of locally evolved techniques.

The work of the anthropologist therefore significantly broadened the knowledge base and the perspective of the project, bringing to light details which had remained 'hidden' to the planners. Perhaps, the social scientists began to argue, there were good reasons why there were no successful hatcheries in this part of the country and these reasons had been largely overlooked by the planners. Some local people were saying that the water was too rich in iron, which made fish breeding difficult, a fact that was starting to be confirmed by the scientists themselves. Perhaps the trading and transportation network which existed was capable of bringing fingerlings into the area by itself and could meet demand effectively, in which case the local production centre was not necessary. At worst, if the hatchery achieved its target output, all the low-income, long-distance fish traders might be made redundant and would lose important income-generating opportunities, thus neutralising or even contradicting the poverty-focused intentions of the project.

Many of these findings were greeted unenthusiastically by project staff, who were faced with the prospect of a relatively straightforward technological intervention (build a hatchery, train local people in its use, produce more fish for everyone) turning into a rather more complicated and less clear-cut venture. Some project staff began to complain privately that the social scientists were getting in the way of the project and that having them around was like 'the tail wagging the dog'. Again, technology was assumed to be the point of the excercise.

At this point, considerable negotiation skills were needed on both sides to overcome misunderstandings and professional pride. For example, it was tempting for the anthropologist to criticise the donors for leaving the social science research until after the project had already been designed and started. This had been a serious mistake, but one which too many professional careers rested upon to allow the error to be openly admitted. The fisheries scientists thought the social research tended towards naivety and negativity, and pounced eagerly upon examples of social scientists' ignorance of specialised technical information whenever it was presented. This was a debate which concerned the 'types' of knowledge considered necessary for development.

The work of the social scientists was eventually used constructively in order to reorient the project in innovative and interesting ways. It was decided to try to encourage the relatively poor fish-fry traders to broaden their resource base by selling advice (after relevant training from project staff) about fishpond cultivation and management to fish farmers as well as selling fish fry, an idea which they found interesting and potentially useful. This fry trader extension strategy was an idea that had emerged from discussions between local staff, farmers and researchers, taking an indigenous system (the network of relationships between fish-seed traders and pond operators) and providing a group of actors in that system with training in pond culture practice. Ethnographic investigation had shown that technical knowledge of fish production was in short supply, since fish culture of this kind was a relatively new activity. This training could then feed into a ready-made distribution and extension system, since it had been learned that pond-owners often asked the fingerling traders for advice on fish culture issues, even though most traders were unable to provide it adequately.

Points for discussion

1. A recurring problem is the non-involvement of anthropologists in the initial planning stages of projects.
2. Anthropological knowledge can be particularly useful in understanding many of the hidden difficulties underlying a set of planner's assumptions, many of which may be biased towards technology rather than towards people.
3. By opening up avenues for discussion with local people, and identifying some of the potentially contradictory interests and needs of different classes and groups, better decisions can be made about responding to felt needs and targeting what the project has to offer to specific categories of person.
4. Far more can be achieved by building upon existing systems than by importing and imposing new technologies and ideas

from outside. For example, locally adapted and highly skilled fish-seed transportation systems, while archaic and 'low-tech', were not a priority for change, whereas particular types of scarce knowledge, which the project could quite easily supply, were in considerable demand.
5. Negotiations with project staff can be just as sensitive as discussion with other 'informants'. Anthropologists may end up being far less sensitive with these people than they are with their more 'traditional' informants (see case 1 on rural cooperative training).

Conclusion

We hope that these case studies illustrate the range of problems and potentials in store for anthropologists who take the professional route and engage in practical development work. Each one raises a set of questions, which can be debated at length. However, we would like to end this chapter with some concluding thoughts about the role of the applied anthropologist in development work.

Grillo (1985: 7) has suggested dispensing altogether with the term 'applied anthropology' and replacing it with 'a much broader notion of contextually defined professional activity', partly because it expresses 'what ought to be' as opposed to what actually happens in practice. Furthermore, as soon as one moves away from a narrow description of applied roles, the distinction between 'applied' and 'pure' anthropology begins to break down. A more accurate and realistic assessment of the anthropologist's potential in development work might be based upon the discipline's ability to 'see beyond' what is initially assumed and explore the complexity of social and economic situations.

Many of those discussing anthropology and development have reached similar kinds of conclusions. Belshaw (1976) stresses the idea of the anthropologist's wider social responsibilities and deploys the metaphor of the 'sorceror's apprentice' to argue his case. The anthropologist is without a 'firm technique' or distinct craft, but may be able to play an advisory role aimed at moderating the temptation, among policy-makers and others with power, to unleash forces over which, in late twentieth-century society, we can expect to have only limited control. Hoben (1982: 366) is less dramatic, but argues convincingly that 'the discipline's theoretical contribution lies in the elucidation of means–end relationships, rather than in the choice of ends themselves'.

Rarely are anthropologists able to agree either among themselves or with development practitioners on a single course of unproblematic action, but they are well equipped to point out the significance of complex, often hidden, relationships; by so doing, they can provide unique and potentially valuable contributions. Following from this, Grillo (1985: 21) suggests that the essence of the anthropological perspective is that it is holistic, in which 'units of study are conceived as complex wholes consisting of a multiplicity of related elements'. Despite the interesting work of anthropological macrotheorists such as Eric Wolf, the anthropological perspective usually retains a significant local dimension, or at least one which begins with individual perceptions and outlooks and then seeks to draw connections and links between experience and wider realities. Anthropologists can describe how people act, think and feel as the world changes.

Despite its important methodological contributions to development work, anthropology remains primarily a 'way of seeing' rather than a specific set of skills or a tool-kit. One of the main ways of applying anthropology, as Wolf (1964) points out, is therefore to teach this distinctive outlook and ideas more widely to people working in other fields. Nowhere is the need more pressing than in the world of development, where prevailing discourses are perhaps now more open to renegotiation and change than ever before.

7 BEYOND DEVELOPMENT?

By now it should be clear that anthropology's relationship to development is riven with contradiction. While on the one hand anthropologists have for many generations worked within governmental and non-governmental organisations, demonstrating how much the discipline has to offer in terms of improving the work of developers, other anthropologists are engaged in a radical critique of the very notion of development, arguing that as a concept it is morally, politically and philosophically corrupt. As we have seen, these different and often conflicting positions have a long history and to an extent simply represent the diversity of views that one would expect to find among any group of individuals: there is no reason why anthropologists and their opinions should be homogeneous.

In the post-modern/post-structuralist context of the 1990s, however, the two approaches appear to be further apart than ever. In this concluding chapter we shall suggest that this need not necessarily be the case. Indeed, while it is absolutely necessary to unravel and deconstruct 'development', if anthropologists are to make politically meaningful contributions to the worlds in which they work they must continue to make the vital connection between knowledge and action. This means that the use of applied anthropology, both within and outside the development industry, must continue to have a role, but in different ways and using different conceptual paradigms than previously.

This 'involved anthropology' is undoubtedly fraught with danger. In this sense it is perhaps the most testing and problematic domain for individual anthropologists to work in, whether as detached critics or as consultants hired by aid agencies. But this should not mean that they shun practical involvement, although they may need to be careful about what form it takes. Anthropologists should also not expect involvement to be easy. If they have any collective responsibility it is endlessly to question and problematise their positions, to be uncomfortable, and with their questions to make others uncomfortable. This is a source of creativity, as well as a form of political engagement. It is also, however, a perilous path to take.

Unpicking development

As Ferguson (1990: xiii) has pointed out:

> Like 'civilisation' in the nineteenth century, 'development' is the name not only for a value, but also for a dominant problematic or interpretive grid through which the impoverished regions of the world are known to us. Within this intepretive grid, a host of everyday observations are rendered intelligible and meaningful.

Laying bare the assumptions behind such 'interpretive grids', and thus indicating the relationship between knowledge, discourse and the reproduction of power, is one of the most important tasks of the contemporary anthropology of development, a project which has burgeoned in recent years.

For example, Hobart (1993: 4) has written about the ways in which development problems are conceptualised in relation to Western 'world-ordering knowledge', while the state of 'ignorance' is not simply the absence of knowledge, but a state of being which is ascribed by those with power to those without. As we saw in the fish traders' case study described in Chapter 6, while foreign aquaculture experts deal in a type of technical knowledge which sees the blanket application of high-technology solutions to problems of fish-seed transportation, local knowledge represents the situation rather differently. People are constituted as actively seeking solutions to the problems of maintaining oxygen levels in water, and their solutions are rooted in *practice* rather than in theory. Although traders knew that they needed to oxygenate the water by hand to keep their fish alive, they did not have a scientific explanation as to *why* this should be done. Such activity is more akin to a set of 'performance skills' with a high level of improvisation involved (P. Richards, 1993), than to a coherent or permanent system of local knowledge.

The new anthropology of development can also be used to deconstruct the knowledge of developers as well as those 'to be developed'. Although often caricatured as simply involving 'scientific rationality', this is also more complex, in much the same way that 'indigenous knowledge' is. As our case studies indicate, development plans are often far from rational, and relationships within development institutions are as hierarchical, unequal and culturally embedded as any of the societies usually studied by anthropologists. The interface between developers and those to be developed is not simply a case of binary oppositions: modern ('scientific') versus traditional ('indigenous') thought. Instead, the paradigms within which developers work are as contextually contingent, culturally specific and contested as those of the social groups whom they target. What must not be lost sight of, however, is that discourses of development are produced by those in power and often result (even if unintentionally) in reproducing power relations between areas of the world and between people.

These perspectives help anthropologists turn a highly critical eye on the assumptions which lie behind those who speak of 'development' in both the resource-rich Northern countries and the economically poor countries of the South. They help reveal how the language used in the North to describe the Third World is not neutral, but reflects the continuing inequalities arising from the histories of colonisation, the need for Northern states to maintain their position of economic dominance and the limited vision that those in richer countries may have of the global future. It also becomes clear how development has been institutionalised, and the people who work within its projects professionalised. Important issues are raised concerning the production and uses of knowledge, about the legitimacy or otherwise of the 'experts' who provide advice, about the level of participation of local people in projects and about the intended and unintended economic and political consequences of the whole development enterprise as it is carried out across the world.

Anthropology and development: moving on

Discomforting, but nonetheless crucial, questions are also asked about the involvement in development work of anthropologists, who are frequently accused of 'buying in' to the dominant discourse and thus perpetuating global inequality even while attempting to 'do good'. As one of its fiercest critics, Arturo Escobar (1991, 674–7), puts it:

Development institutions are part and parcel of how the world is put together so as to ensure certain processes of ruling. Under these conditions, development anthropology almost inevitably upholds the main tenets of development ... for all its claim to relevance to social problems, to cultural sensitivity ... [development anthropology] ... has done no more than recycle and dress in more localised fabrics, the discourses of modernisation and development.

Such perspectives are vital in the ongoing task of rethinking and thus remaking the world. As we have stated, anthropologists must continue to ask difficult questions of themselves and of others. But as well as showing that the very concept of development and all of its discursive paraphernalia (including the role of development anthropology) is deeply problematic, anthropologists in and of development should also be producing ideas on how to change it. For them to criticise the inability of 'development' to deliver is relatively easy; understanding and supporting the alternatives are more difficult.

Why should anthropologists remain involved? Reading through some of the texts produced by post-structuralists it might appear that the problems of Southern countries are simply a construct, a figment of the post-colonial imagination, and a justification for the continuing domination of the South by the North. It is certainly true that every effort must be made to move beyond perceiving the 'Third World' in crude and debilitating stereotypes which negate the agency, dynamism and self-reliance of those who are labelled 'the poor'. It should also be recognised that the 'Third World' – if this is to be understand in terms of marginalisation – also exists within the North; witness the scandal of homelessness and social deprivation within the cities of Britain and the US. Lastly, those from materially richer societies need to recognise the degree to which their views are embedded within their own cultural assumptions.

Yet while it is important to acknowledge that not everyone perceives the world in the same terms, global inequalities and poverty cannot simply be explained away as culturally relative. The first problem with this stance is that it relies upon the notion of bounded and separate cultures, all of which have their own internal logic; in this view there are clearly no universals. Recent discussions of globalisation challenge such ideas (Featherstone 1990; Hannerz, 1992). Indeed, it is increasingly recognised that the world and its cultures are highly interconnected. People are not simply separated by the invisible and impermeable walls of culture. Although there is of course great diversity among societies, there are also great similarities.

Second, while as an ideological position cultural relativism may be 'politically correct', it can lead to complacency, at both an individual and a state level. It may also negate the struggles and perceptions of those fighting to change conditions within their societies, who may request and welcome the solidarity of outsiders. In these cases, the relativism of post-modernist approaches is in danger of collapsing into depoliticised irresponsibility. As Micaela di Leonardo (1991: 24) comments:

In other words, there is no place for any morally evaluative or politically committed stance within the disintegrating logic of post-structuralism. It is fundamentally nihilist ... Ironically, given its sometime association with radical political stances, post-structuralism does not challenge the status quo in an increasingly retrograde era.

Similar issues have been hotly debated within feminism. While the 'politics of difference' (the recognition of the diversity of feminist voices and experience and, by extension, the critique of white, Western feminists' representations) has been central to debates within feminist theory in recent years, some feminists worry that an ideal of endless difference might cause feminism to self-destruct. For the feminist movement to have any meaning, there must therefore be post-modern 'stopping points' (Nicholson, 1990: 8), a recognition that there *are* globalised structures of dominance and subordination. These are not simply a construct (Bordo, 1990: 149).

Another major problem with the deconstructionalist stance is that it makes active involvement in processes of change difficult, for the terms in which such change is thought of are themselves suspicious, as is any Northern involvement in Southern societies (see Glossary). Those from the North[1] therefore become silenced, unable to act beyond producing hostile critiques of the work of those who are involved. But if this is all they do, their contribution becomes reductive: they detract while adding nothing. Although unpicking 'development' is clearly a political as well as an academic act, the irony of post-structuralism is that it can thus also be inherently depoliticising.

If anthropologists are to retain a commitment to improving the world they therefore need to move beyond deconstruction, taking with them its critical insights, but leaving behind the political apathy that it sometimes evokes. There are moral absolutes in the world; people are not merely atomised individuals, endlessly fragmented by diversity, with wholly different perceptions and experiences. People have a right to basic material needs; they also have a right to fulfil their individual potential, whether this involves becoming literate, retaining their cultural identity or their freedom, having the means to generate an income, or whatever. Yet many millions of people throughout the world are denied these rights. We therefore make no apologies for arguing that professionally as well as personally anthropologists should be actively engaged in attempting to change the conditions which produce poverty, inequality and oppression.

One way in which anthropologists can move forward is to shift their focus away from development and on to relations of poverty and inequality. This means that there is still an important role for anthropologists working within development, for from their positions as participants they can continually insist that inequality and poverty – as social relationships – remain at the top of the agenda. As we have argued throughout this book, they can also work on the institutions concerned, whether these are donor agencies, governments or NGOs, insisting that the development discourse itself changes. After all, discourse is a product of those who produce it; it does not simply exist in a vacuum. Anthropologists can therefore be active agents in radically reformulating it. To consider further how this might be done, and the inherent dangers of applied work, let us return to the role of anthropologists in development.

Working from within

As insiders in the aid industry, anthropologists can play a part in ensuring that the issues of equity and participation within the 'development process' (as opposed to the simpler, more measurable notions of economic growth and technological change) are uppermost in the approaches and practices of those working in development. These are in many ways 'anthropological' issues, for the traditional subject matter of anthropology – small-scale, low-income rural communities – has generated a wealth of information about how the different elements of a society fit together, and how, by extension, things could be improved. As we have argued throughout this book, anthropologists ask crucial questions regarding people's access to resources and the differential effects of change. It is vital that these questions stay on the developers' agenda, for, as we have seen, many planners have limited insight into the effects of their work; they need to be constantly reminded that change is inherently social.

One role that anthropologists can play is therefore to keep the developers under control. Mair wrote in her study of anthropology and development that one of the main roles of the social anthropologist is to 'beg the agents of development to keep their eyes open' (1984: 13) and to represent the interests and the discontent of those people passed over by the new order(s) created by economic progress. But Mair's view remains to some extent one of the anthropologist mediating between the developer and the developed along the inevitable path of progress. When she points out that the anthropologist can usefully warn developers of 'resistance likely to be met' (ibid.: 4), this is a far cry from the anthropologist as, ideally, a full participant in questioning development itself or facilitating the participation of people in those processes.

Anthropology has other types of contributions to make beyond being a mediator between the developers and those to be 'developed'. Anthropologists are trained sceptics: they tend to argue that situations and ideas are usually more complicated than is immediately apparent; they believe that no fact or detail is too trivial to be considered; they may prefer quality to quantity; they are rarely ready to offer conclusions or advice in terms of a straightforward course of action. All these qualities are of course of immense value in informing planned change, but they sit uneasily within the time-frames and priorities of the world of development practice. To some development practitioners, anthropologists are therefore an administrative nightmare, because the knowledge and ideas in which they deal seem to have very little practical applicability and, worse still, can raise endless problems. Yet the uneasiness and frustration sometimes created by the presence of an anthropologist can be harnessed in development work and is arguably anthropologists' greatest strength, if it can be deployed constructively.

As we have seen, anthropology can be used in the project setting for a number of purposes. Anthropologists are well equipped to monitor the process of project implementation, which in effect is the task of monitoring social change. To do this, a combination of national and expatriate anthropologists, with both men and women involved, will be able to draw on their different skills and perspectives in order to present different, though mutually reinforcing, analyses of events. Anthropologists in the course of monitoring need to assess whether three-way communication is taking place between planners, implementors and population. This is needed to make projects needs-based and to reduce ethnocentric assumptions.

Anthropologists are trained to see beyond the immediate formal relationships which might exist. While their questions might appear irrelevant to technocrats, they often probe beyond what is immediately apparent. Are the project boundaries drawn too narrowly? For example, are there new or adapting sets of patron–client relationships which are being fed by the project and its resources? What are the distributional effects of the project? Finally, survey data can be supplemented with case studies, which capture dynamism and complexity and therefore add dimension to more static data collection.

On a directly practical level, anthropology has helped to provide a model, through its traditional participatory fieldwork methodology, of information gathering which is more sensitive to people. This not only improves the quality of the information needed by policy-makers and practitioners, but can increase the opportunities for local people to contribute more directly to the evolution of policies and programmes. The use of anthropological methodology in participatory techniques such as PRA is an example. In turn, anthropologists can question and thus help redesign such techniques, ensuring that they do not ossify into rigid exercises which have lost their meaning.

If anthropologists are to become involved in development work in the South, a number of practical issues need to be considered. Before turning to the question of ethics, let us consider these.

How should anthropologists become involved?

There are various practical issues anthropologists should consider before deciding whether to take part in project-based work, as well as compromises which need to be made once a decision to participate has been taken. One important indicator or warning sign which the anthropologist should look out for when considering a practical involvement is the history of a project. Has it been drawn up with the participation of an anthropologist, or is the anthropologist part of an attempt to 'fix up' a project which has run into trouble?

When working in a team, or with other organisations or government agencies, the anthropologist may need to keep in mind the lack of wider knowledge or misconceptions which can exist about anthropology during the work. An important part of such work will be a preparedness to discuss anthropological ideas and outlooks with members of an interdisciplinary team or with project staff or administrators. As we have argued, anthropology is a way of looking at social realities, of looking behind apparently simple situations, and as such can be of value to non-specialists.

The anthropologist needs to be aware of the difference between the way academic anthropology is written up and presented and the more immediate requirements of project or agency reports and documents. Reports will have to be well structured, so that relevant sections can be read separately by those who wish to access information quickly. They should be clearly written, with unfamiliar anthropological terms avoided unless necessary (in which case they must be explained simply), and focused clearly on the specific questions which are being asked by the agency or project. Most anthropologists will generate new sets of questions and issues (unanticipated by their employers); these can then be outlined and addressed after the initial required points have been answered.

It is also important to be constructively critical: it makes little sense if the anthropologist fails to take responsibility for the practical implications of critical points. If certain assumptions or ideas have been shown to be false, alternatives can often be suggested which will create more appropriate courses of action. Many project staff will be pleased to experiment with new ideas, but will be frustrated by relentless negativity. A knowledge of the administrative culture in which many development initiatives take place is an essential prerequisite for this type of applied work.

The ethics of involvement

There can be little doubt that anthropologists can do much to change and improve the work of developers. Their involvement, however, remains deeply problematic. While setting out to reformulate and change from within, the danger is that anthropologists become profoundly compromised. No discussion of anthropology and development can therefore ignore the difficult issue of ethics, an underlying theme throughout the book.

One of the most complex questions for anthropologists concerns on what terms to get involved in development work. Little can be done if the project has been poorly designed or based on unfounded assumptions, and the 'legitimising role' of the anthropologist may indeed make matters worse rather than better. The involvement of the anthropologist will always be a matter of individual conscience, but informed choices can be made by asking some preliminary questions. At what stage is the anthropologist being asked to participate in a project? How much time will the anthropologist have to undertake the research? How much credibility will be given to the findings? By participating in development, does the anthropologist simply become part of the prevailing discourse and help to oil the 'anti-politics machine'?

Another set of ethical issues surrounds the roles of expatriates and nationals. This can lead to the loss of scarce local employment opportunities, and in the longer term may have implications for the development and strengthening of local educational and research institutions. Foreign anthropologists need to ask whether or not there is a critical research tradition in the country where the anthropologist is working, and how the anthropologist's work contributes to strengthening or weakening what exists. Expatriate researchers can easily undermine the work of local practitioners by taking jobs or by using local workers in subordinate positions. Foreign anthropologists need to take responsibility for developing, through their work, the abilities of local researchers to carry out applied and other research. The 'fly in, fly out' expert role is one most anthropologists would wish to avoid, except to provide general support, as such activities can weaken the practice of local research.

For example, in Bangladesh the recent Flood Action Plan (a multi-million dollar project which may be larger than any other development project in the world) has in recent years absorbed large numbers of expatriate and local social scientists in its numerous consultancy studies. This means that a significant part of the country's research agenda is being determined by foreign donors, while a sizeable proportion of Bangladesh's few trained social researchers is 'tied up' with one set of issues. Many other important issues go unresearched and may continue to do so for some time to come. This raises important questions regarding the cooption of research by developers, and the encompassment of anthropological findings within the development discourse.

Cooption by developmental discourse

The increasing use of anthropological research by developers is to be applauded, but we must beware of our work being forced into narrow, institutionally defined boundaries, thus becoming part of the discourse which we should be objectively criticising. Since they may be funding it, the danger is that developers can dictate what type of research is carried out, and on what terms. White, for example, has pointed out how in Bangladesh research has been mostly funded by aid agencies. This means that writings about Bangladesh are largely concerned with a particular set of issues: rural poverty, the social and economic position of women and, of course, development (White, 1992: 15–25). Yet there is far more to Bangladesh than the sum of these issues (Gardner, 1995: 22).

In their insistence that research should be practically 'useful', developers usually presuppose that they know already what the most important issues are. But as we have seen, some of the most interesting anthropology of development does not simply ask questions about policy; it examines change within its wider context. By insisting that the research agenda concentrates on certain issues and that findings are presented in a certain way, development may therefore absorb anthropology – potentially its most radical critic – into the dominant development discourse, which, give or take a few adjustments, remains unchanged.

This has already happened to various important concepts, which have been appropriated for development and watered down to the point of a grotesque parody. The use of the term 'participation' is a good example of the dangers, since it can easily be 'coopted' by those with power and influence. A recent World Bank report (quoted by Paul, 1991: 2) illustrates the terms on which notions of participation have been accepted. Like WID/GAD, the main rationale for the use of participatory methods by the World Bank appears to be that they will increase the 'efficiency' of projects:

Donors and recipients have given too little attention to socio-cultural factors and have not been sufficiently aware of the important role that the poor themselves can play in initiatives designed to assist them. Evidence supports the view that involving the poor in the design, implementation, and evaluation of projects in a range of sectors would make aid more effective. Involvement of women has contributed to the attainment of objectives in many agricultural development projects in Sub-Saharan Africa; participation of local community organisations has improved performance in many urban poverty projects; organisations of beneficiaries in aid-supported irrigation schemes have made important contributions to the maintenance and operation of project works; and involvement of organised groups of low-income borrowers has facilitated repayment of loans in small-scale credit programmes.

Clearly, participation all too easily slips into empty rhetoric, can serve the interests of the status quo and can readily lend itself to the fate of being 'veneered'.

Likewise, the insights of anthropologists working on gender relations have, in some cases, been reformulated to fit into the dominant discourse, thus becoming depoliticised and institutionally 'safe'. By creating posts for WID officers, or adding WID to the list of policy commitments, institutions may feel that they have dealt with the problem, when in reality the changes are little more than cosmetic. Concepts may also get taken up, formalised to fit into the discourse, and thus simplified and changed. Gender training, for example, which is widely used by institutions such as the British ODA in the training of its own employees as well as government and NGO workers in projects which it funds throughout the world, may be easily misinterpreted as a simple formula for understanding gender. While attempting to provide tools to help planners, by presenting women in terms of three roles ('reproductive', 'productive' and 'community management') and simplistically dividing their interests between 'strategic' and 'practical', the danger is that such training provides a homogenising framework, which downplays the importance of cultural context and important differences between women and their interests.[2] This may not have been the original intention of such training; the ideas behind it are certainly more complex (see Moser, 1993). Rather, the institutionalisation of the concepts, and the ways in which they are applied, have been transformed through their absorption by the dominant discourse.

This also happens within project planning and implementation. Since most development work is carefully planned, fitted around bureaucratic tools such as the 'project framework', social change is often forced into the constraints of institutional agendas and phrases. Social development becomes an 'output' to be measured (usually through quantifiable criteria such as numbers of people trained, loans taken out or meetings attended). Likewise, research which points to potential problems in project implementation must be presented in report form, with practical recommendations or 'action points' listed. Reports which are too critical are condemned as being irrelevant or useless and are not acted upon, for they do not fit into the discourse (Ferguson, 1990: 69). It would seem that anthropology is welcomed by some developers, but only on their terms.

Breaking out of the discourse

These tendencies must be continually guarded against by involved anthropologists, and it is here that those working within development and those studying development as discourse may have most to say to each other. We need to reassess endlessly how particular concepts are used, especially perhaps those which seem on the surface to be anthropologically friendly – whether social or community development, WID/GAD, participation, or whatever. This involves research not only into their meanings at the managerial or institutional level, but also into how they are transformed at different stages in the project chain. How do local government workers who have received gender training carry those concepts into their work? What does community development mean to the community development workers employed in projects? How do those participating in projects view things?

It is important to recognise that the agenda is not wholly predetermined. Anthropology can be used to re-radicalise those concepts which have been absorbed by it and stripped of their more progressive connotations: as Rahnema (1992: 122) argues, 'no-one learns who claims to know in advance'. The discourse is already changing to a degree, despite the dangers of cooption. Indeed, by highlighting the problems we do not wish to undermine the contribution of many dedicated professionals working within development agencies and NGOs who are actively engaged in changing it. Perhaps too, we need to be rather more confident. We urge our colleagues working within development agencies to think beyond the immediate constraints of their institutional culture. Are project frameworks really necessary? Must social issues always be treated as a poor relative, allowed to eat at the same table as the economists and technocrats, but only on their terms? Rew (1985) is right to point out the various skills which applied anthropologists must learn (working in a team and writing reports), but let us not be too subservient: the developers too must change.

Beyond 'anthropologists as experts'

Another way of moving forward is to ensure that anthropological insights and methods are not confined to a small elite group of experts. As we have indicated at various points in this book, as a way of seeing, and of working, anthropology does not have to be confined to experts from the North. Anthropology has the potential to be taken up, utilised and 'owned' by people in countries where talk about 'development' is high on the agenda. Anthropological insights need not be solely the property or the domain of academic or professional anthropologists, but can be opened up to those working in different contexts – such as within NGOs.

In Bangladesh, for example, the discipline is a new one, but is already providing a framework through which people can re-examine the development process and indigenise a local anthropology. There is a danger that academic neutrality may be discouraged and that the new field will be controlled by foreign donors, who, by paying for the work, will set its agendas and define the limits of its activities. Anthropologists in the South must not become mere social researchers, funded by foreigners, on the development projects underway in their own countries. They are generating ideas within their own societies and understand and express its needs, but they also need to be supported with opportunities to work elsewhere, in order to bring back ideas and insights. What can these anthropologists and other outsider anthropologists tell us about development issues in both the North and the South?

As we have pointed out throughout this book, anthropological knowledge, and in particular anthropological methodologies, is readily accessible to the non-anthropologist and can be used by development practitioners and indeed everyone. While anthropology shows up the limitations of the popularly used survey methodology for reflecting social and economic realities, what can it offer instead?

The provision of PRA training provides an opportunity for public servants and NGO staff to examine their assumptions and their modes of working in order to make them more people-centred. Even if development projects were to disappear overnight, every society has ongoing relationships and situations in which people interact with outsiders and experts. For example, the agricultural extension worker from the local government office can either 'lord it' over the farmers, relying more on status than on an interest in understanding their possible needs, or she or he can work towards developing a more equal relationship in which a two-way exchange of information takes place, putting her or himself at the service of the clients. A nurse in a local health centre can either patronise his or her patients, or can take time to listen to their needs and develop lasting, two-way relationships. Such methodologies may be adapted or distorted or abused in the process, as when PRA becomes a means of legitimising existing practices with only cursory consultation or forced participation. But ultimately there is no 'proper' way of doing things. More broadly, this type of knowledge and methodology is also useful in its deployment in critical, oppositional, questioning roles, in questioning ethnocentric assumptions and economism.

Meanwhile, many grassroots organisations have been working anthropologically for several decades, without the involvement of experts. As we have seen, NGOs have developed approaches which may be changing the ways in which development is conceived and practised. Their fieldworkers may be drawn from the local community and may provide a sympathetic and accountable link with events and resources locally and more widely. They may be engaged in work which makes outside anthropologists less relevant, but both can have something to learn from each other. Social movements are also potential vehicles for change which may express local aspirations and initiatives. So far, few anthropologists have been involved in such initiatives as either researchers or activists, but this does not mean that potential roles do not exist, although the anthropologist may have to take sides and abandon some customary (and often illusory) detachment.

For the moment at least, the rhetoric of development and to some extent its practice is moving in directions which bring it closer to what might be termed 'anthropological' territory. While a backlash against the participatory model of development cannot be ruled out in future years, it is to be hoped that such changes within development discourse will provide ideas which will feed back into anthropology's own processes of reflection and soul-searching. While the development arena provides anthropologists with a site that is rich in potential for analysing the ways power is exercised and change achieved in the post-modern world, it may also simultaneously contribute, as Johanssen has hinted (1992), to the reimagining of anthropology itself, as local political realites are moved centre-stage.

Conclusion

It would be ridiculous to suggest that anthropology holds all the solutions. Although it may be able to contribute to problematising and changing aspects of development discourse, there are far wider issues involved over which individual anthropologists and their methods have little influence. Ultimately, for the quality of people's lives in poorer countries to improve, global conditions must change. Poverty and inequality are products of a range of global conditions, of which development discourse is only one part. International trade, war, political oppression and so on are all of central importance. Anthropologists traditionally have had little to say about these: while they may comment upon their social and cultural consequences, with a few exceptions they are less practised in analysing them as interconnected phenomena. Instead, they tend to concentrate on the 'micro level' and on face-to-face relations.

Anthropology's contribution to positive post-developmental change is therefore part of a larger effort. But this does not mean that it is not worthwhile. As we have argued throughout the book, development discourse is central to how the world is represented and controlled by those with the most power, and anthropology has much to say about it. As we have seen, it tells us that any causal, engineering model of social change is bound to exclude and indeed repress the richness and diversity of people's lives. We have argued that anthropology offers no simple formula for bringing about positive change. Anthropology cannot bring to bear a set of practical tools to be applied as 'means to ends'.

Instead, anthropology promotes an attitude and an outlook: a stance which encourages those working in development to listen to other people's stories, to pay attention to alternative points of view and to new ways of seeing and doing. This outlook continually questions generalised assumptions that we might draw from our own culture and seek to apply elsewhere, and calls attention to the various alternatives that exist in other cultures. Such a perspective helps to highlight the richness and the diversity of human existence as expressed through different languages, beliefs and other aspects of culture. Anthropology tries to show the interconnectedness of social and economic life and the complex relationships which exist between people under conditions of change. Finally, anthropology encourages us to dig as deeply as possible, to go beyond what is immediately apparent, and to uncover as much of the complexity of social and economic life that we can.

The relationship between anthropology and development will never be a straightforward one. Anthropology cannot simply be put at the service of development or of 'the people', whoever they might be. What anthropology has to offer is a continuous questioning of the processes, assumptions and agencies involved in development. But while they do this, and while they stimulate others to do the same, anthropologists have a role to play in unpicking, analysing and changing development practice over time. There is therefore scope for anthropology to take part in this 'gradualist' challenge, because the problems which development has thrown up, as well as the problems which development seeks to solve, will not be changed or disappear overnight. We do not see the point of simply wishing them away or rejecting them as invalid.

Clearly anthropologists have a choice. We have tried to show in this book the ways in which anthropology exposes the limitations of so much which is done in the name of development – its ethnocentric assumptions, its expression of the imbalance of power, its self-delusion, its economic biases – while at the same time offering ideas for challenging constructively the world of development and suggesting how this can be changed. Are these changes possible, or is an involved anthropology only ever going to reproduce neo-colonial discourses? Should we reject the project of development altogether? We are less pessimistic than this rejectionist position allows, and can see important roles for the anthropologist in reconstructing ideas and practice in order to overcome poverty and improve the quality of life across the world.

NOTES AND REFERENCES

Chapter 1: Anthropology, development and the crisis of modernity

1. In this perspective development discourse is comparable to 'orientalism' – the term used by Edward Said to describe the West's ideological control over Eastern 'others' by representing them in particular ways (Said, 1978). This is discussed in more detail later in the chapter.
2. By 'Western' we refer to ideologies primarily generated in Europe and the 'New World': North America, Australia and New Zealand. Western thought is not, however, confined to these geographical areas alone.
3. See glossary.
4. Escobar argues that economics has been key to development discourse. This too can be understood as the product of culture and within development functions hegemonically (1995: 62).
5. For further discussion of the process of labelling and targeting, see Escobar, 1995: 154–92.
6. Nevertheless, the recent Pergau Dam scandal in Malaysia has kept many of these issues in the public arena and reminds us that they are still in many ways open questions. The UK government allegedly provided aid for a large infrastructural project which contradicted the ODA's poverty-focused aid objectives and led to the transfer of development assistance to a country generally considered not poor enough to qualify. The reason seems to have been to promote sales of British-made military equipment.
7. Texts which explore these debates are Mosley, 1987; Madeley, 1991; and Cassen et al., 1986.
8. See Hoogvelt, 1982; Larrain, 1989; Long, 1977.
9. For a detailed analysis of the Groundnut Scheme, see Morgan, 1980: 226–319.
10. Other central theorists include Cardosa and Immanuel Wallerstein (for detailed discussion of these ideas, see Larrain, 1989: 111–33).
11. This refers to attempts to explain the world through all-encompassing theories or paradigms, such as modernity, structuralism or Marxism. Lyotard, for example, speaks of the replacement of grand narratives by

more localised accounts of reality, thus centrally recognising difference of experience rather than homogeneity (Lyotard, 1984).

12. For further discussion, see McGrew, 1992.
13. As noted above, these categories are in themselves problematic.
14. See, for example, the United Nations Development Programme (UNDP) *Human Development Report*, 1990.
15. See glossary; for a more detailed discussion, see Kuper, 1983.
16. Provoked by texts such as Asad's edited work, *Anthropology and the Colonial Encounter* (1973).

Chapter 2: Applying anthropology – an historical background

1. Some of the more recent literature has therefore used the term 'development anthropology' to describe this type of work (Hoben, 1982; Epstein and Ahmed, 1984). However, we consider development anthropology to be a rather wider category which includes a theoretical critique of development issues – we discuss these in the next chapter.
2. However, evolutionist ideas again became popular in US anthropology after the Second World War and, as we have seen, lived on in the modernisation theories of economic development and cultural change propagated by Rostow (1960b) and others, who talked of 'stages of growth'.
3. Kuper quotes a colonial administrator, Sir Philip Mitchell, who wrote that anthropologists asserted that 'they only were gifted with understanding, busied themselves with enthusiasm about all the minutiae of obscure tribal and personal practices [from which studies] resulted a number of painstaking and often accurate records ... of such length that no-one had time to read them and often, in any case, irrelevant, by the time they became available, to the day to day business of government' (Kuper, 1983:107). Such a comment is not too dissimilar from those sometimes still heard today from non-anthropologist practitioners working in development.
4. This was not always the case, however. M. Harris (1991: 336) recounts how the founder of Mozambique's liberation movement, Dr Eduardo Mondlane, received a PhD in sociology and anthropology from North-western University, Illinois, and was influenced by the idea of combining social science and political action.
5. Angela Cheater's (1986) introduction to anthropology is a good example of a new practical approach developed in the Zimbabwean context.
6. This remains an area of concern in any dicussion of anthropology and development: who is paying for research and why? The issue is returned to in Chapter 5.
7. One example is the Anthropology in Action Workshop, part of the British Association for Social Anthropology in Policy and Practice (BASAPP).

8. This distinction is now regarded as being problematic by many anthropologists today. For example, categories once believed to be scientific or objective can often be shown to be governed by more arbitrary definitions (see Clifford and Marcus, 1986: 180).

9. While working recently on an Asia-wide research project on agricultural technology and NGOs, a series of participatory workshops – at which David Lewis was one of the facilitators – created opportunities for NGO workers (some of whom were themselves farmers) to discuss their agendas with senior government officials away from home within a relatively neutral environment.

Chapter 3: The anthropology of development

1. For an account of structuralism in British social anthropology, see Kuper, 1983.
2. In, for example, his *Political Systems of Highland Burma* (1954).
3. See Bloch, 1983.
4. See also Vatuk, 1972; Breman, 1974.
5. An early example of such an approach is Peter Worsley's *The Trumpet Shall Sound*, an analysis of Melanesian cargo cults, which Worsley argues developed as a reaction to white colonisation during the Second World War (Worsley, 1957).
6. See Mangin, 1967; Turner, 1969.
7. For a summary, see Moore, 1988.
8. Such as Weiner's re-evaluation of Malinowski's work on the Trobriand islanders (1976).
9. For example, Rosaldo and Lamphere, 1974; Reiter, 1975; Ortner and Whitehead, 1981.
10. See, for example, Afshar, 1991.
11. For a wider discussion of this literature, see Kabeer, 1994.
12. While WID refers to women's role in development, GAD refers to the relationship between development and socially constructed gender relations, thus recognising historical and cultural particularities of women's (and men's) social roles and statuses.
13. For a summary of policies aimed at gender relations within development, together with a discussion of gender training, see Moser, 1993 and Kabeer, 1994.
14. Which Escobar calls an 'exemplar of development' (1995: 163).
15. For a critique of discourses of WID, see Kabeer, 1994; Phillips, 1994.

Chapter 4: Subverting the discourse – knowledge and practice

1. Examples might be the reduction of anthropological knowledge of gender relations into training packages such as the 'triple roles framework' (Kabeer, 1994: 294–8), or the solidification into bureaucratically manageable 'indigenous knowledge systems' of complex cultural differences in ways of seeing and understanding.

2. For example, Wolf, 1982; Worsley, 1984.
3. Adapted from Lewis and McGregor, 1992.
4. Adapted from Madeley, 1991: 33–8.
5. As Sen (1981) has argued, famine is not the result of objective scarcity, but a failure in people's entitlement to food, which is always mediated through social and political relationships.
6. Adapted from M. Foster, 1989.
7. Adapted from Rozario, 1992.
8. £1 = approximately 50 taka in 1995.
9. Adapted from Mair, 1984: 110–13.
10. Adapted from ITDG, 1992.
11. We shall be discussing notions of participation in detail in Chapter 5.
12. Personal communication from Proshika workers to Katy Gardner, March 1993.
13. NGOs are discussed in more detail in Chapter 5.
14. Bilateral aid refers to situations where there is only one donor country involved. Multilateral aid involves more than one country and is implemented by multilateral agencies such as the World Bank.
15. Adapted from K. Gardner, forthcoming.
16. Such criteria tend to be quantitative: i.e., so many hospitals built, so many nurses employed. Measuring the success of social policies such as 'empowerment' is extremely difficult, however.
17. As we shall also suggest, such terms need to be treated with some caution.

Chapter 5: New directions – practice and change

1. This discussion refers primarily to national or local NGOs in the South rather than 'Northern' NGOs working in development but based in Europe or North America.
2. See Farrington and Lewis (1993), Bebbington and Thiel (1993), and Wellard and Copestake (1993) for discussion and case studies of NGOs and agriculture in Asia, Latin America and Africa respectively.
3. Adapted from Rahman, 1993.
4. Some of these issues are discussed in the Guatemalan context in an interesting paper by Turbyne and McGregor (1994).
5. Adapted from Jennings, 1990.

Chapter 6: Anthropologists within development

1. This is quite ironic when one considers the ambivalence with which applied anthropologists are often looked upon by their more 'academic' colleagues.
2. A conversation a few years ago in Bangladesh illustrates quite well the confusion which sometimes exists about anthropologists and their role. A senior consultant had been flown out for a few weeks in order to

recruit personnel for quite a large interdisciplinary research project and produced a complex organogram showing about 20 different research posts from nutritionists to water engineers, with a social anthropologist apparently in charge of the whole team. When he was asked what exactly the anthropologist would be doing, he thought for a while and said, 'You know, I've often wondered this, but what exactly *does* a social anthropologist do?' He seemed to hold an opinion of the anthropologist as a general manager who would keep the project together. Although we report this as an example of the haziness surrounding perceptions of anthropologists' precise skills and potential roles in development, on reflection perhaps this consultant did have the right idea about the best place for an anthropologist after all ...

3. ODA jargon is curiously full of sporting metaphors, a reflection perhaps of the public school backgrounds of many of its employees: 'up and running', and 'at close of play' are two other examples.

4. Conversely, some anthropologists have complained that development administrators have ignored freely available work which has potential project relevance. An anthropologist working in Nepal recently told us that, as far as he knew, a large UK project near his fieldwork location had paid no attention to his work, which contained discussions of several highly relevant issues.

Chapter 7: Beyond development?

1. Whatever the criteria for this are. It should be recognised that people's positioning as 'Northern' or 'Southern' is often far from fixed.

2. For a critique, see Kabeer, 1994: 264–305.

BIBLIOGRAPHY

Adnan, S., ed. (1992) *People's Participation, NGOs and the Flood Action Plan: An Independent Review.* Dhaka: Oxfam.

Afshar, H., ed. (1991) *Women, Development and Survival in the Third World.* Harlow: Longman.

Ahmed, A. (1992) *Post-modernism and Islam: Predicament and Promise.* London: Routledge.

Arellano-Lopez, S. and Petras, J.F. (1994) 'Non-governmental organisations and poverty alleviation in Bolivia', *Development and Change* vol. 25, no. 3, pp. 555–68.

Asad, T., ed. (1973) *Anthropology and the Colonial Encounter.* London: Ithaca.

Asad, T. (1987) 'Are there histories of people without Europe? A review article', *Society for Comparative Society and History* pp. 594–97.

Bailey, F.G. (1958) *Caste and the Economic Frontier: A Village in Highland Orissa.* Manchester: Manchester University Press.

Bangladesh Rural Advancement Committee (BRAC) (1979) *The Net: Power Structure in Ten Villages.* Dhaka: Bangladesh Rural Advancement Committee.

Barnett, H.G. (1956) *Anthropology in Administration.* Evanston, IL: Row, Peterson and Company.

Barnett, T. (1977) *The Gezira Scheme: An Illusion of Development.* London: Frank Cass.

Barrios de la Chungara, D. (1983) 'Women and organisation' in Davies, M., ed. *Third World: Second Sex.* London: Zed, pp. 39–61.

Bastide, R. (1973) *Applied Anthropology.* London: Croom Helm.

Beattie, J. (1964) *Other Cultures: Aims, Methods and Achievements in Social Anthropology.* London: Routledge and Kegan Paul.

Bebbington, A. (1991) 'Sharecropping agricultural development: the potential for GSO-government cooperation', *Grassroots Development* vol. 15, no. 2, pp. 21–30.

Bebbington, A. and Farrington, J. (1993) 'Governments, NGOs and agricultural development: perspectives on changing inter-organisational relationships', *Journal of Development Studies* vol. 29, no. 2, pp. 199–219.

Bebbington, A. and Thiele, G. (1993) *Non-governmental organisations and the State in Latin America: Rethinking Roles in Sustainable Agricultural Development*. London: Routledge.

Belshaw, C. (1976) *The Sorceror's Apprentice: An Anthropology of Public Policy*. New York: Pergamon.

Benedict, R. (1934) *Patterns of Culture*. Boston, MA: Houghton Mifflin.

Black, J.K. (1991) *Development in Theory and Practice: Bridging the Gap*. Boulder, CO: Westview.

Blanchard, D. (1979) 'Beyond empathy: the emergence of an action anthropology in the life and career of Sol Tax' in Hinshaw, R., ed. *Currents in Anthropology: Essays in Honor of Sol Tax*. New York: Mouton, pp. 419–43.

Bloch, J. and Bloch, M. (1980) 'Women and the dialectics of nature in eighteenth-century French thought' in MacCormack, C. and Strathern, M., eds. *Nature, Culture and Gender*. Cambridge: Cambridge University Press, pp. 25–42.

Bloch, M. (1983) *Marxism and Anthropology: The History of a Relationship*. Oxford: Clarendon.

Bordo, S. (1990) 'Feminism, post-modernism and gender-scepticism' in Nicholson, L., ed. *Feminism/Post-Modernism*. London: Routledge, pp. 133–53.

Boserup, E. (1970) *Woman's Role in Economic Development*. London: Allen and Unwin.

Brandt et al. (1980) *North-South: A Programme for Survival. The Report of the Independent Commission on International Development Issues*. London: Pan.

Breman, J. (1974) *Patronage and Exploitation: Changing Agrarian Relations in South Gujarat*. Berkeley: University of California Press.

Briody, E. and Chrisman, J.B. (1992) 'Cultural adaptation on overseas assignments', *Human Organisation* vol. 50, no. 3, pp. 264–82.

Brokensha, D. (1966) *Applied Anthropology in English-speaking Africa*. Ithaca, NY: Society for Applied Anthropology Monograph no. 8.

Burghart, R. (1993) 'His lordship at the cobblers' well' in Hobart, M., ed. *An Anthropological Critique of Development: The Growth of Ignorance*. London: Routledge, pp. 79–100.

Carroll, T. (1992) *Intermediary NGOs: The Supporting Link in Grassroots Development*. West Hartford, CN: Kumarian.

Cassen, R.H. (1978) *India: Population, Economy and Society*. London: Macmillan.

Cassen, R. et al. (1986) *Does Aid Work?* Oxford: Clarendon.

Cerna, L. and Miclat-Teves, A. (1993) 'Mag-uugmad Foundation's (MFI) experience of upland technology development in the Philippines: soil and water conservation strategies' in Farrington, J. and Lewis, D.J., eds *Non-government Organisations and the State in Asia: Rethinking Roles in Agricultural Development*. London: Routledge, pp. 248–54.

Chambers, R. (1983) *Rural Development: Putting the Last First*. Harlow: Longman.

Chambers, R. (1992) *Rural Appraisal: Rapid, Relaxed and Participatory*. IDS Discussion Paper 311. Brighton: Institute of Development Studies, University of Sussex.

Chambers, R. (1993) *Challenging the Professions: Frontiers for Rural Development*. London: Intermediate Technology Publications.

Chambers, R., Pacey, A. and Thrupp, L.A., eds. (1989) *Farmer First: Farmer Innovation and Agricultural Research*. London: Intermediate Technology Publications.

Cheater, A. (1986) *Social Anthropology: an Alternative Introduction*. London: Routledge.

Chenery, H.B., Duloy, J. and Jolly, R., eds (1974) *Redistribution with Growth: An Approach to Policy*. Washington, DC: World Bank.

Clark, J. (1990) *Democratising Development: The Role of Voluntary Organisations*. London: Earthscan.

Clifford, J. (1988) *The Predicament of Culture: Twentieth Century Ethnography, Literature and Art*. Cambridge, MA: Harvard University Press.

Clifford, J. and Marcus, G., eds. (1986) *Writing Culture: The Poetics and Politics of Ethnography*. Berkeley: University of California Press.

Cochrane, G., ed. (1976) *What We Can Do for Each Other? An Inter-disciplinary Approach to Development Anthropology*. Amsterdam: B.R. Gruner.

Cochrane, G. (1971) *Development Anthropology*. New York: Oxford University Press.

Cohen, A. (1969) *Custom and Politics in Urban Africa*. London: Routledge and Kegan Paul.

Conlin, S. (1985) 'Anthropological advice in a government context' in Grillo, R. and Rew, A., eds. *Social Anthropology and Development Policy* (ASA Monographs 23). London: Tavistock, pp 73–88.

Comaroff, J. (1985) *Body of Power, Spirit of Resistance: The Culture and History of a South African People*. Chicago: University of Chicago Press.

Conway, G. (1986) *Agrosystem Analysis for Research and Development*. Bangkok: Winrock International.

Cornwall, A. and Lindisfarne, N., eds. (1994) *Dislocating Masculinity: Comparative Ethnographies*. London: Routledge.

Darwin, C. (1956 [first published 1859]) *The Origin of Species*. London: Dent.

Dembo, R., Hughes, P., Jackson, L. and Mieczkowski, T. (1993) 'Crack cocaine dealing by adolescents in two public housing projects: a pilot study', *Human Organisation* vol. 52, no. 1, Spring, pp. 89–98.

Deshen, S. (1992) 'Applied anthropology in international conflict resolution: the case of the Israeli debate on Middle Eastern settlement proposals', *Human Organisation*, vol. 51, no. 2, pp. 180–4.

De Wet, C. (1991) 'Recent deliberations on the state and future of resettlement anthropology', *Human Organisation*, vol. 50. no. 1, pp. 104–9.

Dey, J. (1981) 'Gambian women: unequal partners in rice development projects?' in Nelson, N., ed. *African Women in the Development Process*. London: Frank Cass, pp. 109–22.

Di Leonardo, M. (1991) *Gender at the Crossroads of Knowledge: Feminist Anthropology in the Post-modern Era*. London: Macmillan.

Dos Santos, T. (1973) 'The crisis of development theory and the problem of dependence in Latin America' in Bernstein, H., ed., pp. 57–80. *Underdevelopment and Development*. Harmondsworth: Penguin.

Durkheim, E. (1947 [first published 1893]) *The Division of Labour in Society*. New York: Free Press.

Eades, J., ed. (1987) *Migrants, Workers and the Social Order* (ASA Monograph 26). London: Tavistock.

Edwards, M. and Hulme, D. (1992) *Making a Difference: NGOs and Development in a Changing World*. London: Earthscan.

Engels, F. (1972 [first published 1884]) *The Origin of the Family, Private Property and the State*. New York: International Publishers.

Epstein, A. (1958) *Politics in an Urban African Community*. Manchester: Manchester University Press.

Epstein, T.S. (1962) *Economic Development and Social Change in South India*. Manchester: Manchester University Press.

Epstein, T.S. (1973) *South India: Yesterday, Today, and Tomorrow*. London: Macmillan.

Epstein, T.S. and Ahmed, A. (1984) 'Development anthropology in project implementation' in Partridge, W.L., ed., *Training Manual in Development Anthropology*. Washington, DC: American Anthropological Association, pp. 31–41.

Escobar, A. (1988) 'Power and visibility: development and the intervention and management of the Third World', *Cultural Anthropology* vol. 3, no. 4, pp. 428–43.

Escobar, A. (1991) 'Anthropology and the development encounter: the making and marketing of development anthropology', *American Ethnologist* vol. 18, no. 4, pp. 658–81.

Escobar, A. (1992) 'Culture, practice and politics: anthropology and the study of social movements', *Critique of Anthropology* vol. 12, no. 4, pp. 395–432.

Escobar, A. (1995) *Encountering Development: The Making and Unmaking of the Third World*. Princeton, NJ: Princeton University Press.

Esteva, G (1993) 'Development' in Sachs, W., ed. *The Development Dictionary: A Guide to Knowledge as Power*. London: Zed, pp. 6–26.

Evans-Pritchard, E. (1940) *The Nuer: A Description of the Modes of Livelihood and the Political Institutions of a Nilotic People*. Oxford: Clarendon.

Eyben, R. (1994) 'What can aid do for social development?', *Social Development Newsletter* vol. 2, January.

Farmer, B.H., ed. (1977) *Green Revolution? Technology and Change in Rice Growing Areas of Tamil Nadu and Sri Lanka*. London: Macmillan.

Farrington, J. and Lewis, D.J., eds (1993) *Non-government Organisations and the State in Asia: Rethinking Roles in Agricultural Development*. London: Routledge.

Featherstone, M., ed. (1990) *Global Culture: Nationalism, Globalisation and Modernity*. London: Sage.

Ferguson, J. (1990) *The Anti-Politics Machine: 'Development', Depoliticisation, and Bureaucratic Power in Lesotho*. Cambridge: Cambridge University Press.

Firth, R. (1981) 'Engagement and detachment: reflections on applying social anthropology to social affairs', *Human Organisation*, 40 (3): 193–201.

Folbre, N. (1986) 'Hearts and spades: paradigms of household economics', *World Development* vol. 14, no. 2, 245–55.

Food and Agriculture Organisation (FAO) (1987) *Socio-cultural, socio-economic, bio-environmental and bio-technical aspects of aquaculture in rural development*. Rome: Reports prepared for the Aquaculture for Local Community Development Programme.

Foster, G. (1962) *Traditional Cultures and the Impact of Technological Change*. Evanston, IL: Harper and Row.

Foster, M. (1989) 'Environmental upgrading and intra-urban migration in Calcutta'. Unpublished PhD thesis, University of Nottingham.

Foucault, M. (1970) *The Order of Things: An Archaeology of the Human Sciences* (translated by A. Sheridan-Smith). New York: Random House.

Foucault, M. (1971) 'The order of discourse' in R. Young, ed. *Untying the Text: A Post-structuralist Reader*. London: Routledge and Kegan Paul.

Fowler, A. (1990) 'Doing it better? Where and how NGOs have a comparative advantage in facilitating development', *AERDD Bulletin* 28, February, pp. 11–20.

Frank, A.G. (1967) *Capitalism and Underdevelopment in Latin America*. London: Monthly Review.

Freeman, D. (1983) *Margaret Mead and Samoa: The Making and Unmaking of an Anthropological Myth*. Harmondsworth: Penguin.

Friedmann, J. (1992) *Empowerment: The Politics of Alternative Development*. Oxford: Blackwell.

Friere, P. (1968) *The Pedagogy of the Oppressed*. New York: Seabury.

Garber, B., and Jenden, P. (1993) 'Anthropologists or anthropology? The Band Aid perspective' in Pottier, J., ed. *Practising Developing: Social Science Perspectives*. London: Routledge, pp. 50–71.

Gardner, K. (1991) *Songs at the River's Edge: Stories from a Bangladeshi Village*. London: Virago.

Gardner, K. (1995) *Global Migrants, Local Lives: Travel and Transformation in Rural Bangladesh*. Oxford: Oxford University Press.

Gardner, K. (unpublished) 'Mixed messages: contested development and the Plantation Rehabilitation Project'.

Gatter, P. (1993) 'Anthropology in farming systems research: a participant observer in Zambia' in Pottier, J., ed., *Practising Development: Social Science Perspectives*. London: Routledge, pp. 153–87.

Geertz, C. (1963a) *Agricultural Involution: The Processes of Change in Indonesia*. Berkeley: University of California Press.

Geertz, C. (1963b) *Peddlers and Princes: Social Change and Economic Modernisation in Two Indonesian Towns*. Chicago: University of Chicago Press.

Giddens, A. (1971) *Capitalism and Modern Social Theory: An Analysis of the Writings of Marx, Durkheim, and Weber.* Cambridge: Cambridge University Press.

Goetz, A.M. (1994) 'Who gets the credit? Gender, power and control over loan use in rural credit programmes in Bangladesh'. *IDS Working Paper* no. 8. Brighton: University of Sussex.

Goldschmidt, W., ed. (1979) *The Uses of Anthropology.* Washington, DC: American Anthropological Association.

Grillo, R. (1985) 'Applied anthropology in the 1980s: retrospect and prospect' in Grillo, R. and Rew, A., eds. *Social Anthropology and Development Policy* (ASA Monographs 23). London: Tavistock. pp. 1–36.

Grimshaw, A. and Hart, K. (1993) *Anthropology and the Crisis of the Intellectuals* (Prickly Pear Pamphlet no. 1). Cambridge: Prickly Pear Press.

Gulliver, P. (1985) 'An applied anthropologist in East Africa during the colonial era' in Grillo, R. and Rew, A. eds. *Social Anthropology and Development Policy* (ASA Monographs 23). London: Tavistock. pp. 37–57.

Hancock, G. (1989) *Lords of Poverty.* London: Macmillan.

Hannerz, U. (1980) *Exploring the City: Enquiries towards Urban Anthropology.* New York: Columbia University Press.

Hannerz, U (1992) *Cultural Complexity: Studies in the Social Organisation of Meaning.* New York: Columbia University Press.

Harris, M. (1991) *Cultural Anthropology*, 3rd edn. New York: HarperCollins.

Harris, O. (1984) 'Households as natural units' in Young, K., Wolkowitz, C. and McCullagh, R., eds., 2nd edn. *Of Marriage and the Market: Women's Subordination Internationally and its Lessons.* London: Routledge and Kegan Paul, pp. 136–57.

Harriss, J. (1977) 'Implications of changes in agriculture for social relationships at the village level: the case of Randam' in Farmer, B.H., ed. *Green Revolution? Technology and Change in Rice Growing Areas of Tamil Nadu and Sri Lanka.* London: Macmillan, pp. 225–45.

Hashemi, S.M. (1989) 'NGOs in Bangladesh: alternative development or alternative rhetoric?' Dhaka, mimeo. Institute of Development Policy and Management, University of Manchester.

Haviland, W.A. (1975) *Cultural Anthropology.* New York: Holt, Rinehart and Winston.

Hayter, T. (1971) *Aid as Imperialism.* Harmondsworth: Penguin.

Hill, P. (1986) *Development Economics on Trial: The Anthropological Case for a Prosecution.* Cambridge: Cambridge University Press.

Hobart, M., ed. (1993) *An Anthropological Critique of Development: The Growth of Ignorance.* London: Routledge.

Hoben, A. (1982) 'Anthropologists and development', *Annual Review of Anthropology* 11, pp. 349–75.

Holcombe, S. (1995) *Managing to Empower: The Grameen Bank's Experience of Poverty Alleviation.* London: Zed.

Hoogvelt, A (1982) *The Third World in Global Development.* London: Macmillan.

180   *Anthropology, Development and the Post-modern Challenge*

Howard, M.C. (1993) *Contemporary Cultural Anthropology*, 4th edn. New York: HarperCollins.

Intermediate Technology and Development Group (ITDG) (1992) *Working with Women in Kenya*. London: ITDG.

James, W. (1973) 'The Anthropologist as reluctant imperialist' in Asad, T., ed. *Anthropology and the Colonial Encounter*. London: Ithaca, pp. 41–69.

Jennings, J. (1990) *Adult Literacy: Master or Servant? A Case Study from Rural Bangladesh*. Dhaka: Dhaka University Press.

Johannsen, A.M. (1992) 'Applied anthropology and post-modernist ethnography', *Human Organisation* vol. 51, no. 1, pp. 71–81.

Jordanova, L.J. (1980) 'Natural facts: a historical perspective on science and sexuality' in MacCormack, C. and Strathern, M., eds. *Nature, Culture and Gender*. Cambridge: Cambridge University Press, pp. 42–70.

Kabeer, N. (1994) *Reversed Realities: Gender Hierarchies in Development Thought*. London: Verso.

Kerr, C. et al. (1973) *Industrialisation and Industrial Man: The Problems of Labour and Management in Industrial Growth*. Harmondsworth: Penguin.

Khan, M., Lewis, D.J., Sabri, A.A. and Shahabuddin, M. (1993) 'Proshika's livestock and social forestry programmes' in Farrington, J. and Lewis, D.J., eds *Non-government Organisations and the State in Asia: Rethinking Roles in Agricultural Development*. London: Routledge, pp. 59–66.

Korten, D. (1990) *Getting to the 21st Century: Voluntary Action and the Global Agenda*. West Hartford, CN: Kumarian.

Kramsjo, B. and Wood, G. (1992) *Breaking the Chains: Collective Action for Social Justice among the Rural Poor in Bangladesh*. London: Intermediate Technology.

Kuper, A. (1983) *Anthropology and Anthropologists: The Modern British School*. London: Routledge and Kegan Paul.

Lan, D. (1985) *Guns and Rain: Guerrillas and Spirit Mediums in Zimbabwe*. London: James Currey.

Larrain, J. (1989) *Theories of Development: Capitalism, Colonialism and Dependency*. Cambridge: Polity.

Leacock, E. (1972) 'Introduction' to Engels, F. *The Origin of the Family, Private Property and the State*. New York: International Publishers.

Leach, E. (1954) *The Political Systems of Highland Burma: A Study of Kachin Social Organisation*. London: G. Bell and Sons.

Lewis, D.J. (1991) *Technologies and Transactions: A Study of the Interaction Between Agrarian Structure and New Technology in Bangladesh*. Dhaka: Centre for Social Studies.

Lewis, D.J. (1992) *A Review of the Literature on Corruption*. Consultancy report, Swedish International Development Authority (SIDA), Dhaka, Bangladesh.

Lewis, D.J. (1993) 'Going it Alone: Female-Headed Households, Rights and Resources in Rural Bangladesh', *European Journal of Development Research* vol. 5, no. 2, pp. 23–42.

Lewis, D.J. and McGregor, J.A. (1992) *Change and Impoverishment in Albania: A Report for Oxfam*. Centre for Development Studies Report Series no. 1, University of Bath.

Lewis, D.J. et al. (1993) 'Indigenising extension: farmers, fishseed traders and poverty-focused aquaculture in Bangladesh', *Development Policy Review*, vol. 11, pp. 185–94.

Lewis, O. (1961) *The Children of Sanchez: An Autobiography of a Mexican Family*. New York: Random House .

Lloyd, P. (1979) *Slums of Hope? Shanty Towns of the Third World*. Harmondsworth: Penguin.

Long, N. (1977) *An Introduction to the Sociology of Developing Societies*. London: Tavistock.

Long, N. and Long, A. (1992) *Battlefields of Knowledge: The Interlocking of Theory and Practice in Social Research and Development*. London: Routledge.

Lyotard, J. (1984) *The Post-Modern Condition*. Manchester: Manchester University Press.

McGrew, A. (1992) 'The Third World in the New Global Order' in Allen, T. and Thomas, A. eds, *Poverty and Development in the 1990s*. Oxford: Oxford University Press, pp. 256–7.

Madeley, J. (1991) *When Aid is No Help: How Projects Fail, and How They Could Succeed*. London: Intermediate Technology Publications.

Mair, L. (1969) *Anthropology and Social Change*. (LSE Monographs on Social Anthropology 38) London: Athlone Press.

Mair, L. (1984) *Anthropology and Development*. London: Macmillan.

Malinoswki, B. (1922) *Argonauts of the Western Pacific*. London: Routledge and Kegan Paul.

Malinowski, B. (1929) 'Practical anthropology', in *Africa* vol. 2, no. 1, pp. 28–38.

Mamdani, M. (1972) *The Myth of Population Control: Family, Caste and Class in an Indian Village*. New York: Monthly Review.

Mangin, W. (1967) 'Latin American squatter settlements: a problem and a solution', in *Latin American Research Review* 2, pp. 65–98.

Marcus, G. and Fischer, M. (1986) *Anthropology as Cultural Critique: An Experimental Moment in the Human Sciences*. Chicago: University of Chicago Press.

Mathur, H.M. (1989) *Anthropology and Development in Traditional Societies*. New Delhi: Vikas.

Mead, M. (1977) *Letters from the Field: 1925–75*. New York: Harper and Row.

Midgley, J. (1995) *Social Development: The Developmental Perspective in Social Welfare*. London: Sage.

Miller, M. (1995) *State of the Peoples: A Global Human Rights Report on Societies in Danger*. Boston, MA: Beacon Press and Cultural Survival Inc.

Mintz, S. (1985) *Sweetness and Power: The Place of Sugar in Modern History*. New York: Viking.

Mitchell, C. (1956) *The Kalela Dance* (Rhodes-Livingstone Papers no. 27). Manchester: Manchester University Press.

Montgomery, E. and Bennett, J.W. (1979) 'Anthropological studies of food and nutrition: the 1940s and the 1970s' in Goldschmidt, W., ed. *The Uses of Anthropology*. Washington, DC: American Anthropological Association, pp. 125–34.

Mohanty, C. (1988) 'Under Western eyes: feminist scholarship and colonial discourses', *Feminist Review* no. 30, pp. 61–88.

Moore, H. (1988) *Feminism and Anthropology*. Cambridge: Polity.

Morgan, D.J (1980) *The Official History of Colonial Development: The Origins of British Aid Policy 1924–1945*. Volume 2: *Developing British Colonial Resources 1945–51*. London: Macmillan.

Moser, C. (1989) 'Gender planning in the Third World: meeting practical and strategic gender needs', in *World Development* vol. 17, no. 11, pp. 1799–825.

Moser, C. (1993) *Gender Planning and Development: Theory, Practice and Training*. London: Routledge.

Mosley, P. (1987) *Overseas Aid: Its Defence and Reform*. Brighton: Wheatsheaf.

Murray, C. (1981) *Families Divided: The Impact of Migrant Labour in Lesotho*. Cambridge: Cambridge University Press.

Nash, J. (1979) *We Eat the Mines and the Mines Eat Us: Dependency and Exploitation in Bolivian Tin Mines*. New York: Columbia University Press.

Ng, C. (1991) 'Malay women and rice production in west Malaysia' in Afshar, H., ed. *Women, Development and Survival in the Third World*. Harlow: Longman, pp. 188–210.

Nicholson, L., ed. (1990) *Feminism/Post-Modernism*. London: Routledge.

Ortner, S. and Whitehead, H., eds. (1981) *Sexual Meanings: The Cultural Construction of Gender and Sexuality*. Cambridge: Cambridge University Press.

Ostergaard, L., ed. (1992) *Gender and Development: A Practical Guide*. London: Routledge.

Oxford Dictionary of Current English (ed. Allen, R.E) (1988) Oxford: Oxford University Press.

Parsons, T. (1949) 'The Social Structure of the Family' in Anshen, R., ed. *The Family: Its Function and Destiny*. New York: Harper and Row, pp. 173–201.

Paul, S. (1991) 'Non-governmental organisations and the World Bank: an overview' in Paul, S. and Israel, A. eds *Non-governmental Organisations and the World Bank: Co-operation for Development*. Washington, DC: World Bank, pp. 1–19.

Pearse, A. (1980) *Seeds of Plenty, Seeds of Want: Social and Economic Implications of the Green Revolution*. Oxford: Clarendon.

Perlman, J. (1976) *The Myth of Marginality: Urban Poverty and Politics in Rio de Janeiro*. Berkeley: University of California Press.

Phillips, S. (1994) 'Anthropology of development: how current theory can inform social development practice', *Social Development Newsletter* vol. 2, January.

Polgar, S. (1979) 'Applied, action, radical, and committed anthropology' in Hinshaw, R., ed. *Currents in Anthropology: Essays in Honor of Sol Tax*. New York: Mouton, pp. 409–18.

Pottier, J., ed. (1993) *Practising Development: Social Science Perspectives.* London: Routledge.

Rabinow, P. (1986) 'Representations are social facts: modernity and post-modernity in anthropology' in Clifford, J. and Marcus, G., eds. *Writing Culture: The Poetics and Politics of Ethnography.* Berkeley: University of California Press, pp. 234–62.

Rahman, A. (1993) *People's Self-development: Perspectives on Participatory Action Research.* London: Zed.

Rahnema, M. (1992) 'Participation' in Sachs, W., ed. *The Development Dictionary: A Guide to Knowledge as Power.* London: Zed, pp. 116–32.

Reiter, R., ed. (1975) *Toward an Anthropology of Women.* New York: Monthly Review.

Rew, A. (1985) 'The organizational connection: multi-disciplinary practice and anthropological theory' in Grillo, R. and Rew, A., eds. *Social Anthropology and Development Policy* (ASA Monographs 23). London: Tavistock, pp. 185–98.

Rhoades, R.E. (1984) *Breaking New Ground: Agricultural Anthropology.* Lima: International Potato Center.

Richards, A. (1939) *Land, Labour and Diet in Northern Rhodesia.* London: Oxford University Press.

Richards, P. (1993) 'Cultivation: knowledge or performance?' in Hobart, M., ed. *An Anthropological Critique of Development: The Growth of Ignorance.* London: Routledge, pp. 61–79.

Riddell, R. and Bebbington, A. (1995) *Developing Country NGOs and Donor Governments: Report to the Overseas Development Administration.* London: Overseas Development Institute.

Robertson, A.F. (1984) *The People and the State: An Anthropology of Planned Development.* Cambridge: Cambridge University Press.

Rogers, B. (1980) *The Domestication of Women: Discrimination in Developing Societies.* London: Kogan Page.

Rosaldo, M. and Lamphere, L., eds. (1974) *Woman, Culture and Society.* Stanford, CA: Stanford University Press.

Rostow, W.W. (1960a) *The Process of Economic Growth,* 2nd edn. London: Clarendon.

Rostow, W.W. (1960b) *The Stages of Economic Growth: A Non-communist Manifesto.* Cambridge: Cambridge University Press.

Rozario, S. (1992) *Purity and Communal Boundaries: Women and Social Change in a Bangladeshi Village.* London: Zed.

Sachs, W. ed. (1992) *The Development Dictionary: A Guide to Knowledge as Power.* London: Zed.

Sacks, K. (1975) 'Engels revisited: women, the organisation of production and private property' in Reiter, R., ed. *Toward an Anthropology of Women.* New York; Monthly Review, pp. 211–35.

Said, E. (1978) *Orientalism.* Harmondsworth: Penguin.

Schapera, I. (1947) *Migration and Tribal Life.* Oxford: Oxford University Press.

Schumacher, E.F. (1973) *Small is Beautiful.* London: Blond and Briggs.

Scoones, I. and Thompson, J. (1993) *Challenging the Populist Perspective: Rural Peoples' Knowledge, Agricultural Research and Extension Practice.* Institute of Development Studies Discussion Paper 332. Sussex: Institute of Development Studies.

Scoones, I. and Thompson, J. (1994) *Beyond Farmer First: Rural Peoples' Knowledge, Agricultural Research and Extension Practice.* London: Intermediate Technology Publications.

Scudder, T. (1980) 'Policy implications of complusory relocation in river basin development projects', in Cernea, M. and Hammond, P.B., eds. *Projects for Rural Development: The Human Dimension.* Baltimore, MD: Johns Hopkins University Press.

Seddon, D. (1993) 'Anthropology and appraisal: the preparation of two IFAD pastoral development projects in Niger and Mali' in Pottier, J., ed. *Practising Development: Social Science Perspectives.* London: Routledge, pp. 71–110.

Sen, A. (1981) *Poverty and Famines: an Essay on Entitlement and Deprivation.* Oxford: Oxford University Press.

Sen, G. and Grown, C. (1987) *Development Crises and Alternative Visions: Third World Women's Perspectives.* New York: Monthly Review.

Shiva, V. (1988) *Staying Alive: Women, Ecology and Survival in India.* London: Zed.

Sobhan, R. (1989) 'Bangladesh and the world economic system: the crisis of external dependence' in Alavi, H. and Harriss, J., eds. *Sociology of 'Developing Societies': South Asia.* London: Macmillan.

Spencer, J. (1989) 'Anthropology as a kind of writing', *Man: The Journal of the Royal Anthropological Institute* vol. 24, no. 1, pp. 145–64.

Sponsel, L.E. (1992) 'Information asymmetry and the democratisation of anthropology', *Human Organisation* vol. 51, no. 3, pp. 299–301.

Staudt, K., ed. (1990) *Women, International Development and Politics: The Bureaucratic Mire.* Philadelphia, PA: Temple University Press.

Staudt, K. (1991) *Managing Development: State, Society, and International Contexts.* Newbury Park, CA: Sage.

Stavenhagen, R. (1971) 'Decolonising applied social sciences', *Human Organisation* no. 30, pp. 333–44.

Strathern, A. (1993) *Landmarks: Reflections on Anthropology.* Kent, Ohio: Kent State University Press.

Taussig, M. (1980) *The Devil and Commodity Fetishism in South America.* Chapel Hill, SC: South Carolina Press.

Tendler, J. (1982) *Turning Private Voluntary Organisations into Development Agencies: Questions for Evaluation.* Washington, DC: United States Agency for International Development.

Turbyne, J. and McGregor, J.A. (1994) 'Time and money: a critical review of participatory rural appraisal', Anthropology in Action Conference paper (unpublished).

Turner, J. (1969) 'Uncontrolled urban settlements: problems and policies' in Breese, G., ed. *The City in Newly Developing Countries: Readings on Urbanism and Urbanisation.* New York: Prentice Hall, pp. 507–31.

Tvedt, T. (1995) *Non-Governmental Organisations as a Channel in Development Assistance: The Norwegian System*. Report to Norwegian Development Agency by the Centre for Development Studies, University of Bergen (mimeo).

United Nations Development Programme (UNDP) (1990), *Human Development Report*. New York: UNDP.

Vatuk, S. (1972) *Kinship and Urbanisation: White Collar Migrants in North India*. London: University of California Press.

Vincke, J., Mak, R., Bolton, R. and Jurica, P. (1993) 'Factors affecting AIDS-related sexual behaviour change among Flemish gay men', *Human Organisation* vol. 52, no. 3, pp. 260–71.

Wallerstein, I. (1974) *The Modern World System: Capitalist Agriculture and the Origins of the European World Economy in the Sixteenth Century*. New York: Academic Press.

Warry, W. (1992) 'The eleventh thesis: applied anthropology as praxis', *Human Organisation* vol. 51, no. 2, pp. 153–63.

Weiner, A. (1976) *Women of Value, Men of Renown*. Austin: University of Texas Press.

Wellard, K. and Copestake, J., eds (1993) *NGOs and the State in Africa: Rethinking Roles in Sustainable Agricultural Development*. London: Routledge.

White, S. (1992) *Arguing with the Crocodile: Gender and Class in Bangladesh*. London: Zed.

Whitehead, A. (1981) 'I'm hungry Mum: the politics of domestic budgeting', in Young, K., Wolkowitz, C. and McCullagh, R., eds. *Of Marriage and the Market: Women's Subordination Internationally and its Lessons*. London: Routledge and Kegan Paul, pp. 93–117.

Wilson, G. (1941) *An Essay on the Economics of Detribalisation of Northern Rhodesia. Part I*. Rhodes Livingstone Papers, no. 5. Livingstone: Rhodes Livingstone Institute.

Wilson, G. (1942) *An Essay on the Economics of Detribalisation of Northern Rhodesia. Part II*. Rhodes Livingstone Papers, no. 6. Livingstone: Rhodes Livingstone Institute.

Wolf, E. (1964) *Anthropology*. London: Prentice-Hall.

Wolf, E. (1982) *Europe and the People without History*. Berkeley: University of California Press.

Wood, A. (1950) *The Ground-Nut Affair*. London: Bodley Head.

Wood, G.D (1985) *Labelling in Development Policy*. London: Sage.

Wood, G.D. and Palmer-Jones, R. (1990) *The Water Sellers*. London: Intermediate Technology Publications.

Worby, E. (1984) 'The politics of dispossession: livestock development policy and the transformation of property relations in Botswana'. Unpublished MA thesis, Department of Anthropology, McGill University, Montreal.

Worsley, P. (1957) *The Trumpet Shall Sound: a study of 'cargo cults' in Melanesia*. London: Macgibbon.

Worsley, P. (1984) *The Three Worlds: Culture and World Development*. London: Weidenfeld and Nicholson.

INDEX